PARADOX

The Spiritual Path to Transformation

BERNARD TICKERHOOF

TWENTY-THIRD PUBLICATIONS
185 WILLOW STREET • PO BOX 180 • MYSTIC, CT 06355
TEL: 1-800-321-0411 • FAX: 1-800-572-0788
E-MAIL: ttpubs@aol.com • www.twentythirdpublications.com

Twenty-Third Publications
A Division of Bayard
185 Willow Street
P.O. Box 180
Mystic, CT 063 55
(860) 536-2611
(800) 321-0411
www.twentythirdpublications.com

ISBN:1-58595-216-8
Library of Congress Catalog Card Number: 2002110054
Printed in the U.S.A.

Acknowledgments

At one point in this book, I describe my father's formative role in my understanding of paradox. At the time of its printing, he lies bedridden and in constant care. My sister, Ruthayn, is his guardian and angel of mercy. My dad's life continues to reveal a great deal to me about the paradoxes of aging and diminished capacity, and my sister's current situation speaks of grace in the midst of role reversal. At the beginning of this book I wish to acknowledge my indebtedness for the lessons they both teach me in different ways.

For me, the ideas present in this work have gone through a long process of development that stretches back almost ten years. I wish to thank the publisher for allowing it to finally come into concrete form. In a special way, I also want to thank my friend, Susan Burke, who helped me through much of its development with her skills of editing and her holding me accountable to clarity and conciseness of thought. There have been many others who have contributed in various ways throughout the process of the book's coming to birth. In singling out Fr. Peter Lyons, TOR, Sr. Cecilia Liberatore, SND, and Sr. J. Lora Dambroski, OSF, I do not mean to imply that they have been the only ones who have offered me insights and reflections that have made their way into its pages. I especially want to thank my many spiritual directees over the years, who probably without even knowing it, showed me so much about how the dynamics of paradox function in the daily living out of human spirituality.

Contents

Introduction

"Take a deep breath, and hold it," the doctor says, as he listens to my heart. "Now another…good. And another." He is moving his stethoscope around my chest, alert to any irregularities. I am dutifully trying to breathe deeply and rhythmically. I am also fascinated that he does not say, "Take a deep breath, and then let it out." He is presuming I will exhale, of course. I cannot sit there constantly inhaling. I must breathe in and breathe out. Or perhaps the breath does not occur with the in or the out. Perhaps breathing is only complete once both the inhaling and the exhaling have been accomplished.

As you begin this book, I want you to know that you are breathing. Perhaps you had not thought much about that fact, but now as you reflect on the matter, you will no doubt be aware that you are continuously taking breath and letting it go in some sort of rhythmic pattern. You are inhaling and exhaling, and, in between, you make the slightest of pauses in order to switch from one to the other. So which is actually the breath? Breathing in is an action. Breathing out is also an action. They are opposite actions. But in which action is breath contained? In which one is life sustained? Perhaps life is not contained in either one, but only in the rhythm of both. Could it be the *rhythm* of breathing that sustains life?

Let us perform together this simplest of exercises. Take a deep breath, and as the air passes into your lungs, imagine that you are being filled also with the Spirit of God. It is the promise of continued life, physical but now also spiritual. But to try holding on to either the air or the Spirit indefinitely would be to invite inevitable collapse. You will have to let them both go: otherwise neither the air nor the Spirit

1

will be able to flow forth. When they do, they go out into the world, and they are no longer in your possession. At that moment you are left depleted, empty. For an instant there is the semblance of death. But then once again you inhale, and the air comes back in. Let us imagine the Spirit does as well. It is this return of air and Spirit that saves you. The return could be seen as a life-saving gift, and so you receive this breath with renewed gratitude. But then you realize that the whole process is gift, and in this essential breath life is initiated and continuously sustained. Finally you realize that, while the experiences of inhaling and exhaling seem to be as different as they can possibly be, they are both necessary if your essential breath is to exist at all.

I want to suggest this image of breath as a metaphor for paradox and transformation, the primary subjects of this book. While at first we might think of breathing as basically an effort to take in oxygen through the lungs in order to get it to our bloodstream, a little reflection shows us that this is only half the process. Just as important as what comes into us is what must then go out of us. These two actions, inhaling and exhaling, would seem to be opposite to each other. In most other realms of life, opposite actions that seem to create countereffects would be deemed *contradictions*. That here they come together to form another reality we call *breathing* makes them a metaphor for what I see as *paradox*, a reconciling of opposites. That the process of their coming together can sustain life hints at the transformation I will suggest is always present in a true paradox.

While the subjects of this book are paradox and transformation, it is concerned with many other things as well. Among them are prayer and healing, discernment and surrender, virtue and sin. These topics are treated in their proper place. Beyond these thematic presentations, however, this book is also concerned with *evangelization*, though not so much as a specific topic. Evangelization is really more the intention that lies behind the book's writing. The word *evangelization* is concerned with spreading the Good News. Our Good News, of course, is primarily about Jesus Christ and the hope of salvation he offers. But the Good News of Jesus never comes in a vacuum; it is always delivered in some real world context. This book, therefore, is intended for the context of our modern world at the beginning of a new millennium. It is intended for a world that struggles with belief—not just belief in Jesus, but belief in general. When we look at the amount of spiritual hunger around us, we sense that our world wants to believe, but there is something in its experience that makes it hold back. There is a doubt in the world that causes hesitation, suspicion, and cynicism.

This doubt arises because those who seem to already believe (the churches) appear at one time to offer simple answers and then to retract them when life becomes complicated. God, or Jesus, or religion, or spirituality is offered as *the* answer, but to many people the questions all appear muddled, or confused, or contradictory. As a result, many have headed off on their own quest, sewing together a patchwork of spiritual elements into what they hope is a new synthesis with new answers. Others have stayed within the traditions but remain unsettled in their belief. Still others have fallen back on simple answers for simple questions and are staunchly content to ignore any challenges, legitimate or otherwise, that this real world of complications presents.

One result of these tendencies has been the creation of a great deal of polarization within the communities of faith. People who hold essentially the same belief have entrenched themselves in languages that appear either heretical, divisive, or superstitious to those who hold other positions. To this point it seems that many believers have been unable or unwilling to get beyond this polarization. To some, however, there is the sense that the problem lies deeper than simple differences in language. It seems to be a struggle with what belief itself consists of. Perhaps there is a need to bring faith and all that it entails to reflection at a new level.

So this book is concerned with evangelization, but it does not deal with *apologetics*. It does not seek to systematically present the tenets of belief, or defend doctrine by using either old formulas or new language. Instead it hopes to establish a new foundation upon which belief can rest in the context of the world we know and live in. It does not presume an audience of believers—or of unbelievers. Instead it seeks to address those who hunger for firmer foundations upon which to build a faith context in the first place. The foundation

I suggest for this new faith context lies in approaching life through paradox. In recognizing the paradoxical nature of reality and coming to terms with it, I suggest, the world opens to us in a new way, transformation happens, and belief is seen as not only possible, but desirable—and not only desirable, but tangibly present.

It seems there is no escaping contradiction in the experiences of our lives. Everyone has to deal with life that continuously presents itself as two-sided. Our individual unfolding stories are tied up in struggles, frustrations, grievings, and confusions that arise because the events of life sometimes seem to be one way and at other times seem to be the opposite, and many times seem to be both together. Some suffer through these experiences, taking them more or less for granted or shrugging them off as part of life's mystery. Some take a more cynical approach, suggesting that the presence of many of life's contradictions is ultimately attributable to human perversity. Some expect religion to come up with the answers to these kinds of problems, and when it doesn't, or when the answers are not satisfying, they become disheartened or bitter. If paradox can present a way out of the dilemma of contradiction, then it is something everyone needs to know and experience. We need to recognize the times when our dreams are shattered and when our paths are blocked, so that we can not only deal with the contradictions and move on with our lives, but also envision our dreams anew and find new paths that are opening up.

This book seeks to identify and build on some basic distinctions between contradiction and paradox. In its pages contradiction is never seen as a fruitful thing; it is instead an experience of being somehow stuck in life. On the other hand, this book recognizes true paradox as always being fruitful. Paradox, unlike contradiction, is rich and mysterious. As a spiritual reality, it is always experiential. To really understand paradox means learning to live with it in life's experiences, to act out of this new world view, and to be willing to accept the transformations that such actions present. That is what a spirituality of paradox is about—always more about *life* than about mere ideas or perceptions.

The following chapters suggest and develop these essential statements of a spirituality of paradox:

- Every aspect of life can be experienced in relation to an opposite aspect. These opposing aspects pervade life and can be found in life forces (a time to be born and a time to die), in events (a time to mourn and a time to dance), or in elements of opposition within events (a time to love and a time to hate).

- We most often encounter elements of opposition as contradictions in life. Some of these contradictions, such as life and death, good and evil, punishment and reward, joy and suffering, to name a few, have been at the center of the human agenda from the very beginning.

- Many oppositions in life cannot be solved, but every opposition can be transformed, if we are truly willing to pursue this transformation.

- The potential for transformation is what distinguishes paradox from contradiction. Paradox offers us a way through contradiction.

- This transformation is not found in the two elements of opposition. It presents itself as a distinct reality, different from either of the two opposing forces. This new reality is not ours to manufacture.

- We should not expect that this transformation will be obvious, or that it will lie on the same plane as the elements of opposition. Transformation will move us somewhere else, frequently surprising us when we find where we have ended up.

- To discover this transformation, we should be ready to let go of our resistances against it. This is an action that I will call surrender. It could have other names as well. The experience is more important than what we end up calling it.

- The transformation of opposing forces does not usually eliminate the polarities—it transforms them.

- Every transformation has a purpose, which is not necessarily our stated purpose. Every transformation furthers a process and contributes to a greater plan. We have only a shadowy conception of what that plan is all about.

- When we not only can recognize that all these principles are true at a theoretical level, but also are able to integrate them at a daily experiential level, where they are allowed to have a permanent impact on our attitudes, choices, decisions, and actions, we live in something I call transforming consciousness.

- Transforming consciousness is, by its nature, a graced reality, that is, it is the result of our cooperation, and not of our construction. Its nature is essentially that of gift, which we participate in, but do not merit.

- In transforming consciousness, life's contradictions finally come to be recognized as illusions, while paradox is seen as the truer reality.

These twelve statements form the heart of this book. Each chapter, I hope, will make its own contribution to our understanding of them; I hope to build upon this structure of understanding to the point where our own experiences of life become for us the clearest statements of paradox and transforming consciousness that can be made.

Chapter one attempts to "lay out the problem," if you will, explaining the difference between contradiction and paradox, and giving a few basic definitions. Chapter two grounds us in the Christian experience by exploring both the life and the death of Jesus, the one who embodies the challenge, the hope, and the fulfillment of paradox. Chapter three focuses on the need for a stance of surrender, which ties paradox to conversion. Chapter four offers some theoretical underpinnings of my view of paradox. The final chapters offer a survey of the impact of paradox on some of the major aspects of the spiritual life. Chapter five explores some basic dichotomies in the spiritual life, such as transcendence and immanence, community and solitude, and others. In chapters six through eight I examine virtue, prayer, discernment, dream work, and healing through an understanding of paradox. The final chapter alerts us to the need to concretize conversion and transformation through action in order to manifest their connection with the Reign of God, the greater plan that is at work. Some of these chapters begin with original stories, which I hope will add a further dimension of illustration to the chapter's topic.

I

Contradiction and Paradox

I begin this chapter with a remembrance from my childhood. This event took place a number of times, which is probably what makes it so ingrained in my mind, and now that I look back on it, simple event that it was, I see more and more significance to it.

The scene is my family's living room early in the evening or over a weekend. I am a boy of seven or eight, and I am doing my religion homework. At that time in parochial school, this task consisted primarily of memorizing certain sections of the Baltimore Catechism, the standard tool for teaching young Catholics about their religion. The Baltimore Catechism, as many Catholics still remember, had a very simple format. It asked a question, and then it gave the answer. It then asked another question that built upon the previous one, and gave the answer, and so on. In first grade the questions were simple, such as "Who is God?" and "Why did God make me?" Of course, by now I was a second- or third-grader, already prepared for first communion and for the sacrament of confession. I had left such simple questions behind.

As I studied my catechism questions, memorizing them for recitation the next day, I could think of twenty things I would rather be doing. I didn't dare stop, however, because it just wouldn't do to be caught unprepared during religion class. However, I had given myself permission to silently lament my predicament, and there usually settled over me on these occasions a growing frustration. Into this scene of restlessness and building irritability would enter my father, a man who had a national reputation for teasing kids. Seeing what I was doing, he would say, "Oh, I'll help you with your catechism." As soon as I heard this, I would know what was coming, because it was a kind of ritual that never changed. My protests notwithstanding, both he and I knew that the ritual, once begun, must necessarily follow through to its preordained end.

He would ask, "Who made me?" Now, of course, this had nothing to do with what I was studying, and under other circumstances it would have been a question far below the dignity of a second- or third-grader. Still, I would dutifully answer, "God made me." Then he would ask, "Can God do all things?" Well, anyone knew the answer to that. "Yes, God can do all things." There, I had done it. Once more I had set him up, as I knew I would all along.

"Can he make a stone so big that he can't lift it?"

What was I to do? No matter how I answered, he would say, "Well, then, God can't do all things." I would try reasoning, and third-grade logic (known for its erudite subtleties), and protestation. But it was all to no avail. I could not "convince" my father of God's omnipotence.

Eventually the game would end, and I would go back to studying for the real world. This ritual left its mark upon me, however—a mark beyond anything my father ever intended. First of all, I was left to ponder the fact that there were contradictions, at least in our language, that could not be easily argued away. These contradictions embraced even ultimate reality. And as much as I knew that somewhere there was a fallacy in my dad's logic, I was still left, I believe, with as clear a grasp of paradox as a third-grader could handle.

Beyond this, however, was a greater realization, unformed at the time, but that now has come into conscious focus. In my dad's irreverent humor, no less a power than God had been subjected to the scrutiny of unanswerable questions. God was made to be held accountable to our human inquiry, challenged by my dad in a way that none of my teachers would dare. Unlike the Baltimore Catechism, my dad never gave me the answer; we both knew there was none. I was left to sort it all out after the fact. Nor was there any need to come to God's defense. And amazingly, God survived the scrutiny...and triumphed.

God triumphed for me despite the contradictions, and for my dad too. He always was a man of deep and quiet faith. Both he and I knew this was a joke. It turned out, however, that the joke was not on me, or him, or even God. It was on our own overly serious religious pretensions that leave us little room to maneuver.

A World of Contradictions

My dad's catechism questions were not the first encounter I had with contradiction. I, and you, and every other human child were born into a world where things do not always seem to flow, or make sense, or follow the path we expect. Children know this, although they do not always understand why it is this way. We adults patiently tell them, although we do not really know why ourselves. It is hard to explain to a child something that we ourselves do not understand, or to explain it to each other, for that matter. One thing we know is that contradiction surrounds us. We don't have to look very far in life to get in touch with the experience of it.

Life and death are often one of the first contradictions we must encounter on this earth. Fittingly enough, they are also among the last. It is hard to know just when the child first comes to an experience of death. As far as we can assess, some awareness of life is with us from the very beginning. Then one day death enters into the picture. It might come in the form of the death of a close relative, a grandparent, or elderly uncle. Or it might be the traumatic loss of a family pet, or the discovery of a dead animal in the yard. It might even be the tragic death of a parent or a playmate. Even in the absence of these real life experiences, there is plenty of death in the pages of fairy tales, and it is to be found everywhere on television. Death will not be escaped, even by the young at heart.

In *The Broken Connection: On Death and the Continuity of Life*, Robert

Jay Lifton claims that the images of death begin to form in the child at birth. He maintains that these "death equivalent" images pair themselves alongside primordial images of life or vitality. He specifically names three pairings of opposites: the vital images of *connection, integrity,* and *movement* contrasted with *separation, disintegration,* and *stasis.* The images of death serve as "psychic precursors and models for later feelings about actual death." Once the reality of death has come to our awareness, it never leaves us. We might try to run from it, or ignore it, or even glorify it, but death traveling alongside life continues to journey with us. I have heard it said that the purpose of religion is ultimately to answer our questions about life and death. I'm sure that is true, even if it is not the only purpose.

But our felt contradictions do not stop here. Another contradiction that occurs to us early on deals with life's rewards in the face of our behaviors. If I am good, why am I not always rewarded? If I am bad, why am I not always punished? These are timeless questions. Through much of the development of the Old Testament, it was the overriding opinion that, in fact, reward and punishment were in keeping with our behavior. God blessed with prosperity those who were faithful servants, and fortune frowned on the wicked. Although it might sometimes appear that wickedness is rewarded, that is only an illusion that God will eventually rectify. While there were still vestiges of this thinking at the time of Jesus (see Lk 13:1–5; Jn 9:1–2), it was the Book of Job that finally asked Israel to confront what was obvious from its experience—that good and evil, reward and punishment were all bound up in contradiction.

It gets worse, or at least more pervasive. Life seems to be filled to overflowing with a two-sidedness. Are we free to choose our own path, or is our life determined by events beyond our control? Are we responsible for our every action, or are we recipients (some would say victims) of environmental factors whose complexity removes us from accountability? If we assume our responsibility, does that extend to our very salvation, or are we "justified by faith," as the classical terminology contends?

These, of course, all seem like ultimate questions. But we bump into and stumble over contradictions all the time, even in the most ordinary aspects of life. We find ourselves constantly pondering the contradictions within us as we go through our daily lives.

"Why am I always trying to please everyone, even when I know that most often it seems that everyone, including me, ends up being disappointed?"

"Why am I able to breeze through all the unimportant things of my day, but I never seem to get around to the one thing I should really be doing?"

"Why is it that when I try so hard to do the right thing, I always seem to get criticized for it?"

"Why is it that the people I'm closest to seem to be the hardest to get along with?"

The list could go on and on. There appears to be no escaping our two-sidedness. Nor are we likely to perceive these two sides strictly from a neutral, objective position. We are not like the statue of justice, blindly holding the scales of our experiences in a balance. Usually there is one side of contradiction we quickly align ourselves with. Most of us want good over bad, at least making the conscious attempt to follow what we understand as correct behavior. Certainly we prefer happiness to sadness, joy to despair, pleasure to pain, and success to failure. The problem is that while we want these things, we cannot escape their counterpoint completely. The things that we call negative, mostly shunned by our desire, follow us like so many yapping dogs. Occasionally they become raging monsters that seem to devour us. While we struggle against our pain and our failures, we also grapple with the human condition that demands that we deal with them in the first place.

Most of us find ourselves unable to function well with contradiction. We lament it and rail against it, and frequently find that it has immobilized us. It is at the heart of the common feeling that we have just not settled with life. It remains like an open wound that cannot be healed. Contradiction is worked into the fabric of our lives. It is inside of us, and that makes it all the more frustrating. It can be found in the *attitudes* and *perceptions* that we have brought with us into adult life. We discover them in the messages we receive from our families. We are confronted by them in the attitudes we hear in church and in society.

We are asked to ponder them throughout our education.

Look for a moment at some of these attitudes. How do we feel, for instance, about God? Some of us have a great ambivalence toward God. For many people, God seems to be both loving and cruel, judgmental and indifferent, present and absent, all at the same time. We look to God for help in times of trial, but we continue to question God's role in human suffering. We want to draw close to God, but we fear what will have to change if we do so. God, if you will, brings out the best and the worst in us.

We also have contradictory attitudes about others. We feel trust and mistrust toward others, a desire to be with them and a desire to get away from them. We feel an urge to open ourselves up to other people while at the same time experiencing a reticence about revealing ourselves. We look at the people around us, and they themselves seem to be walking containers of contradictions. Certainly we could not have so many contradictions within us. In our more honest moments, of course, we realize that we probably do, but the contradictions of others seem to be so much more apparent.

The world in general seems like a contradictory place in our perceptions. We live in the best of times and the worst of times, to use Dickens's phrase. Our world always seems to be changing, and yet nothing really new ever shows up. The same old problems keep resurfacing. Politics seems to continue along its inevitable track. Reformers don't deliver substantially on their promises, and business goes along pretty much as usual. Especially today, with instant communication and intense coverage by the media, all our heroes seem to have feet of clay. Their lives appear as contradictory as *ours* are.

And in fact, the longer we live, the more we end up perceiving that the greatest contradictions in our experience are the ones that lie within ourselves. Most of us, in a moment of truth, would likely say that we see ourselves as the supreme example of contradiction. Almost every part of who I am lives in irreconcilable tension with another part of me. We remember Paul's comment to the Romans: "I do not understand my own actions. For I do not do what I want, but I do the very thing I hate."(Rom 7:15) And we respond, "Well, yes, that happens to me all the time."

There are basically three responses to contradiction: extremism, indecision, and compromise. Perhaps the three of them are all intrinsically related, and underneath they are all some kind of response to fear, but we perceive them differently and they play themselves out in significantly different ways.

Extremism is the confrontational response to contradiction. If we think of contradiction as bipolar, extremism is the shift to an ultimate position on one of those poles. In making that shift, I credit that one pole with the sole possession of the truth. I assign goodness, justice, and some form of superior intelligence to this one position. Of course, I will necessarily see the element that lies at the opposite pole as embodying the worst of all attributes. It will be the position of falsehood, evil, and ignorance. It is a short step from here to the idea that I and those who think like me (who make up the correct position) are somehow being called to convince, convict, or eradicate the opposition. Extremism plays into the hands of hatred and violence, as we have seen innumerable times throughout the course of human history. Reflect for a moment on whom you consider to be extremists. What position is it that opposes them?

Indecision is the nonconfrontational and, really, inactive response to contradiction. When it takes on the form of indifference, it becomes itself the polar opposite to extremism. Indecision is basically an immobility, temporary or permanent, that refuses to deal with either pole. Sometimes there is the hope in indecision that the contradiction will just go away. More often it springs from a desire to choose the "correct"position, but there is an abiding lack of certitude as to which pole offers that correctness. The position of "I'm damned if I do, and damned if I don't" shows the frustration and bitterness that occur when the lack of certitude becomes pervasive or long-term. Indecision in its various forms of immobility ultimately stands aside while other forces choose the course of action. Because we cannot claim the truth with certainty in whatever possible action we take, indecision usually turns into fear, doubt, and resentment.

Compromise is at least a course of action, to a degree. It is an attempt to eliminate the tension between the poles, either by stating that no tension really exists, or by settling for common ground between the two at the expense of elements of both. But usually either of these responses will be felt to be unsatisfactory.

To say that no tension exists, that it is all, for instance, just a matter of different perception, usually creates feelings of anger in those who sense their perceptions have been dismissed. It also frequently betrays a subtle lack of integrity, for while I might propose that there is no tension, at another level of self-honesty I know this is not totally true. The final outcome of denying the tension is really not much different than the results of indecision.

The other response of compromise, settling for common ground, usually offers better possibilities. This is because at least it acknowledges some truth, that there are tensions present and resolution is coming only with great difficulty. If all parties can come to this position, there is some hope for a course of action that will work at least for the time being. Compromise rises and falls on the ability of all parties to give up some part of their position. This seems to happen with greatest frequency in smaller rather than larger forums. At the smallest forum, the inner self, this sense of compromise is how we most often deal with the minor contradictions of our lives. It also works pretty well for small cohesive groups that share other common bonds. As we see again and again, it does *not* work particularly well at the global level between different countries, religions, or ethnic groups.

Compromise, however, is at best a stopgap measure. It can bring about a tenuous peace, but it is not likely to sustain it. At the same time all parties have the felt sense that at some level they have sold out. Values have been relinquished, or at least diluted. To live in compromise is somehow to live with the awareness that I have given up a part of what I considered the truth. If I feel that I have sold the truth for the purchase of an absence of conflict, it will not only be hard maintaining the compromise. It will be hard living with myself.

The question then arises: is compromise all we've got? Is compromise the best way of dealing with contradictions in life? Do we just have to admit that we live in an imperfect world, and make do with what seems to be the best solution? Except for the extremists in our midst, that is how most of us try to respond to the contradictions that we meet in life. We can each judge for ourselves our collective success.

We could, however, ask a deeper question. Is our perception that reality is contradictory actually correct in the first place?

Paradox: The World Beyond Contradiction

This book is not about contradictions in life. It is about life as *paradox*. The two are not the same, although at first they might appear to be very close. As you read the previous pages you might have even found yourself saying, "Well, after all, life is paradoxical." It is true that life is paradoxical, but not because it is filled with contradictions. In fact, my basic premise here is that paradox is about as far from contradiction as you can get.

It would not be worth drawing the distinction if this were just a semantic difference. I have no doubt that most people use the two words interchangeably, and that linguistically they are more or less considered to be synonyms. I wish to draw a distinction because it is important to recognize that there are two completely separate experiences behind these two words. We have seen what contradiction is. I now want to introduce an understanding of paradox. It is my belief that in recognizing paradox and integrating it into our lives, we have a primary key, perhaps *the* primary key, to learning how to live fully the life and destiny we were called to. It is a golden key that enables us to understand our problems, then to understand our lives, and finally to understand something powerful and transforming at the heart of reality.

What is a paradox? Merriam Webster's Collegiate Dictionary offers several definitions, among them:

- a statement that is seemingly contradictory or opposed to common sense and yet is perhaps true.

- a self-contradictory statement that at first seems true.

- something or someone with seemingly contradictory qualities or phases.

While none of these definitions in themselves will be adequate for how I intend to speak of paradox, they alert us to something about our general understanding of the word. First, they all seek to define paradox by way of contradiction. Second, there is a sense of ambivalence as to whether paradox should be considered true or not. As I intend to use the word paradox, I hope the reader would not assume that there is anything untrue about it.

From the point of view of philosophy, there cannot really be a distinction between paradox and contradiction, based on what logic calls the law of contradiction. This law states that a thing cannot *be* and *not be* at the same time under the same formal aspect. If a paradox claims that something is true, and then claims that the very opposite is also true at the same time, logically this is an impossibility, and there must be a contradiction present. Philosophy understands the idea of paradox as a problem of knowledge and of language. Either my process of knowledge or reasoning is faulty and the paradox would be resolved if I had better or more complete information, or the paradox exists because of my limited use or understanding of words. Often it is presumed that a paradox exists solely as word play, and to eliminate the language is to eliminate the contradiction.

Paradox as understood in spirituality also presents a problem with the limitations of our knowledge and our language. It is, however, a problem that will not be solved by either expanding our knowledge or eliminating the language. The reason is that paradox also presents a problem with the limitations of our experiences. To say, for instance, that transcendence and immanence are paradoxical is not calling for the elimination of these words. Perhaps we have none better. We can admit that the words transcendence and immanence are limited; they are attempting to describe something that is beyond the meaning of either word. Furthermore, the experience of either transcendence or immanence is open to innumerable shades of meaning. Sometimes their presence flows together, frequently being perceived simultaneously by the same person at the same time during a single experience. We ask these words to hold more than they are able, not because we have not taken the time to be more specific or more honest, but because we have no choice.

We could say that our human mind reflecting on its experience of spirit generates paradox simply because its subject is not totally within our grasp. The limitations of knowledge, language, and experience as basic characteristics of paradox, therefore, will necessarily force us to face the experience of Mystery. That is ultimately why paradox is spiritual; it leads us invariably into the abyss, the nothingness, the cloud of unknowing. In the experience of Mystery I am reduced to insignificance and raised to the greatest value. Suddenly I know nothing and yet have boundless wisdom. As I am speaking of paradox in this book, I am also speaking of Mystery. We meet it at every turn. What is it? Is it God, or Ground, or Being? Is it Brahman, or the Tao? Is it the Great Spirit, or Enlightenment? These questions are not the questions of paradox. They seek only definition, while paradox longs for presence and relationship. Mystery and paradox become one. Perhaps every mystery is a paradox waiting to be discovered.

What is the essential difference, then, between contradiction and paradox? How can we distinguish between the two experiences? The difference is this: contradiction is a closed system between two opposing entities. These two entities form a duality wherein each is defined as the negation of the other. Yet as long as that duality remains, the contradiction continues endlessly, without resolution. Paradox, however, in keeping with its being rooted in Mystery, is not closed. It is inherently open to the addition of an outside force at a crucial moment. In paradox there is a kind of breakthrough, but it is as much a breaking in as a breaking out. It is an action of grace. This is a very clear difference in understanding between contradiction and paradox, but not nearly so clear in the observable experience. Under observation it might even look like little has changed, or that nothing has been added. While I am suggesting that paradox presents the introduction of another force or element, I do not mean to imply that this force is obvious. In fact, I believe that this third element is almost always obscure or hidden.

If that is the case, how can we even posit the presence of this new element? The major task of this book will be to raise our consciousness not only to recognize this new element, this new force, but also to help us release its power in our lives. At this point I simply wish to say that it will always appear as a transforming reality. Transformation has something to do with change, but not just change from one form to another. Transformation is a change to a new level, to a new reality. And this transforming presence makes its impact felt across the widest spectrum of our existence. It literally has the power to change everything, from how we greet a casual acquaintance to how we experience our own lives to how we live in the presence of God.

This transformation makes the differences between paradox and contradiction apparent, at least for now at the theoretical level. To experience contradiction in our lives leads first to opposition, then to some form of disintegration (through either extremism, indecision, or compromise, as stated above). Paradox, on the other hand, presents us with a different process. The experience of paradox first leads us to opposition, but then something happens. This opposition is not met with fear; instead it is embraced by openness and trust. There is a surrender to a hidden force, and a kind of breakthrough occurs. This breakthrough manifests itself as some kind of transformation. This transformation is not fleeting. It endures in some permanent form. And as we become accustomed to recognizing paradox in our lives and allowing it to transform us more and more completely, we become aware of ourselves and everything else in a new way. We come to live at a deeper and deeper level of transforming consciousness.

A Change of Perspective

To recognize this transforming consciousness, however, requires a fundamental shift in perspective. This shift is so basic that at first it might not even be recognized or appreciated. Yet without this shift in perspective much of what is said in the following chapters could well be missed. To demonstrate this shift I must first say a word about what we could call standard consciousness. That is our consciousness from the ordinary perspective of life, which includes our pervasive awareness of contradictions. Let us say that in standard consciousness we perceive the end or goal of life as happiness. True enough, for the person of faith this is understood to be happiness with God. Yet even the nonbeliever is pursuing what he or she understands to be some kind of enduring state of well-being. This happiness is seen as something worth actively pursuing, and most of our decisions are made with a view toward moving us in the direction of its attainment.

When good things happen to us in standard consciousness, it is generally recognized as furthering our goal. We celebrate it and enjoy it, and it fits in well with our understanding of religion or our search for meaning. When good things happen, happiness either seems to have arrived, or at least it is believed to be that much closer. A problem arises, however, when bad things happen to us, for these do not easily fit with our perception of the goal. Yet if we can see the bad things as somehow being of our own making, either through a mistake we have made or a sin we have committed, then we can more or less reconcile these bad things with our standard perspective. The difficulty comes when the bad things that happen to us cannot be seen as being in any way our fault or failure. Then we grapple with why these things are happening to us. We wonder why God is letting them happen, or making them happen. We experience suffering, and we see this as a frustration or even a destruction of the happiness that we feel should ultimately be ours. Even though bad things happen to us on a regular basis, from this standard perspective we are always to some degree surprised that they should. In standard consciousness, therefore, mystery is rooted in suffering and pain. Everything else, including God, generally seems to fit into our overall perspective.

In transforming consciousness, however, everything radically shifts. First of all, happiness as we normally understand it is not the primary goal of life. The goal of life is transformation, the total reconfiguration of the self and all of life into a new and dynamic relationship with and presence to God. This reconfiguration to God is as close as I intend to get to an articulation of the Reign of God, a phrase that was central to the teaching of Jesus, but one he refused to define in the gospels, and one that we must likely concede has no final definition. From this new perspective, it is transformation that is to be actively pursued, and our decisions are to be made with this new end in mind. But in transforming consciousness our goal of transformation can be realized not only through the good things that come to us, through the things that cause us happiness, but also through the bad things, whether they are of our creation or not.

Suffering and pain are not disruptions of our goal, but are, in fact, every bit as much the means to transformation as are our joys and successes. They are not something to be shunned or denied (even though our feelings toward them will remain the same), but to be embraced and explored. And they are nothing to be surprised about. Suffering and pain can be expected as frequent visitors. They are not the source of mystery. Instead, Mystery lies in the reconfiguration; Mystery is embraced in the Reign of God. And because transformation can be experienced through both good and bad, through the joyful and the sorrowful, through the successes and the failures, it seems that Mystery uses the paradoxes of life as one of its most fruitful components.

Allow me, therefore, to conclude this chapter by offering my own more complete definition of paradox, one that I hope will remain consistent throughout this book. Paradox is the harmonizing of two opposing experiences or aspects of an experience that in themselves are irreconcilable but, through another force acting upon them at a crucial moment, are created into a new or transformed reality. But what paradox is will not really be as important as what paradox can bring about. My overriding purpose in this book is to help allow our experiences of paradoxical reality to bring about a transforming consciousness within us.

II

The Paradox
of Jesus

A Story: Who Do You Say That I Am?
—Inspired by Mark 8:27–38

James looked back along the dusty road. Behind him a few of his companions trekked along, deep in conversation, stirring up enough dust that he could hardly see beyond them. He turned his face back to the front. At some distance he could see Thomas, setting the group's pace with a dogged determination James could not understand. It was characteristic of Thomas, but it was not as if they were in any great hurry. He happened to know their immediate destination, and they were already drawing close to it. He was not sure if Thomas knew where they were going or not. He chuckled to himself; he just might end up walking right past it.

James focused his eyes a short distance ahead of him where Jesus walked, conversing with James bar Alphaeus. Not long before, Jesus had caught his eye, and he noticed what he took for a concerned look in the master's expression. He thought he could guess what was on Jesus' mind; it had been on his for the last couple of days.

He turned again to peer back through the dust. Beyond the main body of disciples he could make out the one figure that brought up the rear. It was Simon, whom Jesus had taken to calling Peter, one who is rock-like. Simon didn't look too solid at the moment, however. His eyes cast down, he walked hunched over, barely keeping up with the pace. There he was, at the periphery of the group, where he had been most of this week. James had tried to talk to him before they set out this morning, but Simon had only mumbled something incoherent and pulled away. Perhaps eating a few pounds of dust on the journey had made him a bit more sociable.

James stopped and allowed most of the others to pass him by. He noticed Simon slow down a bit when he realized that James was planning on joining him.

"It's a wonder you can even see the road back here, Simon. I can't remember when the air has been so dry and dusty." Simon didn't respond, but James felt that his expression still held a kind of openness, as if he might be ready for some companionship.

"Simon, I must tell you that I'm becoming concerned. I know most of the others feel the same way. And I know Jesus does too. What is it? What's the matter?"

Although James had asked Simon the question, he felt that he probably already knew the answer. It was six days ago that Simon's fortunes in the company suddenly seemed to spin down like a desert whirlwind. Within one short hour James had seen his friend rise to a peak of exuberance only to crash to the brink of despondency. The group had been walking much like they were today, but the dust was down, and Jesus was asking them questions about himself as the focus of local gossip. Most of the disciples were not paying that much attention to what Jesus was asking. It had been a long walk, and many of them were fatigued. Some, however, were trying to tell him what they had heard in some of the synagogues and in the markets. There was actually a great deal of speculation in the local towns about who Jesus was. Some seemed to be dismissing him or at least were suspicious, but others had obviously given great thought as to his identity. Perhaps a prophet, perhaps even an Elijah-type figure.

Then Jesus had asked them who they thought he was. At that

point he and the others fell silent. The truth was that most of them didn't know what to make of Jesus.

But while the others hesitated, Simon had blurted out, "You are the messiah." Everyone was stunned. Surely it had been in the back of their minds. That was why most of them had thrown their lot in with this ragged group to begin with. But that Simon would actually say it, that had overwhelmed the rest of them. It was, however, the answer that Jesus seemed to be looking for, and James had seen the others' esteem for Simon suddenly climb. He could see it in Simon's own eyes as well. Most of the others already looked upon Simon as a spokesman of sorts, but suddenly it seemed that "Peter" was claiming this for himself.

Well, it wasn't an hour later that everything turned around dramatically, at least as it must have seemed to Simon. Jesus had gone on to talk about something James could not understand. It had something to do with Jesus being the messiah, but he was also talking about some kind of suffering and rejection, which didn't seem to make sense. He also began speaking about his death and about resurrection of the body, which most of the disciples believed in, but which Jesus seemed to expect very soon. They were all feeling very uneasy at that point, and Simon must have felt that way too. He pulled Jesus aside, and seemed to be protesting, gesturing in such a way that it seemed he was trying to convince him of something. But Jesus almost immediately turned on him. They could all feel his anger. They heard him call Simon a satan, a tester sent from the evil one. Simon was obviously humiliated, and everyone felt very sorry for him, because his heart had been in the right place. He had, in fact, acted in a way most of the others wished they had the courage to do. Anyway, since then Simon had pulled away, and it seemed no one, not even Jesus, had been able to reach him.

"Simon," James continued, since Simon had remained silent, "I know you're humiliated because of what happened the other day. Listen, you have to snap out of this. No one holds any of that against you. I know Jesus doesn't. He's even more concerned about you than the rest of us. It's not the end of the world."

Simon stopped walking and looked intently at James.

"James, did you understand what Jesus was talking about the other day, when he was speaking about his death?"

James was happy to finally hear him speak, but he had to admit, "Well, not really. But I have to say that it wasn't the first time his words confused me."

Simon spoke as if he already knew what James's answer would be. "I don't feel humiliated, James, at least not now. I mean I surely was at first, but you know me. Well, I've been saying things I've regretted my whole life. I've learned to bounce back by now. There is something else, though. It's kept me awake the last few nights. Maybe what you said is true. Perhaps it is the end of the world."

"Simon, the dust has made you delirious. What is this talk I hear?"

"James, I know you don't understand Jesus. None of us do. Maybe I know him less than anyone. But when he was talking about his death the other day, there were two things that seemed to be hitting me square in the face. First, I can't remember when I was ever so afraid. It was a fear I just couldn't shake. I had to make him stop talking about it. But at the same time I was also realizing something. I came to see something I can't explain. I came to see that with Jesus nothing is ever going to be the same for me again. You and I, James,…and John and Andrew and the others…it's not going to be the same for us. I don't think it's going to be the same for anyone…," his voice drifted off, "ever again."

James wasn't quite sure what Simon was saying, but at least he didn't seem despondent anymore.

"Well, of course it won't be the same. Now come along with me to the front. We will soon be approaching Mount Tabor. John told me a little while ago that Jesus wants the three of us to accompany him when he climbs to the top to pray."

James pulled Simon along with him. He felt his friend was finally coming out of it. He knew Simon; he was a rugged man. He would soon be back to normal.

Contradiction, the Bible, and Jesus

Trying to understand Jesus has been a fundamental Christian endeavor from the very beginning. The gospels attest to the fact that the earliest disciples, even the ones closest to Jesus, probably didn't understand what he was really about. They tended to take Jesus and his teachings and try to fit them into their own expectations and theological presuppositions. They projected onto him their own hopes for how God would bring about salvation. When he seemed to be saying something different from what they expected, they usually censored out the part that didn't fit, or applied their own categories to what he said, or just didn't hear him at all.

After two thousand years we are still taking the same kind of approach to Jesus and his message. We still tend to pick the image of Jesus that "fits" for us. When I say that our image of Jesus must fit, I mean that we desire to feel comfortable with what we believe to be his teachings and want to believe that by and large we have met his demands. To be comfortable with Jesus, however, is to be selective with Jesus. A good rule of thumb would be: if my concepts of what Jesus taught and did are always in keeping with my own perspective, then my image of Jesus is probably tailor-made to fit my own mind, not an image of the real Jesus but to some degree my own fabrication. This kind of image is no more than a projection of my own ideals and values.

You might have heard the expression "cafeteria Christianity." It usually indicates a religious atmosphere that has sufficiently blurred theological and doctrinal lines so that any individual, almost regardless of beliefs and values, can find a comfortable fit. We can walk through the line and all the teachings are laid out for us. There is enough variety that all of us can fill our plates. No one need go away hungry. We each pick the parts that are most appealing, and we let the rest go. What we can do doctrinally we can also do scripturally; the cafeteria line also has a Bible bar. In this process certain parts of the Bible become a source of comfort, and the rest is essentially ignored.

But we might also ask what the alternative is. From a fundamentalist perspective there is nothing worse than this type of cafeteria Christianity. The fundamentalist solution, however, would seem to be a set menu where everyone gets the same dish. And who is to determine whose idea of Jesus and his message is the correct one? It seems easy and so very peaceful and secure to bring an end to the debate, but in our two-thousand-year history, this approach does not have a very good track record. We might take a lesson from Peter, who thought he knew better than Jesus the meaning of messiah. This approach is usually filled with arrogance and self-righteousness. It is no less a projection, and the results are just as disastrous.

Then is there no escape? Are we doomed one way or the other to construct our own projected religion? Is there no other position? There is, but fair warning: it is a minefield of contradictions. The overriding impression many people have of the Bible is of a book that says one thing at one minute and then turns around and says the opposite. Some say that you can find something in Scripture to back any position. It's true that groups with opposing views can come up with proof texts around any issue. But at least it would seem that as long as we stay on either extreme of the spectrum, either "anything goes cafeteria style" or "the one true path of self-righteousness," we can still hold a tenable position. The problem is that both of these sound less and less like positions of integrity.

But why is the Bible so contradictory in the first place? If it is the word of God, why can't it be consistent? The reason is primarily that the Bible was not constructed in the same way that, for instance, a modern political philosophy might be formulated by the consensual efforts of its proponents. It is not a text that was set down by a group of like-minded people who hoped to use it to clarify their own beliefs and values. Instead, it reflects the faith journey of a very complex people over a great number of centuries. They went through the suddenness of traumatic experiences and the gradual unfolding of ordinary life. Their culture changed dramatically, not just once but many times. And with each trauma and each upheaval there were many voices that attempted to interpret the events in light of their faith. To do so they used different literary forms and different rhetorical styles, all the while trying to make the events of the world around them meaningful for the community. In the process, this people saw its faith awareness grow and develop, becoming richer but also less simplistic.

From that perspective most of us could understand, or at least tolerate, some degree of contradiction in the Bible. But shouldn't the gospels at least be consistent? True, the four gospels were also woven together by many hands, certainly many more than four. And yes, that process took place over a number of decades. Furthermore, they were constructed out of the experience and development of several faith communities, communities surrounded to some degree by different cultures and different religious environments. Certainly a case could be made that this multiplicity in itself would account for much of what seems contradictory in the four gospels.

That still leaves us unsettled, however. If that were all there was to it, then shouldn't there at least be some consistency within each gospel individually? Wouldn't the final redactor of each gospel—the one whose hand last touched the text—have made the effort to clean up the text, eliminating the contradictions and resolving the inconsistencies? Why would inconsistent and contradictory language remain even within an individual gospel? The answer is, of course, that the individual redactors didn't feel they had the freedom to make those kinds of changes. They held in great reverence what had been handed down to them. While they could perhaps shape a passage to fit the context of their communities, there is still present in the gospel texts the strong impression that they had to remain somehow faithful to what they had received.

We could ask, then, reverence of what? Faithful to what? Why was this material, handed down within a relatively short time span, held to be so important that its mysterious and contradictory language had to be preserved? The only answer to these questions that would seem to fit is that the material was felt to reveal the person of Jesus. The material that eventually made its way into the gospels, often through oral tradition, frequently from liturgical sources, was believed to be offering some witness to the life and the death of Jesus of Nazareth. It was certainly recorded by many hands, and it obviously went through a thorough reshaping, but in the end these faith communities, and eventually the Church as a whole, felt that they had in their possession four works that contained as much of the truth about Jesus as they could find.

Still, despite all this, the gospels are filled with contradictory language and contradictory thought, language and thought that specifically revolve around the presence and teaching of Jesus. If we can understand the contradictions of the Bible as a whole to be due to the complex way it was formed, how do we account for these apparent contradictions in the gospels? When we hear Jesus say in John's gospel, "Peace I leave with you; my peace I give to you. I do not give to you as the world gives. Do not let your hearts be troubled, and do not let them be afraid" (Jn 14:27), how are we to reconcile this with Matthew 10:34? "Do not think that I have come to bring peace to the earth; I have not come to bring peace, but a sword." Are the authors of John and Matthew so far apart that they totally missed this part of Jesus' teaching? Or is one right and the other wrong? Or do their communities have such divergent views that they perceive the peace of Jesus in such totally different ways, as in fact practically opposite?

But what if these two statements do in some way each accurately reflect the thought of Jesus as handed down to the communities? What if, in fact, the gospels for the most part present a very consistent picture of Jesus, not as competing theological portraits constructed by the different evangelists but as an overall accurate presentation of the one man? We can, I believe, look at the four gospels with all their differing theological perspectives, and recognize that they are speaking about the same individual.[1]

But if this is true, are we still faced with a new problem? Are the accounts of Jesus in the gospels accounts of a spiritual teacher who spoke and acted in very contradictory and arbitrary ways? Was Jesus not clear about what he thought? Or was he purposely trying to confuse his disciples and the crowd around them? And wouldn't that make the contradictions in the gospels seem even more disheartening than those in the Bible as a whole? Some people might feel this way. Perhaps they become frustrated by the contradictory language of Jesus, and so they simply tune out a part of the message of Jesus, the part that does not fit into their general framework of life. Or maybe they feel that it is just too difficult to try to recognize what Jesus really thought about something. Or maybe they feel that Christianity has manipulated Jesus to arrive at its own contradictory ends.

If none of these conclusions satisfies us, then we could finally pursue the possibility that Jesus and his teachings are essentially rooted in paradox. In that case we would not actually be speaking of contradiction in the sense that this book has understood that word. Instead we would be looking at Jesus as speaking from an entirely different level of consciousness, a transforming level. In this I am not implying that a view of the gospels through the lens of paradox will solve every problem of redaction criticism or form criticism. I am saying that the actions and the teaching of Jesus are by their nature paradoxical, and no amount of literary criticism can fully explain the gospels otherwise. In fact, an understanding of how we humans struggle with paradox might further help us get a sense of why the early faith communities could come up with such different portraits of Jesus in the first place.

The sacred writers of the New Testament understood that the paradoxical nature of Jesus was not recognized primarily through the things he said and did, but it was more seen in the person he was. Each gospel writer had a way of presenting this, even if they did not have the specific language. Perhaps the synoptics, Matthew, Mark, and Luke, were hoping that the ambiguous concept of the Reign of God would help explain what could not in any way be fully answered. Perhaps John's use of contrasting symbolic language, such as light and darkness, and the frequent introduction of ironic constructions were meant to portray an image of Jesus that could not be otherwise contained. As we will see, the gospels in general found in the resurrection a transformed reality springing from the opposition of life and death. But all of this still needed to be demonstrated to those who approached the earliest communities, hoping to find in Jesus the salvation they were seeking. His words and actions again became significant to the gospel writers because they pointed to and helped illustrate the reality his followers believed him to be.

In looking at Jesus from the point of view of paradox and transforming consciousness, I want to explore some of the basic categories through which he might have been seen at first in the eyes of his contemporaries. While we bring two thousand years of Christology into our understanding of Jesus, his contemporaries had their own categories, the theological categories of the Jewish tradition. They also had their own contemporary culture through which to filter their experience of him. How did they encounter this man, and how did he present himself in comparison with other religious leaders of their age? I want to begin by looking at ways in which Jesus might have been understood as a prophet, a teacher, and a healer.

Jesus the Prophet

It is probable that the Old Testament role in which Jesus most closely fit in the eyes of his contemporaries was that of prophet. Prophets were not common at the time of Jesus, and in fact, with the noted exception of John the Baptist, Judaism had not had a recognized prophet in its midst since the time of the prophet Malachi around 460 BC. Though not common, they were expected. The reappearance of a prophet was tied to the longed-for revival of the nation. The Qumran community had prophetic expectations, and the gospels indicate that both John and Jesus were acclaimed by at least some people to be prophets. Some might have held out the hope that Jesus would be the messiah. Yet the messiah was to be a unique manifestation; there was no recognizable type of messiah that was expected to arise periodically. It would have indicated a deep personal commitment to proclaim an individual to be the messiah. Prophets, on the other hand, had a clearly defined role in the history of the people of Israel. It was not unthinkable that they would make an appearance.

A prophet was one who spoke God's word to the people. The prophetic word was seen as revealing God's will and intention. While the prophet delivered this word through the vehicle of his or her own personality, once the community had sufficiently tested it, that word was accepted as having a divine source. The testing and accepting of the prophetic word was not as streamlined as it might seem. Often the prophet was challenged, even ridiculed. Some were accused of being false prophets. On more than one occasion in the Old Testament, two individuals with prophetic reputations faced off against one another with contrasting messages. Sometimes the prophet was totally rejected, and it was only later, perhaps much later, that the prophet's word was proven true, and the prophetic mission universally acknowledged.

Most often the prophetic word was a pretty straightforward one. That is, in fact, one of the major attributes of the prophet, the clarity of the message. Often the prophetic utterance had to do with correct worship, or social justice, or the nation's reliance on God rather than human salvation. There was much of this kind of language in the message of Jesus, and it would seem that Jesus claimed a role for himself out of the prophetic tradition. In chapter four (vs. 18–19), Luke has Jesus come to his hometown of Nazareth, where he proclaimed in the synagogue, "The Spirit of the Lord is upon me, because he has anointed me to bring good news to the poor. He has sent me to proclaim release to the captives and recovery of sight to the blind, to let the oppressed go free, to proclaim the year of the Lord's favor" (see Is 61:1–2).

This straightforward proclamation of Jesus got mixed reviews. Some were accepting; some were dubious. That is to be expected in the nature of the prophetic type. But Jesus did not long maintain this direct style. Was it the rejection that he encountered in Nazareth and in other towns that made him shift to a more cryptic and paradoxical manner? If it was, the style to which he adapted was no more successful at avoiding rejection. Possibly the shift had more to do with the type of message that Jesus was delivering. The basic prophetic word that came from the lips of Jesus was about the Reign of God. This ultimate sovereignty of God on earth, already coming forth in the person of its messenger, transforming every dimension of life as it was accepted in faith, was not the most obvious or facile reality to grasp. It was, in fact, a kind of topsy-turvy reality that seemed to have as its primary feature the element of reversal.

The prophetic statements of the Reign of God as proclaimed by Jesus were aimed at those who felt that they had their deliverance well in hand. What you expect, Jesus seemed to be saying to them, is not what is coming forth; do not presume that you understand how God intends to act. It could be just the reverse. The paradoxical nature of reversal of fortune went right to the heart of a society that seemed to feel that, being the chosen people, it had a handle on the spiritual and religious agenda. "There will be weeping and gnashing of teeth when you see Abraham and Isaac and Jacob and all the prophets in the kingdom of God, and you yourselves thrown out. Then people will come from east and west, from north and south, and will eat in the kingdom of God. Indeed, some are last who will be first, and some are first who will be last."(Lk 13:28–30) God would be generous, but that generosity did not simply come with a bloodline or a tradition. It was given, but in some way it also had to be earned. "For to those who have, more will be given; and from those who have nothing, even what they have will be taken away."(Mk 4:25)

This reversal of fortune was connected with a common prophetic theme, that of conversion. "The time is fulfilled, and the kingdom of God has come near; repent, and believe in the good news."(Mk 1:15) As the Greek word for conversion or repentance, *metanoia*, would suggest, this exhortation of Jesus was calling for a completely new heart and mind on the part of the hearer. Things could not remain as they were. Conversion, therefore, was itself to be understood as a sign of reversal. While many were looking for miraculous works as proofs of Jesus' divine mission, Jesus offered them a paradoxical sign instead. "This generation is an evil generation; it asks for a sign, but no sign will be given to it except the sign of Jonah. For just as Jonah became a sign to the people of Nineveh, so the Son of Man will be to this generation….The people of Nineveh will rise up at the judgment with this generation and will condemn it, because they repented at the proclamation of Jonah, and see, something greater than Jonah is here!" (Lk 11:29–30, 32)

Jesus spoke out prophetically about many of the same things as did the prophets of old. Often he chose to do this with irony, contrast, and hyperbole, figures of speech that highlighted the paradoxical nature of his message. In regard to cult and worship, Jesus' favorite target was the scribes and Pharisees, groupings of active and educated laity who in their zeal for religious piety had replaced a religion of interiority with a religion of form. While these influential leaders seemed to hold Jesus in a wary respect, his actions and behaviors, so many of which seemed to purposely challenge their own religious practices, were a continual source of consternation and anger. When they chided his disciples for picking and eating grain on the Sabbath, he retorted, "But if you had known what this means, 'I desire mercy and not sacrifice,' you would not have condemned the guiltless. For the Son of Man is lord of the Sabbath."(Mt 12:7–8)

Again he entered the synagogue, and a man was there who had a withered hand. They watched him to see whether he would cure him on the Sabbath, so that they might accuse him. And he said to the man who had the withered hand, "Come forward." Then he said to them, "Is it lawful to do good or to do harm on the Sabbath, to save life or to kill?" But they were silent. He looked around at them with anger; he was grieved at their hardness of heart and said to the man, "Stretch out your hand." He stretched it out, and his hand was restored. The Pharisees went out and immediately conspired with the Herodians against him, how to destroy him. (Mk 3:1–6)

Jesus also spoke out against the lifestyle of the rich, who had no concern for those who were less fortunate than they. With irony he described the situation of a rich man whose prosperity continued to increase. The man decided to tear down his barns and build still bigger ones, where he could store his wealth. Self-contented, he planned to eat, drink, and be merry. "But God said to him, 'You fool! This very night your life is being demanded of you. And the things you have prepared, whose will they be?' So it is with those who store up treasures for themselves but are not rich toward God." (Lk 12: 20–21) Nor did he seem to hold out much hope that the rich would ever be able to repent on their own power. "It is easier for a camel to go through the eye of a needle than for someone who is rich to enter the kingdom of God." (Mk 10:25)

It is frequently the nature of the prophet to make people feel uncomfortable. That is why prophets are called the conscience of Israel. In this regard Jesus seemed to fit well into the prophetic role. He made those around him, especially the powerful, so uncomfortable that eventually they had to find some means to get him out of the way. The fear that he had come to change things radically was more than they could bear. Yet Jesus did not see himself as a destroyer. His criticism of the rich and powerful was ultimately meant for their benefit. While his detractors might accuse him of undermining the law of their ancestors, Jesus saw himself as the true keeper of the law. "I have not come to abolish the law, but to fulfill it." (Mt 5:17)

Jesus the Teacher

While prophets were rare in Judea and Galilee at the time of Jesus, teachers were not. Judaism is a religion that holds religious education in high esteem, and there were any number of learned individuals who were recognized as teachers. The title of teacher was not an official position, but was instead a title given to show respect or to acknowledge wisdom and learning. In the New Testament the Greek word that is used for teacher is *didaskalos*. It is likely, as stated in John's gospel, that it represents the Hebrew word *rabbi*, which at the time of Jesus would not have carried the official status that it would later take on. Jesus is frequently addressed in this way. His acceptance of the title, however, is paradoxical. In Mt 10:24–25 ("it is enough for the disciple to be like the teacher, and the slave like the master.") Jesus speaks of a teacher in a way that would seem to refer to himself. He very clearly accepts the title in chapter thirteen of John in the context of washing the feet of his disciples. But in Mt 23:8 ("But you are not to be called rabbi, for you have one teacher, and you are all students") he seems to prohibit the title's use in a passage that quite possibly reflects the community's later disagreements with their Jewish neighbors.

The approach that Jesus takes to teaching is in a sense like concentric circles. While he continually taught the crowds that gathered around him, he would reserve some special teachings for his disciples, and within that number it would seem that the Twelve received special attention. His teaching had a wide range. He explained the law and the prophets, he addressed both personal and social morality, and he generally taught how to attain a right relationship with God and to grow in it. He taught by word and by example, both of which carried with them great power. The teaching of Jesus, we are told, was not like that of his contemporaries. Mark, for instance, tells us that the people of Capernaum "were astounded at his teaching, for he taught them as one having authority, and not as the scribes." (Mk 1:22)

It is hard to determine if Jesus purposely developed paradox as a rhetorical style. Certainly not all his teachings are paradoxical, for he was not really interested in paradox as an overarching methodology. It was more that Jesus naturally thought with the kind of transforming consciousness that made his teaching transcend the usual mental dualities through which most of us tend to think. "The eye is the lamp of the body. So if your eye is healthy, your whole body will be full of light; but if your eye is unhealthy, your whole body will be full of darkness. If then the light in you is darkness, how great is the darkness." (Mt 6:22–23) This passage about moral discernment and life orientation leaves us wondering in the end. We who so often smugly believe we understand the nature of health and unhealth, of light and darkness, how are we to judge our own actions and the motivations hidden within them?

One of the outcomes of transforming thought is the ability to differentiate between the essentials and the nonessentials. This is brought out nowhere better than in the Sermon on the Mount (Mt 5–7). It is widely considered to contain some of the deepest core of Jesus' teaching, but it is a discourse that is filled with extreme statements. "If your right eye causes you to sin, tear it out and throw it away; it is better for you to lose one of your members than for your whole body to be thrown into hell. And if your right hand causes you to sin, cut it off and throw it away; it is better for you to lose one of your members than for your whole body to go into hell." (Mt 5:29–30) By and large the Christian tradition has not felt this passage should be taken literally. But are we to say the same about this passage? "But I say to you, Do not resist an evildoer. But if anyone strikes you on the right cheek, turn the other also; and if anyone wants to sue you and take your coat, give your cloak as well; and if anyone forces you to go one mile, go also the second mile." (Mt 5:39–41) This passage is just as challenging, just as uncompromising.

These passages and so many others like them, while not paradoxical per se, can only be spoken healthily by someone who lives at the level of transforming consciousness. Otherwise they could represent a distorted and dangerous view of life. In themselves they are extreme statements. The first appears to encourage self-mutilation, while the second could be interpreted as cowardly appeasement. To lift either of them out of the context of the Sermon on the Mount, or, more properly, out of the context that Jesus himself provides for them, is a very risky thing. If a family member did such things, would we not likely suggest they needed some help, perhaps critical help?

And yet Jesus does not have a distorted sense of reality. He is not insane, nor is he unbalanced. He does, however, live with an acute sense of paradox. This awareness of paradox and transforming thought gives him a freedom of expression shared by very few. Because Jesus experiences reality with a profound understanding of paradox, he can make extreme statements without being an extremist. Can we make the same claim? We live in a world that is inundated with the language of extremism, but it does not possess the same kind of freedom. It is used by those who wish to express hatred or prejudice, or by people who are attempting to put themselves in the spotlight, or by those whose own unbalance has brought violence and chaos onto others. In the twentieth century extremism literally brought the world to its knees. It has been neither free nor transforming. How far is our common experience of social extremism from the profound extremism of this "simple" Jewish teacher!

One of the extremes that we find in the teaching of Jesus revolves around power. Jesus claims extreme power for himself on many occasions. We have seen above how he claimed to be lord of the Sabbath. Even more contentiously, he claimed to have authority over the temple, as seen in accounts found in the synoptic gospels where Jesus drives from the temple those who had gathered there to carry out business related to temple sacrifice. "It is written, 'My house shall be a house of prayer'; but you have made it a den of robbers." (Lk 19:46) He delivers a scathing attack against the scribes and Pharisees in chapter twenty-three of Matthew's gospel, calling them blind guides, hypocrites, and whitewashed tombs full of the bones of the dead. These influential people fare no better in chapters eight and nine of John's gospel. This gospel even has Jesus standing toe to toe with Pilate, the Roman procurator, at the scene of Jesus' trial. "You would have no power over me,"Jesus says, "unless it had been given you from above." (Jn 19:11)

Yet Jesus' teachings on power are basically the shunning of power. "You know that among the Gentiles those whom they recognize as their rulers lord it over them, and their great ones are tyrants over them. But it is not so among you; but whoever wishes to become great among you must be your servant, and whoever wishes to be first among you must be slave of all. For the Son of Man came not to be served but to serve, and to give his life a ransom for many." (Mk 10:42–45) When asked by his disciples who would be greatest in the Reign of God, Jesus stood a child, dependent and without status, before them. "Truly I tell you, unless you change and become like children, you will never enter the kingdom of heaven. Whoever becomes humble like this child is the greatest in the kingdom of heaven."(Mt 18:3–4) In a similar way in John's gospel, at the scene of the last supper, Jesus washes the feet of his disciples. He explains to them, "Do you know what I have done to you? You call me Teacher and Lord—and you are right, for that is what I am. So if I, your Lord and Teacher, have washed your feet, you also ought to wash one another's feet."(Jn 13:12–14)

Just as the basic message of Jesus was the appearance of the Reign of God, so the core of his teaching was centered around discipleship as it was understood from the perspective of the Reign. We might already have the sense that, paradoxically, Jesus, the one who showed unlimited compassion to all he met, healing the sick and forgiving the sinner, set almost impossible standards for his disciples to meet. They were expected to undergo radical renunciation. "If any want to become my followers, let them deny themselves and take up their cross and follow me. For those who want to save their life will lose it, and those who lose their life for my sake will find it. For what will it profit them if they gain the whole world but forfeit their life? Or what will they give in return for their life?" (Mt 16:24–26) This renunciation was to affect every dimension of their lives. "Whoever loves father or mother more than me is not worthy of me; and whoever loves son or daughter more than me is not worthy of me; and whoever does not take up the cross and follow me is not worthy of me." (Mt 10:37–38)

The difficulty of this renunciation is brought out clearly in the story of the rich young man in Matthew's gospel (Mt 19:16–30). The young man does not come seeking discipleship but some guarantee of eternal life. He tells Jesus that he already keeps the law, but he needs some further assurance. What Jesus gives him instead is a challenge. "If you wish to be perfect, go, sell your possessions, and give the money to the poor, and you will have treasure in heaven; then come follow me."

The young man turns away disappointed, but Jesus uses the occasion to teach about the power that riches can have over us. The disciples are surprised, because in their tradition riches are usually associated with God's blessing. But Peter, who has understood the nature of renunciation that Jesus demands, in effect asks for a clarification. "Look, we have left everything and followed you. What then will we have?"

We can understand Peter's question. Jesus is asking them to leave not only greed and wealth and power behind. He is asking them to give up many things that traditional Jews would understand to be part of their spirituality, family ties, ancestral inheritance, parental responsibilities, and the opportunity to be a gainful provider for their dependents. What indeed will they have left? Jesus then, in paradoxical reversal, offers them back everything they have let go of. He tells them that "everyone who has left houses or brothers or sisters or father or mother or children or fields, for my name's sake, will receive a hundredfold, and will inherit eternal life. But many who are first will be last, and the last will be first."

This reversal of discipleship is enshrined in the two accounts of the beatitudes that we have from the gospels of Matthew and Luke. The accounts are somewhat different. Matthew's account in the Sermon on the Mount (5:1–12) has to some degree spiritualized that of Luke (6:20–26). Nor does Matthew have the accompanying woes that we find in Luke. The general tenor of the two passages is the same, however. What now seems like a curse in life will be reversed, and those who live in various forms of misery will find their lives a blessing. It is interesting that the beatitudes do not see this as simply offering a new perspective to those in need. There is no sense of anything such as "Look on the bright side; things aren't as bad as they seem." They offer, instead, the prospect of real change, of restructured reality. This is the prospect of living in the Reign of God. This is transforming consciousness. It is not about seeing things in the best possible light. It is the experience of a new creation.

Jesus the Storyteller

One of the most interesting features of the teaching style of Jesus is that much of it took the form of storytelling. Storytelling is one of the most universal means by which humans convey important ideas to one another. Every culture, no matter how primitive or advanced, has its stories and its storytellers. Stories are not simply ways we have found to entertain children, or even adults. Whether it is through forms we call myths or fairy tales or fables or the "great American novel," meaning and purpose are explained and carried on in a culture by means of its stories. In many cultures the story-teller holds a revered position, the one who is keeper of that society's greatest treasures, its origins, its values, its identity, its soul.

There are as many different kinds of stories and storytellers as there are cultures. Jesus was not the same kind of storyteller as the African tribesman or the European troubadour or the Oriental Zen master. Nor are the parables of Jesus very similar to the fairy tales of Grimm or the yarns of Mark Twain. The word parable, the word that designates the kind of stories Jesus told, suggests a comparison, an extended simile. Most commentators understand the basis of the parable to spring from everyday life. The material that Jesus uses is not fabulous or even miraculous; it is drawn from elements of life within the experience of his hearers.

That does not mean, however, that Jesus' parables are in any way ordinary. At times they are disarming, at times disorienting; they can lead along, and then suddenly trip you up. They were often perplex-ing for their original hearers, and sometimes infuriating. Their para-doxical nature has only recently come to be widely appreciated. In patristic and medieval times the parables were primarily seen as alle-gories, where the individual elements in the stories stood for corre-sponding spiritual truths or realities. From the end of the nineteenth century well into the twentieth, the parables were mostly treated as moral narratives essentially presenting one basic message. Today it is more widely recognized that, like most stories, the parables of Jesus can speak from many levels.

Why was it that Jesus chose to teach the crowds by using such sto-ries? If we can accept what we hear in chapter 13 of Matthew's gospel when his disciples asked just that question (13:10–17), it was a matter of recognizing different levels of knowledge. Jesus expected the crowds to be bewildered by his parables, but he also desired that his

disciples would possess more understanding of the truths he was trying to articulate through these metaphors. He tells them paradoxically, "For to those who have, more will be given, and they will have an
abundance; but from those who have nothing, even what they have
will be taken away."(vs. 12) It is questionable how much more than
the crowds the disciples actually understood at that point, but at least
they remembered the parables because the gospels have recorded a
good number of them.

Matthew's chapter thirteen is itself a treasure chest of parables,
collected around a common theme, the description of the Reign of
God. Jesus never offered a verbal definition of the Reign; it was,
instead, through the use of such parables and other enigmatic teachings that he attempted to describe it clearly enough that the disciples
would recognize it when they stumbled over it. The parables of
chapter 13 offer a wealth of information about the Reign, information about its pervasiveness, its transmission, and its ultimate success. A number of the parables, however, give us special insight into
its hidden or secret nature. In the first two parables of the chapter,
the parable of the sower and the parable of the wheat and the weeds,
Jesus offered a common image of growing seeds, an image that must
have held great mystery for the agrarian world he lived in. In both
parables, even though they have different themes, the dark and hidden nature of seed growth provides the backdrop for examining
some of the "quirks" of the Reign, for instance, its fragile relationship to the world and its willingness to coexist with evil. We could
compare the similarity of the nature of the seed's growth in these
parables to that of the parable in Mark 4:26–29, the parable of the
seed growing secretly. The man in Mark's parable, like the house-
holder in the parable of the weeds, gathers the fruit of the harvest he
has planted, but he hasn't the slightest idea of how it came about. A
similar mystery of vegetative growth is present in the parable of the
mustard seed in Matthew 13:31–32. The Reign of God grows, but no
one can fully comprehend its mystery.

The parable of the leaven in vs. 33 of Matthew's chapter thirteen
offers a related image. The woman in the parable hides the leaven in
the dough, and once there, unseen, it causes the entire mixture to

rise. In vs. 44 Jesus offers the parable of the hidden treasure. The man in the parable finds the treasure by accident, but then must himself hide it again in order to keep it secure while he makes his preparations to legally possess it by renouncing (selling) all else. All of these parables present us with various features of the hiddenness of the Reign of God.

But what, if anything, does hiddenness have to do with paradox? While these parables do not directly present the Reign as being paradoxical in nature (except for the instruction Jesus offers in vs. 12 as to why he uses them to begin with), we could say that the presence of paradox is implied in each one. The parables might suggest to us that paradox itself is a hidden way to come into possession of the Reign. While living through the paradoxes of life, we do not fully understand them, and the fruit that we harvest in their transformation is at once ours and not ours. Or conversely, the parables might suggest that the Reign is in some way best approached through paradox and mystery. It is something right before us that we do not see; it is a valuable treasure that we possess but do not control.

At the end of Jesus' teaching in chapter thirteen he turns again to his disciples. "'Have you understood all this?' They answered, 'Yes.' And he said to them, 'Therefore every scribe who has been trained for the kingdom of heaven is like the master of a household who brings out of his treasure what is new and what is old.'" (Mt 13:51–52) There is, in other words, a value to both sides, in this case to what is traditional and what is innovative. A question remains for the disciples, however. How were they to get what is necessary to enable them to make the essential discernment that will release the treasure, the presence and the power of the Reign? Did they already possess this training of which Jesus speaks as emphatically as their response suggests? The weight of the gospel would indicate that they did not, at least not yet. And of course, we are so much like the disciples in this regard. We are frequently so quick to say we understand the process of the Reign of God in our lives as well. But the parables teach us that, in the face of paradox and mystery, patience is necessary in order to see the fruit God wishes to bring forth.

Jesus the Healer

If we can understand reversal as a central aspect of Jesus' prophetic mission and renunciation as a key factor in his teachings on discipleship, how are we to understand the nature of paradox in the other clearly demonstrable aspect of the mission of Jesus, that of healing? In the view we receive from the gospels, the healing ministry of Jesus was the most dramatic feature of his mission. It was the primary aspect of his ministry that seemed to initially attract people to Jesus. Perhaps this attraction would later be deepened by his prophetic ministry, and broadened by his powerful teaching, but it was the presence of Jesus as a healing force that made the crowds first follow after him with an enthusiasm and determination that frequently caused him and his disciples great physical discomfort.

The paradox of healing in the mission of Jesus lay in its sign value. While refusing to perform signs upon request, the healings of Jesus had clear features of the very type of work that many were demanding to see from him. By a sign, I mean some type of manifestation that is at once pointing to a deeper reality in some way present in the work but still not fully or completely present. As signs, the healings he performed were never ends in themselves, but were always pointing to something beyond their immediate aspect, no matter how dramatic. This would be clear if for no other reason than that he healed selectively. Jesus cured, but Jesus did not cure all. Instead, as a sign, the healing pointed to something not yet present. It was to reflect the reality of transformed life in the Reign. Those who were healed and those who witnessed the healing were to recognize the transforming power that would be made available to all in the new age. That is why Jesus would give this power to his disciples as he sent them out to preach (Mt 10:1). It was not something to be identified with him but with the Reign.

But while healing was a sign of the Reign, in the Reign itself there would actually be no healing. This was because at that time everything would already be transformed. While the gospels did not have the language, they imaged Jesus as something of an energy field. As he goes out in mission, that field increases. His preaching and teaching expand the Reign by the very presence of his person. So too, when

Jesus heals, the energy of the Reign extends itself. The healing is a public display of the nature of the Reign.

In Mark and Luke, Jesus experiences healing as a kind of power that goes out from him (Mk 5:30; Lk 8:46). Healing, however, is also power that is limited. Jesus has the power to heal, but his healing cannot in itself change the inner heart. For that, a kind of power is necessary in the recipient and the observers: that is, the power of faith. Sometimes that power is present and sometimes it isn't. In chapter six of Mark, Jesus comes into his own neighborhood and begins to teach in the synagogue. But many there know him, and begin to question how this "known quantity" can be anything special. "And they took offense at him. Then Jesus said to them, 'Prophets are not without honor except in their hometown, and among their own kin, and in their own house.' And he could do no deed of power there, except that he laid his hands on a few sick people and cured them. And he was amazed at their unbelief." (Mk 6:3–6)

The gospel of Luke gives us another way in which the power of healing can be ineffective, even when it is "successful." In chapter seventeen we hear of the story of the ten lepers. They come to Jesus and call upon him to have compassion upon them. He does, and tells them to go show themselves to a priest in fulfillment of the Mosaic law. On their way they are healed. The story does not tell us whether they ever fulfill that request, for it focuses on the one leper who returns to Jesus praising God. Jesus credits the faith of this individual, who happens to be a Samaritan, but takes offense at the ingratitude of the other nine (Lk 17:11–19). While the healing itself is a sign of the Reign, the reality of the Reign can be resisted in this case by human self-centeredness.

Healing has a communal dimension to it. In Mark 2:1–12 Jesus heals a paralytic who is lowered through the roof by his friends because the crowd was too great to get to him in any other way. Jesus sees their faith, and this causes him to grant both healing and forgiveness. It is also the faith of the father (vs. 24) in the story of healing in Mark chapter nine that causes him to heal the man's epileptic son.

But sometimes the healing is a sign against the community. In Luke 13:10–17, while teaching in a synagogue, Jesus heals a woman who has been crippled for eighteen years, but because it is on the Sabbath the leader of the synagogue chides the people for agreeing to submit to healing on this day. Perhaps the man's inability to directly confront him causes Jesus to answer back. His rebuttal is telling. "You hypocrites! Does not each of you on the Sabbath untie his ox or his donkey from the manger, and lead it away to give it water? And ought not this woman, a daughter of Abraham whom Satan bound for eighteen long years, be set free from this bondage on the Sabbath day?" (vs. 15–16) The use of the plural, "hypocrites,"would tend to indicate that Jesus' anger is not primarily at the official but at all those who support the system of cultic worship. Along with Satan they have done their share in holding this woman bound. By referring to her as a daughter of Abraham, Jesus is saying that she is a child of the covenant and should enjoy the protection of the law. But while exceptions are widely made for beasts of burden on the Sabbath, no one seems to be paying much attention to her humanness or to the right of inheritance she has by way of the covenant. Here the healing of the woman also becomes a prophetic statement.

The same kind of message is given in chapter nine of John's gospel with the healing of the man born blind (vs. 1–41). In this chapter, which reads almost like a comedy, Jesus heals a man who has been blind from birth "so that God's work might be revealed in him." One would think that everyone would rejoice, but because it is the Sabbath, the Pharisees who are present seek to get to the heart of the matter and discover how this sacrilege could have happened. Through a series of interviews with the man and his parents they are made to look foolish, for they cannot bring themselves to admit that the hand of God was at work. In a paradoxical statement of reversal Jesus says, "I came into this world for judgment so that those who do not see may see, and those who do see may become blind." (vs. 39)

All of this tends to make us view healing as a very fragile reality. While it displays the power of God, it has no power to effectively bring God into a faithless human heart. While it can usher in the Reign, it can also bring down judgment upon those who refuse its sign. Nor is any instance of healing final and definitive. In reference to the casting out of unclean spirits, Jesus offers the image of one uprooted spirit who roams through the wastelands of the world looking for someplace to rest. Eventually it returns to its original host with seven other spirits more evil than itself, "and the last state of that person is worse than the first." (Mt 12:45) In the same way in John's gospel, having cured the man at the pool of Bethesda, Jesus exhorts him, "See, you have been made well! Do not sin any more, so that nothing worse happens to you." (Jn 5:14) Healing is a gift from God, but like all God's gifts, it seems we receive it into our hands, which then can either support it or crush it.

Outrageous Mystery

We can see the thread of paradox running through the mission of Jesus as portrayed through the roles of prophet, teacher, and healer. None of these religious roles, at least as Jesus lives them out in the gospels, would be called commonplace religious functions. The average person might have prophetic moments, or moments of wisdom and insight, or might occasionally be an agent of healing, but relatively few make claim to be identified in one of these roles. In my presentation of paradox in the mission of Jesus, they have served as definable contemporary religious categories that offer some reference point from which to speak about Jesus. However, none of these categories holds the full ministry of Jesus. Nor does their combination sum up what we experience of him in the gospels. There is something left over, something still indefinable that remains to be explored.

Perhaps it lies in the fact that the gospels also make claim to Jesus as the messiah. As I mentioned above, this is a claim of unique proportions. While not everyone in Judaism was waiting for the messiah (some were looking for various other eschatological figures), the messianic appearance was still regarded as a definitive event. Originally the term designated the heir to the Davidic throne, the new king who was anointed to lead the people. In time it came to indicate a future king, one who would again establish the royal house of Judah. Still later the messiah came to be connected to the belief in God's conclusive intervention in order to make right a world gone wrong.

There is no doubt that the gospels make the claim that Jesus is the messiah that the people are waiting for. But can even the title of messiah contain what the gospels present to us of Jesus? We saw reflected in the story at the beginning of this chapter that Peter and the other disciples closest to Jesus were not able to neatly fit their expectations of the messiah into their experiences of this man. This story was an adaptation from the gospel of Mark (8:27–38), but the underlying mystery of Jesus is not just present in Mark; it is reflected in various ways in all the gospels. In actuality each gospel to some degree makes a far greater claim for the person of Jesus. John's prologue is probably the clearest expression of this. In what has come to be called high Christology, John makes the direct claim of divinity for Jesus. "In the beginning was the Word, and the Word was with God, and the Word was God. He was in the beginning with God."(Jn 1:1–2) While the synoptic gospels do not make such a direct claim, there are a number of ways in which we can see this alluded to indirectly. One very common way is for the evangelist to attribute to Jesus what was understood to apply to God in the Old Testament (cf. Mk 2:7; Lk 8:24–25; Mt 23:37, to mention a few).

Still, the gospels are documents of faith, and their claims as to who Jesus was remain in the realm of faith. Perhaps the old adage holds truest here: for those with faith, no proof is necessary; for those without faith, no proof is possible. Indeed for the early church the gospels were not meant to be proof texts at all. They were meant to be good news. The proof would come specifically from the community's experience of the risen Jesus and from the work of the Spirit among the believers, manifested for all to see.

It might be necessary to clarify something about paradox and belief in the divinity of Christ. I do not wish to imply that the view of Jesus I have presented, as one steeped in paradox and transforming consciousness, would automatically indicate a claim to anything beyond the human. On the contrary, it is my view that all of us should be seeking to live our lives at this level. We would expect, however, that one for whom claims of divinity were made, at the least, would manifest this kind of consciousness. That Jesus perceived the world through paradox, and directly and indirectly articulated that world view in his words and actions, is certainly not a proof of divinity, but it is a reinforcement of our view of Jesus as one who had at least reached the greatest human potential we can imagine. It would also be expected that, since paradox opens out into mystery, it could in fact be seen as a steppingstone beyond human potential. In other words, the presence of paradox and transforming consciousness in Jesus are consistent with the Church's claim.

In the end, therefore, we might be left only with mystery. Those of us with faith as well as many of those without it would perhaps be able to recognize that, as the gospels describe Jesus, there is something in him that remains undefined. He is a mystery, and in that he is a paradox in himself. But if he is a mystery, Jesus is an outrageous mystery. A person can be mysterious in many ways—by remaining aloof and hidden, or by doing odd or unusual things, or by speaking in cryptic and esoteric language, or by performing rituals that in some way veil what is held to be true. But Jesus was mysterious in speaking plainly and openly of his perceptions of the Reign of God.

We certainly could not say that Jesus attempted to hide himself or make himself unavailable. Although at times danger or fatigue required that he withdraw from the public view, Jesus had a very high profile. He was with people, teaching them, healing them, ministering to them with compassion. But Jesus did not "fit right in." He always seemed to be the center of a swirl of activity, partly because of his effective ministry, but also partly because of his controversial presence. Jesus presented himself to others in an outrageous manner. The gospel of Mark suggests that this was a source of deep embarrassment for his family, who at one point sought to restrain him (3:21). Jesus, however, used the occasion to teach about the Reign and about discipleship. "'Who are my mother and my brothers?' And looking at those who sat around him, he said, 'Here are my mother and my brothers! Whoever does the will of God is my brother and sister and mother.'"(Mk 3:33–35)

John's gospel records an incident close to the end of Jesus' ministry (Jn 12:1–8). He is in Bethany in the home of Martha and Mary and Lazarus (whom he had recently raised from the dead). Mary takes a costly perfume and begins to anoint the feet of Jesus and dry them with her hair. Judas Iscariot, who is about to betray him and whom the gospel portrays as something of a thief, objects that the perfume was used for this wasteful purpose. It could have been sold, and the money given to the poor. At face value this does not seem to be an unreasonable observation. Jesus, however, anticipating his death, says, "Leave her alone. She bought it so that she might keep it for the day of my burial. You always have the poor with you, but you do not always have me." This response seems to be the reverse of so many teachings of Jesus, where he identifies with the poor and encourages renunciation. It seems to be opposite to Jesus' own action of washing his disciples' feet in the next chapter of John. Whatever the moral state of Judas, we are still left wondering about this apparent reversal in Jesus. While this passage clearly has to do with the importance of Jesus in the course of God's plan, we are still left puzzled by his divergence from our expectations of him.

Jesus seems to be fully aware that he presents himself as a shocking figure to just about everybody at one time or other. No less a person than John the Baptist is not sure what to make of him. From prison John sends disciples to inquire about Jesus. Jesus sends them back to John, telling them to report out of their own experiences. "Go and tell John what you hear and see: the blind receive their sight, the lame walk, the lepers are cleansed, the deaf hear, the dead are raised, and the poor have good news brought to them." But he then concludes with something of a challenge to John and to us. "And blessed is anyone who takes no offense at me." (Mt 11:2–6) Jesus then goes on to praise John, a man of controversy himself. Comparing their two different styles, Jesus notes that both of them were occasions of scandal for those who had closed their ears to God's message delivered through them. "For John came neither eating nor drinking, and they say, 'He has a demon'; the Son of Man came eating and drinking, and they say, 'Look, a glutton and a drunkard, a friend of tax collectors and sinners!' Yet wisdom is vindicated by her deeds."(vs. 18–19)

Perhaps, therefore, the greatest paradox in the mission of Jesus is that we are asked to embrace both him and the Reign, a package deal, without being able to fully understand either. Through these two thousand years of the Christian message, despite the scholastic analysis of the great theologians, the scepticism of the scientific world of the Enlightenment, and even the contemporary arrogance of the quest for the historical Jesus, we are still confronted with the mystery of who Jesus is and what it is he desires to bring about for our world. We are, it seems, always like the Samaritan woman in chapter four of John's gospel. We do not recognize who it is who has entered into our reality, nor do we know how to respond to his request. Jesus asks the woman for a drink of water, and she takes him at one level, not realizing that he speaks to her out of an entirely different consciousness. He says, "If you knew the gift of God, and who it is that is saying to you, 'Give me a drink,' you would have asked him, and he would have given you living water." (Jn 4:10)

The Death of Jesus

After everything said to this point, it is paradoxical in itself that the height of the enigma surrounding Jesus was little concerned, if at all, with anything that he did, but revolved around something that happened to him. Even though the ministry of Jesus was filled with paradox in his words, his actions, and even his self-presentation, it was the death of Jesus that became the formative (and transformative) event of the Christian faith. Jesus lived at the level of transforming consciousness, even though he found himself mostly unable to convey this awareness to others, including some of his closest disciples. At the end of his life they still tended to experience him and the Reign he preached very literally and very dualistically. Paradox overtook them, however, in the events of his death and its aftermath. What Jesus lived in his earthly life took on transformative dimensions in his dying.

How are we to understand the death of Jesus? We would first have to consider what we understand death to be. At its most observable level it is the end of our biological life—the final chapter, we might say in a more poetic sense, in the novel we have spent our lives writing. In our normal linguistic usage, it is often placed in contrast to life. "It was a life or death decision,"we say. While our own death is usually projected somewhere into the future, our life is generally perceived to be a present experience…that is, until death snatches it away. Does life continue after death? We have the hope that it does. Most religions, although not all, have incorporated some form of life after death into their core of beliefs. Still, at an observable level, life continues only in what we might call legacy, what each of us leaves behind.

In the time following the events of Calvary, however, it became the belief of the earliest disciples that it was more than the legacy of Jesus that continued beyond his death. It became, and continues to be, the belief of the Christian community that Jesus experienced a full and complete resurrection. That is, life did not end for Jesus, nor did it simply remain the same as it was. This resurrection was new life, but not just for Jesus; it also meant new life for us. We were to share in the resurrection event of Jesus. "But if we have died with Christ, we believe that we will also live with him. We know that Christ, being raised from the dead, will never die again; death no longer has dominion over him. The death he died, he died to sin, once for all; but the life he lives, he lives to God. So you also must consider yourselves dead to sin and alive to God in Christ Jesus." (Rom 6:8–11)

This faith in the resurrection of Jesus became the core belief in the life and self-understanding of the Christian community. It remains so today. Celebrated liturgically during the three days between Good Friday and Easter Sunday, the resurrection of Jesus is tied to just about every belief that Christians hold, from the means by which we receive forgiveness of sin to the hope we hold in our own new life. Take away the resurrection of Jesus, and there is not much left to hold onto. Writing to the community at Corinth concerning some members who were denying their own eventual resurrection, Paul states,

> If there is no resurrection of the dead, then Christ has not been raised; and if Christ has not been raised, then our proclamation has been in vain and your faith has been in vain. We are even found to be misrepresenting God, because we testified of God that he raised Christ—whom he did not raise if it is true that the dead are not raised. For if the dead are not raised, then Christ has not been raised. If Christ has not been raised, your faith is futile and you are still in your sins. Then those also who have died in Christ have perished. If for this life only we have hoped in Christ, we are of all people most to be pitied. (1 Cor 15:13–19)

But how can we understand something so unobservable, so incomprehensible, so paradoxical? What was there about the death of Jesus and its aftermath that led his followers to the conviction that resurrection had happened?

The death of Jesus is one of the few events in his life that is verified in extra-biblical sources. There is not much doubt about what happened. He was killed by the Roman garrison in Jerusalem upon the order of Pontius Pilate, who was procurator of Judea. The form of execution was known as crucifixion, a custom Semitic in its origins rather than Roman. The cause of death would probably have been asphyxiation, which likely occurred quickly because Jesus would have been exhausted by the severe torture that preceded it.

There has, however, always been speculation about what happened after his death. In a relatively short period of time there was no longer a body to point to in order to verify that Jesus had remained dead. His disciples came to believe that this was because he had been raised from the dead. Opponents of this new Way found other explanations for the loss of the body; for instance, that it had been carried off by his disciples and hidden. The community of believers developed two different scriptural traditions as proof that Jesus was in fact raised. The first was the tradition of the empty tomb, which in itself offered no proof of resurrection as such, but was a necessary prerequisite. But the second, a tradition of various appearances by Jesus following his death, was witnessed by a substantial number of people, according to Paul (1 Cor 15:5–8), all of whom happened to be believers.

There are a variety of opinions on how early these traditions emerged. They were well in place by the writing of the four canonical gospels, with the possible exception of the earliest form of Mark. The timetable presented in the gospels would suggest that these traditions began immediately on the first day of the week following the crucifixion with the discovery of the empty tomb by some of the women disciples of Jesus, followed that same day by the appearances of Jesus to them and to the eleven remaining apostles. In today's age of historical criticism and the developing "quest" for what can be verified historically through textual and extra-textual sources, many people have a tendency to hold to a very strict standard of what can be historically provable. This movement by and large has been very profitable for modern biblical scholarship, as long as it is recognized that to be unable to prove something historically is not the same as disproving it. Some would therefore claim that the tradition of the appearances of Jesus was much slower to develop in the faith community than the gospels suggest. This, however, is not the same thing as saying the resurrection did not take place. It might have more to do with the disciples' own process of awareness.

Whatever the actual development of the community's understanding of the resurrection, there are a number of aspects of what this occurrence was and was not that have always been part of the Church's tradition. First, the resurrection was not the resuscitation of the pre-crucifixion body of Jesus. It was not the same kind of event, in other words, that had happened to Lazarus or the son of the widow of Naim. Furthermore, the resurrection was transformative. It made Jesus different than he was, even to the point of being unrecognizable at times. Finally, the resurrection was something that happened to the entire person of Jesus. It was not just a raising of Jesus' spirit, much less a kind of symbolic affirmation of his spiritual and ethical teachings.

Along with a concern for what the resurrection was comes the importance of what it meant. How did the early Church understand it? This again hinges on how it understood the meaning of Jesus' death. Was it something necessary? Did God require it and freely accept it as a death for others, a sacrifice for human sinfulness, as Jesus had indicated at the last supper accounts (in which case resurrection was the sign of God's acceptance)? Or was Jesus' death not acceptable to God, something that was wrong and needed to be overturned by resurrection in order for the life of Jesus to be vindicated? Or was the early community unsure and divided on the issue? Perhaps in the accounts of the gospels the death of Jesus contains within it what appears to be a fundamental contradiction. Was the death of Jesus a tragedy or a triumph; did it need to be vindicated or celebrated? As with the nature of contradiction, we are then left with a sense that the passion narratives in the gospels are somehow a delicately balanced mobile, a patchwork of theological opinions attempting to hold together a young community deeply squared off in opposition. Were the predictions of death that Jesus makes in the gospels ultimately a tool that the gospel writers used to weave together a solution that would rectify the two contradictory positions?

There is another way of understanding this dilemma. Maybe the reason that the evangelists did not completely choose between these two opposing positions about the death of Jesus was that they and their communities came to understand that they could both be true. Perhaps instead of seeing them as contradictions, the community of disciples in the light of Easter faith came to recognize them as a paradox. They had lived with this man of paradox through the years of Jesus' ministry; had the transforming power of his death finally been the event that broke open their resistances and broke through to a new level of awareness? To say that Jesus' death was a sacrificial death for others and freely accepted by God would appear to stand in contrast to the belief that his death was a closing of accessibility to God and needed to be overturned. But in effect the faith community has always held that both of these statements are true at one and the same time.

From this understanding the resurrection is the event that brings together these two opposing statements about the death of Jesus. Yet it is of great importance to see that it is not the same as either. Nor, since these two understandings of his death stand in opposition to each other, can the resurrection simply be the sum of the two. Nor is it a compromise position between them. It is, in other words, a new reality. It does not take away from either understanding, nor does it change their truth. Instead, it lifts our understanding of Jesus' death to a new level. This new reality, however, is not simply an idea. It is in fact the continuation of this person, Jesus risen from death. It is the Jesus whose mission it was to proclaim the Reign, but it is also the Jesus who has given new meaning to what that Reign looks like and how it comes about. It is the Jesus who remains a permanent symbol of both redemptive suffering love and active nonviolent truth, making them both viable at the same time.

The death and resurrection of Jesus becomes *the* Christian paradigm. The first letter of Peter proclaims, "Blessed be the God and Father of our Lord Jesus Christ! By his great mercy he has given us a new birth into a living hope through the resurrection of Jesus Christ from the dead, and into an inheritance that is imperishable, undefiled, and unfading, kept in heaven for you who are being protected by the power of God through faith for a salvation ready to be revealed in the last time." (1 Pet 1:3–5) The resurrection of Jesus, however, can also serve as an important paradigm for our under-standing of paradox itself. It teaches us something crucial about the process by which paradox takes place. In the first place, we can see from the resurrection that the transforming event in paradox is a new reality, different from either of the two opposing forces. We can also see that the two forces of opposition are not destroyed by the transformation, but are each raised to a kind of new level where they receive new meaning from the transformative event that took place.

We can understand this event in yet another way, as a reconcilia-tion between life and death. At the moment of Calvary, life and death stand in stark contrast. The life of Jesus in all that he did—his teachings, his healings, his compassion—is a witness to the light. "As long as I am in the world, I am the light of the world."(Jn 9:5) The death of Jesus, by contrast, is an abandonment to the darkness. Death, the ending of all that we know of ourselves and our world, is not a welcome guest, and Jesus approaches it with grave misgivings. He struggles with it at Gethsemane, and he voices his feelings of abandonment on the cross. But in dying, Jesus is also becoming truly human, for it is a necessary ingredient to the human condition. In his death Jesus fully comes to terms with God's desire that he be one with us. The Easter event is as much the fulfillment of Christmas, the feast of Incarnation, as it is of Good Friday.

When the breakthrough of resurrection comes for Jesus, it comes for him in only one way, through a complete surrendering to God's will. It is the surrendering of Jesus that allows the resurrection to happen. That is why the remembrance of his time in the garden of Gethsemane, which we commemorate as part of the events of Holy Thursday, has always been personally of great importance to me. At Gethsemane Jesus is aware that events are coming to a head, and that the outcome has become a matter of his very survival. He strug-gles with that reality and questions if there are not other options, but in the end he says, "Yet, not what I want, but what you want." (Mk 14:36) His surrendering only reaches its apex at the event of Calvary, but it had begun before that. And it is on Calvary where the resur-rection of Jesus begins. John's gospel account of the death attempts to show this by having Jesus breathe out his spirit from the cross. In the giving over of his spirit, Jesus begins to rise even as death and life meet in their inevitable embrace.

In the spirituality of paradox, death is neither the end of life nor is it the contradiction of life. Death and life are both transformed into something else, something marvelously alive in God's plan. But the key to it all is the willingness to enter into the act of surrendering. There is nothing automatic about resurrection. We all "die" many times before we die. Our lives are filled with moments of darkness— loneliness, failure, loss and grief, pain and illness, to name a few. It would be comforting to believe that all of these are transformed— comforting, but not true. Their transformation is possible, but not guaranteed. That depends on our willingness and cooperation. We must explore more deeply the experience of surrendering, the ability to let go into transformation.

ENDNOTES

1. I do not mean to imply by this that I think all four gospels are attempting to portray Jesus in the same way. It is very clear that each gospel has its own intention when presenting its image of Jesus. Each evangelist has a clear theological purpose in painting the personality of Jesus as it appears in each work. I am saying that while this is true, there is still a consistent impression of Jesus that runs through the four gospels as a whole. If this were not the case, we would seem to be hearing accounts of four different lives.

III

The Keystone
of Paradox

A Dream: Into the Bowels of the Earth

What follows is a dream that I recorded in my journal on June 13, 1987:

> I am in my hometown of Johnstown, PA. I am with a woman I
> can't identify. We are walking down into the center of the city
> from the hills that surround the city. My sense is that we are
> descending a steep grade, perhaps down what would be
> Bedford Street, but the specific location is indistinct. I stop at
> one point and look at the hills around me. The two of us final-
> ly come into the center of the city, specifically into the industri-
> al section of town. We meet a man the woman knows, who, it
> turns out, is a miner. He is going to take us into a mine. Entry
> into this mine is through two small holes in a floor, like two
> manholes positioned side by side. The holes are filled to the
> surface with water. Without waiting for an invitation, the
> woman dives headfirst into one of the holes. I hesitate to follow.
> I ask the man if it is safe to take any valuables with me. He is
> surprised I haven't been told that I have to leave them above
> ground or they will be ruined. I leave my money and my pass-

port in a jacket. I ask him if there is room to breathe. He vaguely assures me that I will be fine, but that it is way over my head. I plan on going in a little at a time. Supporting myself by my arms on either side of the hole, I enter in up to my waist, but then I hesitate. It is here that the dream ends.

After I had the dream I titled it "Into the Bowels of the Earth"for no conscious reason. Upon later reflection it occurred to me that the title was most likely drawn from the emotional level of my experience of the dream. The bowels are the deepest part of us, but they are not a seemly part. They are smelly and filled with waste. It would be much more pleasant to enter into the "heart" of the earth—more pleasant, but not nearly as honest a rendition of the dream. While no one is forcing me to enter into this mine, I am disturbed that I feel I have to undergo this venture. My disturbance is primarily one of fear, I suspect, but only partly a fear for my life. It is also a fear for my life-as-I-know-it, for the way I have become comfortable and have found my adjustments to life's circumstances. Thus the hesitation even after I have been reassured of my survival.

Jungian spirituality refers to my female companion as an anima figure. She comes from that less-identified-with side of my personality that holds traditionally recognized "feminine" traits. It is characteristic that she would function in the role of a guide, and also a model. Her lack of hesitation stands in sharp contrast to my own procrastination. In the course of my dream journey through the years, my anima had not always been so positive and encouraging, and I had not always willingly followed her lead. It occurs to me that my growing willingness to trust her was one of the primary reasons this dream could come to light at that point in my life. It also, of course, starkly demonstrated that my trust still had some growing to do.

The figure of the miner functions in a very familiar role for me. Many of my dreams have such positive male helpers, mentor figures, in a sense. I reflect that many of them are "hands-on" types of people—miners, foresters, construction foremen. In Jungian terminology, they are all predominantly sensate, skilled workers. I, who am a strongly intuitive person, have only in recent years sought to develop my more sensate side. There is a clue here for me as to what this dive into the depths is likely to consist of. It will necessitate entering into my inferior side, where the dream shows that I am still hesitant to proceed. To do so I must leave behind what has up to now been of great value to me, how I have made my way, how I have paid my way. It is the miner who gives me the important information I need.

How significant that all this happens in my "hometown," in a sense going back to the beginning place of my life journey, and back to its "industrial district." Johnstown traditionally is a steel town, but when I was growing up, the mines surrounded it and provided the mills with their raw material. To be a miner is to be a discoverer within the earth. And of course mines hold the precious metals and earthy resources that possess much more lasting riches than currency, the value of which is much more simply a matter of convention.

But even with a clear guide, a gifted teacher, and the potential for something of more lasting value, it is still hard to let go and "enter in over my head." I still hold onto the sides, hoping I can ease my way into the experience. But perhaps I can only accomplish this task by letting go and plunging in. Perhaps I cannot know ahead of time what it will all entail, or work out my strategy intellectually so I can maintain control of the situation. Perhaps I will have to learn how to breathe under water, something seemingly impossible from my ordinary earthly perspective. Some pertinent questions come to mind. Do I dare take such a risk? Do I dare to risk such a loss of control? What if I am not able to find my way back to the surface again? What if I won't be able to retrieve what I believe to be valuable? What if I don't survive such a plunge, despite all the reassurances to the contrary?

The Experience of Surrender

It is my hope that this dream conveys something of the emotional atmosphere of the experience of surrender as we meet it in the course of our lives. There is the hesitancy that is born of fear, and the ambiguous feeling of wanting to do something but not being able to take the plunge. There is also the feeling of potential loss, as well as apprehension built around the prospects of an uncertain future.

The challenge of surrender can arise over just about any life circumstance. It can be concerned with a big event or a small one. As we will see, it can look like innumerable things and be called by many names. I chose to use this dream because it seemed to identify some very common elements in the general experience of surrender. In its time and place in my life it had a specific context relating to events that were unfolding for me, but in its general imagery I believe it also offers a good taste of what surrender entails as a universal experience.

As the dream imagery suggests, with the first invitation to enter into the experience of surrender there frequently is felt, first of all, the need to become lighter or less encumbered. This can look like having to discard old and fixed values, particularly some that might still seem highly valuable or useful from several of points of view. Then we might find a sense of letting go of something that is held on to, a security point of some sort that appears fixed and stable, and a falling into something that seems in some way dark, unknown, or uncharted. This dark quality removes the semblance of control from us, and it can appear as if we were being set adrift. Consequently there is almost always present within us some quality of resistance to the direction that seems to be emerging. This could have many appearances.

All of this, however, hinges on the fact that in the final analysis surrender is an act of the will, and is therefore something that must be freely chosen. This is very important. There might be a strong invitation to surrender present in an experience, but ultimately there can never be coercion. To coerce is to remove freedom, which critically changes the experience. If in my dream, for instance, the miner had pulled a gun, and said, "Jump in!" we would no longer be dealing with surrender as I intend to use the word. You might object, and say that in this case I would be "surrendering" to the miner and his gun. Linguistically that is correct, but it is giving surrender a different meaning than I intend. We must later explore the difference between letting go and giving up.

The questions at the end of the dream section are questions frequently asked in the midst of the invitation to surrender as it might often occur in our lives. Do I dare to take a risk? This is the recognition that with freedom always comes risk. I could break the bank or I could lose my shirt. Or more appropriately, I could discover transformation or I could find out it was all a delusion. Even if we could say, as I believe, that every situation or happening is transformable, there is no guarantee that I am in a position to experience it. I might pass by the opportunity for transformation. The risk that accompanies freedom can never be totally eliminated.

Do I dare to risk such a loss of control? There are several common ways whereby I hope to control my environment (wherein I also must include myself). I can seek control of my environment through my head, analytically. I might also hope to control it emotionally. I can finally seek some kind of physical control—or a combination of all three. Whatever my control of a given situation looks like, it is important that I understand that surrender will ask me to relinquish it. If the particular control is perceived to be too important or vital to me, I will not consent to surrender myself, even if I know for a fact that it is to my benefit to do so. I think we find this frequently in addictive behavior, where at some level I might see through the delusion of the addiction, but I am not yet ready to let go of it.

What if I am not able to find my way back to the surface again? In the act of surrender one of the great fears is that of losing my way. Mythically it is the effort Hansel and Gretel make to drop bread crumbs on the path in the forest so that they might find their way home at the end of the day. Perhaps I would let go if I knew I had a lifeline back to the surface. It is a happy fault of the process, a *felix culpa*, that our bearings are among the first things to go in the act of surrender. There is no going back; the path dissolves behind us, the ladder disappears. If in my dream I finally let go of the sides of the manhole, I would likely discover that there no longer was a manhole. But, of course, this raises another question related to what it was I left back there above ground.

What if I won't be able to retrieve what I believe to be valuable? In our lives this is a real concern. Perhaps circumstances will be such that I will be able to go back and retrieve it; perhaps they won't. But there are a few things to take note of in relation to the valuables we leave behind. If I don't recover them on the other side of my act of surrender, it might be that I no longer recognize them as possessing the value that I once thought was theirs. If I do get them back beyond surrender, I will surely find them changed. It could also be, however, that these valuables are lost to me. Part of the experience of surrender is what is called sacrifice. Sacrifice is the act of letting go of something important. It could be big or small (the smallest things can be very important to us, as we know from looking at most arguments). Surrender, however, is born of the trust that loss itself is transformable. At the very least it is transformed into freedom.

In his book titled *Transformation*, John Bennett spells out the connection between freedom and sacrifice:

> The fruit of sacrifice is freedom. Freedom is a very wonderful state of existence, for it is no less than the possibility of a creative act. True freedom is so rare in our human experience that few people can ever recognize its taste....No one is free who is not inwardly free and this inner freedom comes in the moment of sacrifice. As our sacrifices are only partial sacrifices—that is, involving the attachment of only a part of ourselves—the inner freedom we can get does not last long. But so long as it lasts it is unmistakable. (p. 43)

What if I don't survive such a plunge, even despite all the reassurances to the contrary? With this question we have finally reached the crux of the problem with surrender, and that is that it looks like death. We do not usually receive this information as good news. Most people spend much of their lives running from various death experiences. To now say that surrender will ask us to turn around and confront the very thing we were trying so desperately to escape is, to say the least, disheartening. We would like someone to say to us, "Oh, don't worry. Of course you'll survive!" But the reality is that in a real act of surrender something is going to die. Even if we ourselves survive the experience, which is not guaranteed, something in relation to us or the experience will necessarily fall away. This is true because if nothing dies, nothing was surrendered. It is the essential nature of a free choice; every choice is a death. To say yes to something is to say no to everything else. If I say yes to something, expecting to get everything else as well, I have not really chosen anything. I have just created a time sequence which I expect will eventually allow me to have it all. When we are dealing with freedom and surrender, we are not dealing with "having it all."

While on the subject of surrender and death, there is something else important to mention. This is that death is everything it is cracked up to be. The kind of death that is connected to the experience of surrender is not some kind of romantic loss that really insulates me from the real world. The surrender I am presenting is not "tragic" in the sense that it makes my loss bigger than life. "Come and see if my suffering is not the greatest of sufferings!" Nor, on the contrary, is it death that is so small as to be insignificant. The death of surrender is the death of grief and mourning. What is lost in the surrendering is something that is missed. I will feel its loss painfully. And if I or a part of me is what is lost in the surrendering, then I or that part of me will be grieved over, by myself, if only in an anticipatory fashion, but also possibly by those who love me, and maybe by creation itself. The grieving has to do with the value of what has died. Real tragedy lies in the fact that what has died was seen as being painfully valuable.

If surrender is so integrally bound up with death, then why would anyone want to choose to do it? Why seek out death? Or is surrender only for the morbidly minded? First of all, the death in surrender has nothing to do with morbidity. It has everything to do with vitality, growth, and freedom. But it is not really a question of seeking death out to begin with. I am no advocate of that. Enough death comes into our lives each day; there is no real need to go looking for it. The death of the experience of surrender is the death that is tied to life; it is the death of paradox.

We have seen this kind of death mentioned in the gospel of John (12:24–26). The grain of wheat must fall to the ground and die, or it cannot really live. It was never intended to remain grain or seed in the first place. It was intended to become fruit. If it does not die, it remains in living death. So it is with us. We were made for transformation, actually for a process of transformation. Without surrender we are stopped at the door. We are caught between the dualities of life and death, and the options of extremism, indifference, and compromise are all that remain for us. The willingness to surrender is the key to going beyond the duality. That is why I call surrender the fundamental spiritual experience, and that is why this chapter is entitled "the keystone of paradox."

Paradox and Surrender

It might be good at this point to recall the definition of paradox that I presented in chapter one. Paradox is the harmonization of two opposing experiences or aspects of an experience that in themselves are irreconcilable, but through another force acting upon them at a crucial moment are created into a new or transformed reality. I do not believe it is hard to get in touch with what this definition means when it speaks about two opposing experiences or aspects of reality, for life is filled with examples. But this definition raises three other questions about paradox that are not so obvious. First, what is this force that acts upon the opposing elements? Second, can we see, or at least name, the new reality that is supposed to come forth in trans-formation? And finally, how are we to understand what is meant by a crucial moment?

The first question draws a line in the sand of reality. What is this force that acts upon the opposing elements? In suggesting that this force raises paradox to a new level and in the process in some way creates a new reality, there is the strong indication that this force lies at another level itself. I have already referred to this force as grace. But, of course, grace is not a neutral word. Believers and nonbeli-evers will react predictably to its use. Believers will likely bring into the equation a long string of assumptions and presuppositions that they have come to associate with grace. This is unfortunate, for it may keep the believer from understanding some aspects of para-dox. On the other hand, there is the very real danger that the non-believer will hear this word as a "stopper." It will be perceived as superstitious, delusional, or at least unempirical, and therefore beyond the scope of our observation. It occurs to me that I can do nothing to safeguard against either of these possible reactions. It might be that I will have to rely on grace itself to aid the believer and the nonbeliever alike, to help them suspend their judgments and treat the concept of grace afresh, in order that we may proceed from here without harmful presupposition.

By grace I mean something that is, of course, mysterious, because it involves us with Mystery. I do not, however, mean something that is uncommon, unavailable, or even unnatural. It is my presumption that grace must be a natural thing, because we feel its impact in the natural world around us. This is true even if we look at what has traditionally been called supernatural grace. Such traditional designations as supernatural, actual, habitual, etc., help us realize that grace does not come in a generic package. It happens in very different ways in very different circumstances. I am, however, more inclined to speak here of grace as a single reality, probably because I am slow to want to name Mystery or its attributes, as if we really understood them.

I indicated that grace is available, even common. That should not surprise us, since there is the sense that God would wish to make it so. Since grace is really God's communication, God's relationship with us, why would we not presume that it is available for us to take advantage of? In fact, grace abounds (Rom 5:15). If grace is what transforms contradiction into paradox, then there would have to be a great deal of it around (as if metaphorically it were a substance), since there is no end to the possibilities of transformation. Of course, if God's grace is available to us in the sense that there is the divine desire to relate and communicate, then paradoxically it could be true that grace is not available to us—in the sense of its being in our control. This is why I mentioned among my general principles in the Introduction that grace is the result of our cooperation, and not of our construction. Grace reaches us through this cooperation. While our cooperation is not sufficient in that we can then demand grace, it is still necessary in order to avail ourselves of it. More will have to be said about this cooperation momentarily.

If our first question drew a line in the sand, the second question is where the edge of the sand falls off. Is it possible for us to see, or at least name, the new reality that is supposed to come forth in transformation? The answer to this must be: sometimes, but not always. It is more likely that the new reality, the transforming aspect of paradox, remains most often hidden or obscure. It is sometimes, but not often, seen—that is, objectively identified. It is even less likely to be named, although sometimes it can be, and when that happens it can be a powerful experience, both individually and communally.

I do feel, however, that this transforming reality can quite frequently be experienced. This lies most often in the recognition of a quality that I call fruitfulness. Fruitfulness as a biblical concept is derived, among other passages, from our citation on the grain of wheat in John 12. Paul also speaks of the qualities of life that come forth from the Spirit as being fruitful (Gal 5:22–23). Fruitfulness has the supreme advantage of being distinguished from both productivity and success. These two terms are such loaded cultural concepts for us, and so tied to perfectionism, that it is perhaps unlikely that today we can use them in any healthy spiritual sense whatsoever. Productivity and success are measurable quantities and qualities of our Western culture, and we especially love to measure them. We usually begin to do so from childhood on. They are loaded with judgment—judgment of both ourselves and others. Fruitfulness is not so measurable. For one thing, something can become fruitful in ways that we could never initially imagine. It could be fruitful for me or you or us or them or even for life in general. We do not even have to recognize an experience's fruitfulness to understand that it still could be so. The earth, for instance, is fruitful in ways that never come under human observation, ways that are never channeled into the means of production, ways that never show up on progress charts. The fruit remains, nonetheless.

But to experience fruitfulness, that part of it that is ours to experience, requires something extra of us. It requires a quality of awareness that does not just happen automatically. The fruitfulness that is born of the transformation that grace brings about is everywhere, if we could only develop the kind of sight that would enable us to recognize it. We can be trained to some extent to make this kind of spiritual sight available to us. This has always been the domain of the mystic or the spiritual master. Every spiritual tradition seeks to provide a way for its disciples to come to the awareness of life's fruitfulness. It is a kind of contemplative seeing. It is in some way the kind of "seeing" that Annie Dillard writes about in *Pilgrim at Tinker Creek*:

The secret of seeing is, then, the pearl of great price. If I thought he could teach me to find it and keep it forever I would stagger barefoot across a hundred deserts after any lunatic at all. But although the pearl may be found, it may not be sought. The literature of illumination reveals this above all: although it comes to those who wait for it, it is always, even to the most practiced and adept, a gift and a total surprise....I cannot cause light; the most I can do is try to put myself in the path of its beam. (pp. 34-35)

So in true paradox grace acts upon opposing forces, the contradictory forces of life, to transform them and make them fruitful. This takes place at a crucial moment. This brings us to our third question. How are we to understand what is meant by this crucial moment? If grace is always present, we could ask, then why isn't the transforming nature of paradox just spontaneously happening? Why don't the contradictions in our lives simply resolve themselves as soon as they appear? The ironic thing is, there is a part of us that feels they should. Even though contradictions in life have been with us throughout the years of our existence, and even though we have had to face the same ones over and over again, there is a part of us that is surprised, and, we must admit, personally affronted, when we are forced to deal with them again. "Why is this happening to me?" "Why does this always happen to me?"

One would think that sooner or later we would come to the conclusion that life's contradictions don't just go away. Joys and sorrows, gains and losses, advancement and diminishment, clarity and confusion—they are always there. At some point do we then say, "That's life"? We might come to the conclusion that it will not get any better. "Just live with it." But then grace shouts out "This needn't be!" Contradictions don't just go away, but they can be transformed—if I choose to let it happen! The breakthrough comes, I believe, in the experience that I am calling surrender. And as I mentioned, surrender always involves a free choice; it is an act of the will. Surrender is the choice I make to cooperate with grace.

As I have described surrender, it involves the willingness to become less encumbered, to let go of some of my cherished securities, to give up my illusions about control, and to fall into the uncharted darkness of the paradox. It also means overcoming my resistance to all of the above. But this does not mean that I go through life in a permanent passive mode. We are not called to back our way through life. The surrender I am speaking about is a free choice that I make at a very particular moment. That is the crucial moment of my definition. This crucial moment is what Scripture refers to as the *kairos* moment, the moment of immediate opportunity, the moment when the Reign of God is breaking in. This moment is not to be missed, for it may not come again.

It is in the kairos moment that the letting go of surrender takes place. But paradoxically, letting go frequently looks like holding on. While we let go of our securities, our resistance, and our control, at the same time we must learn to hold on to our awareness, our courage, and our perseverance. The Sufis tells the story of a man who arrives at the gates of paradise. It is because of the life that he has followed that he has thus far been rewarded. However, he is unable to enter paradise because the gates are tightly closed. They open only once in a hundred years. So he settles in to wait for his opportunity. Time goes by (and there is not much to do at these particular gates) and so he begins to nod, then momentarily falls asleep. At just that moment the gates swing open ...but only for that moment. They just as swiftly close, the story concludes, with a crash that would wake the dead.[1] Here his letting go into sleep was no surrender.

A similar recognition of the importance of the active dimension of kairos shows up frequently in the parables of Jesus. The faithful steward watches for the master's return (Mt 24:44–47), the wise virgins have made adequate preparation for the coming of the bridegroom (Mt 25:1–13), and the poor widow persists in her demands upon the unjust judge (Lk 18:1–5). It is true that frequently we have to make kairos happen. This is seen most dramatically in the parable of the Good Samaritan (Lk 10:25–37), where the foreign traveler goes out of his way at great personal risk and expense to respond to the demands of the moment. The remarkable thing is that all of these examples are incidents of surrender, although they don't fit the usual understanding of that term.

The Problem with Language

All of this demands that we face squarely the difficulty with language. It should not be surprising that paradox would give us problems when it comes to the attempts we make at expression. After all, it deals with opposites to begin with. Then paradox leads us over the edge of our understanding of opposing terms into new ground that really has no expression. But we must also realize that there is a paradox present in language itself. This paradox, like so many others, will cause us endless problems if it goes unrecognized. In fact, it is already doing so in our parishes, congregations, and religious communities. It causes innumerable problems in society as well.

It seems necessary to me that we recognize both the importance and the unimportance (call it the limits) of language. First of all, language is extremely important to us, not only because by definition it enables us to communicate. Certainly that is directly true. But there is a special indirect truth to the importance of language. It structures reality. If we consistently speak about an object or an experience in a certain way, we will begin to think of that object or experience in terms of how it is structured in that language. We will presume that the language encompasses the reality.

This can be illustrated to some degree in terms of our society's language about death. Specifically, we find that "to kill" is spoken about quite ambiguously in our culture. For the sake of sensationalism in media and entertainment, killing is still presented in its stark and sometimes brutal forms, but there are some ways in which the expression of "killing" is considered most unacceptable. Another language set is therefore invented. We speak of "neutralizing the village," "terminating the fetus," and "carrying out capital punishment." The reason for introducing this language is an attempt to restructure the reality of what we are doing. And although we cannot change the physical events, we do succeed in anesthetizing our awareness. The new language seeks to create a separate morality which says, "We must look at this differently from how we view killing." We should derive little comfort from the fact that those folks we like to call liberals and conservatives both participate in this restructuring of language—and reality.

All this, of course, makes language very important, particularly since we seldom stop to assess the impact that our language has upon us. We take language for granted, and therefore we give it permission to maintain control over us. On the other hand, those who do not take it for granted, who consciously recognize its power, are all the better able to use language to further their ends, for better or for worse. The history of the twentieth century has given us a feel for the word "propaganda," which is perceived as language that is used to further one's cause. We are all ministers of propaganda as well as simultaneously subjected to it. We need only look at all our possessions, at the "necessities" of consumerism, to realize how susceptible we are to the power of language.

On the other hand we must paradoxically maintain that frequently we have made language too important. Having given all this power to language, we must now take it back. We have to recognize that in the final analysis it is only a symbolic representation of something. It is not the reality itself. To equate language with reality will ultimately place us in a delusional world. Look, for instance, at a line of sportswear that recently was promoted by famous athletes, who proclaimed to us, "Image is everything." To make language and reality coterminous is to create a world where image is glorified and real things become no more than our most naive and subjective constructions. This then becomes the breakdown of communication. Reality deals only with the agreement of expression and not the deeper search for truth.

This dilemma over language is most noticeable when what we are trying to express is already beyond the realm of expression. That includes most of the language we use about religion. The contradictions of language have had no more harmful manifestations than in the realm of faith and theology. The most enduring example from the experience of Christianity is the dilemma between the language of justification by works and justification by faith. This dichotomy arose around historical circumstances that called Christians to reflect on what they understood as differences between the theological positions of James and Paul. These reflections, and the attitudes of entrenchment that followed, ultimately fractured the Christian community in the sixteenth century in what is known as the Reformation. Much of the bitterness born from that experience remains in the Church, and it is only now after four hundred years that the Christian community is in a position to begin looking at ways of bringing itself back together.

Such experiences call us to the awareness of the stakes involved in the contradictions of language. We need to keep in focus that most of the wars that have been fought, and continue to be fought, are waged under the banner of religious truth. The problem is that most of the religious bloodshed of the centuries has not really been about truth at all. It has indeed been about power, and fear, and greed, and violence, and prejudice—but it has also been perpetrated in the name of articulated belief, faith language, our expressions of what we think truth is. If we honestly look at the record, we would have to say that truth has not been served much in the process.

All this is by way of saying that our word "surrender" presents us with just such a linguistic conflict.[2] We need to recognize that this word is problematic for many people, and the problem is inversely proportional to the perception of one's own personal or communal power. For those who have a deeply felt experience of integrated power, to name surrender as a keystone of transformation is not so personally challenging. That does not mean it is an easy thing to do. Letting myself go into my insecurities and loss of control is always difficult, but at least I can come to see the need for just such an action. This is especially true if I can recognize that it is the resistance to letting go that is keeping my life from becoming fruitful or vital.

This awareness is quite different, however, if for some reason I am coming into the experience feeling a lack of power. For any powerless individual or oppressed segment of the population, the word "surrender" will carry a great deal of baggage with it. The first response will be to say it feels like I have done that my whole life, and the results have not been particularly fruitful. Quite the contrary, it seems as if it is the attitude of surrender itself that has kept me in my circumstances of oppression. To say to oppressed minorities, for instance, that they have to attain an attitude of surrender to bring about their transformation sounds very much like urging them to remain in a state of oppression and powerlessness. This in fact has been done over and over again by oppressors, and often in the name of God and religion.

Why should a young black male in American society, for instance, hear the need for surrender as good news? Why should a survivor of the Holocaust or someone who has escaped one of our current experiences of "ethnic cleansing,"our modern euphemism for genocide, rush to embrace a spirituality that calls for surrender? Why should women who are consistently underpaid for equal work and looked upon as physical objects to be used, and frequently abused, need or want such a spirituality? How can women, for instance, be expected to assert the need for surrender when these conditions described by Kathleen Norris and an unnamed Benedictine sister persist:

> Women in American society are conditioned to deny their pain, and to smooth over or ignore the effects of violence, even when it is directed against them. As one sister said to me, "Women seem to have trouble drawing the line between what is passive acceptance of suffering and what can transform it." (*The Cloister Walk*, p. 94)

We could say, "Oh, but there is a difference. The kind of surrender that is an experience of letting go is totally different from that of giving up." No doubt, that is true, but in saying this we have failed to recognize the importance of language. Language is shaped by experience, and in turn it structures reality. If my experience of surrender is born out of a life that has been abusive and oppressive, my perception of that word will not change because someone asks me to redefine it. Surrender will continue to carry connotations of defeat, passivity, victimization, and hopelessness. Perhaps in such a case it would be better to throw out the word "surrender" and find a word that better captures the experience for all. The important thing is not the word, it is understanding the experience that whatever word we use is meant to describe.

While I have no vested interest in the word "surrender," on the other hand I do have a great deal of interest in clarifying the experience that I am saying is the most fundamental experience we can have in the spiritual life. Whatever we choose to call it, it is not giving up, nor is it giving in to defeat or victimization. It is as far from hopelessness as one can get. We could say that it is a letting go, but that can also present a further problem, for it still conveys the sense that what I am doing is a passive operation. The experience of surrender I am referring to is, in the true paradoxical sense of the word, both active and passive, but perhaps not always at the same time.

There are indeed times when to surrender will require passivity, as when I have been actively resisting something that I need to do in order to grow. In this kind of a situation the only way through my resistance is to let go of my need to control a particular aspect of the reality. My actions have been the means I have used to frustrate any hope of transformation. I could perhaps find twenty new kinds of activity in which to get lost so that I do not have to face the one thing that is blocking me. Here my only recourse is passivity; I will have to stop all else I am doing and give up the fight.

It is probably true, however, that more often than not my surrender will require a high degree of action. The reason for this is, as I stated earlier, that surrender is ultimately an act of the will. Quite frequently, for instance, my surrender will have a strong confrontational sense to it. We can presume that practically every act of surrender will in some way call me to confront myself. It is also not unlikely that surrender will ask me to confront parties beyond me. I might be called, as the early martyrs were, to stand against forces directly opposed to my faith. I might be called, as many contemporary martyrs have been, to actively resist injustice and human oppression. These responses will call forth surrender from within me in a very active way.

In the dream with which I started this chapter, we can see both an active and a passive understanding of surrender. In the passive sense of the word, my dream was calling me to learn how to follow my own inner resources, to give up resistances, and to let go. In the active sense of the word, the dream was asking me to make a conscious decision of the will to lose control, a decision that was going to lay out for me a course of action I would have to undertake. The dream was not coercive, however. There is no doubt that, if I chose, I could muster the persistence to resist taking the plunge of surrender. To actually do so, on the other hand, would clearly require an active effort on my part.

Because of the subtle nature of the surrender experience, there are a number of words and expressions that could substitute for the word "surrender." I offer you the following list, which is not meant to be exhaustive. Each expression probably has its advantages and disadvantages. That there are so many words available underscores the breadth of the experience that underlies them.

1. *Abandonment.* This has the sense of forsaking or deserting something that I once held in my possession. This could particularly involve letting go of the claim I have on something or of the opportunity to exercise my rights. To abandon my will would indicate forsaking the claim to plot my own path or agenda. Abandonment also has the sense of desisting from some action I was doing. In that sense I could abandon a certain line of behavior that was not transformative.

In abandonment there is the further sense of yielding completely, particularly to emotions. This gives a very different sense of the word. Here abandonment is a surrendering of head control to trust perhaps a more intuitive feeling or instinctual level. In this sense abandonment has been used in the past to indicate the letting go of my inhibitions.

2. *Detachment or nonattachment.* We find in these two related concepts the designation of a process of disconnecting or separating. Detachment suggests a disassociation with my surroundings or with the concerns of others. Because of this, like many of our alternative words, it is just as ambiguous as surrender or even more so. Perhaps nonattachment has a bit less negative connotation, and probably exists as an attempt to bring a more favorable ring to detachment. Detachment, however, does suggest an absence of prejudice, or a disinterest with things that might distract me from pursuing a genuine spiritual agenda. They both suggest an attitude of abstinence from things that might automatically capture my interest.

3. *Apatheia.* This is a Greek word popular in early Church asceticism. Evagrius Ponticus used the word to indicate a state of moral perfection. It literally means to be without feeling or emotion. It carries the connotation of spiritual surrender to the extent that I have died to my "passions," the dark inclinations that keep me from transformation. Because it is the word from which we derive our English

word "apathy," it carries perhaps too much baggage to be useful except in the most highly nuanced contexts.

4. *Kenosis*. This is also a Greek word, but one that is rooted in scriptural theology. It designates a process of self-emptying or letting go of inner content. We find the idea of a spiritual kenosis presented in Paul's letter to the Philippians. "Let the same mind be in you that was in Christ Jesus, who, though he was in the form of God, did not regard equality with God as something to be exploited, but emptied himself, taking the form of a slave, being born in human likeness. And being found in human form, he humbled himself and became obedient to the point of death—even death on a cross."(Phil 2:5–8) So kenosis carries not only the sense of being emptied, but also the quality of humility and obedience to the greater will.

Because it is not an English word, kenosis is able to escape much of the negative baggage that many of our alternative words still carry. Particularly when bonded to the self-giving attitude of Christ, it can be a powerful expression of self-surrendering. However, like apatheia, it must always be contextualized and interpreted; it can seldom stand on its own without further explanation.

5. *Release*. This word suggests being set free from confinement. There is in release a connotation of deliverance or liberation, also an unfastening of something that has caught me. It is the word preferred by Ernest Kurtz and Katherine Ketcham in their book, *The Spirituality of Imperfection*. They speak of release in the following way: "The experience of Release has been described as 'the chains falling away,' 'a light going on,' 'a weight lifted,' 'something giving way.' The very language attests that the experience is not one of triumph ('I did it!') but one of awe and wonder ('I somehow see what I never saw before!'). The awareness that we do not earn this experience, but are given it, reveals life itself and the experiences within it as gift." Kurtz and Ketcham specifically equate release with a sense of surrender:

> In the experience of Release, as just about everywhere else in the realm of spirituality, the fundamental truth of mutuality holds. We are able to "get" only what we are willing to give. Thus it is that we can experience release only if we have released—only if

we have let go. We do not find Release by letting go, for that would still involve the manipulative attempt to control. When we truly release, when we really let go, we abdicate control, and it is this surrender of control that is so terrifying. (p. 165)

6. *Relinquishment.* This word suggests putting something aside or releasing my hold on it or desisting from pursuing a certain course of action. There is suggested the quality of renouncing something, particularly something that has been prized or desirable. In that sense we could say that relinquishment is very scriptural, especially in the sense of the gospel renunciation that in chapter two was suggested to be essential to our understanding of discipleship. It is perhaps this gospel renunciation, so much a part of the inspiration of the Franciscan charism, that has led the authors[3] of *St. Francis and the Foolishness of God* to choose relinquishment as the word they connect with Francis's ongoing conversion.

Relinquishment is much more than giving up material goods. It means giving up prestige and privilege, learning to listen and accept criticism and learning how to use our power differently and ultimately to share our power. At the very least, our task as the non-poor is to share the power available to us—our resources of wealth, education, influence, and access—with those who lack these things. This is not charity or "noblesse oblige." It is a fundamental letting go to allow the very structures that benefit us to be transformed so that they will no longer impede but will include and benefit others. (pp. 35-36)

7. *Submission.* Perhaps of all our alternative words, submission carries the most negative connotation. It suggests becoming subject to an outside power, but in our culture it carries the further sense of a willingness to be dominated. This could be accompanied by an attitude of resignation, meekness, or even in some circumstances masochistic tendencies. It is, therefore, all the more worth reflecting that submission and surrender are the two most frequent renderings of Islam, the word that designates a religion we would not be quick to equate with resignation. The important question becomes: to whom or what is the submission given? It need not indicate a totally passive stance at all. The submission in this case is seen to be a

complete surrendering to God.

However, this might still be the decisive factor that would make surrender preferable to submission. Whereas submission to God is highly commendable, almost any other act of submission is expected to be highly qualified by circumstances before our culture would see it as a positive action. Surrender, on the other hand, has a greater flexibility. I can surrender to God, but I can also surrender in many other ways that do not indicate a passive acceptance of domination. To surrender to a lover, for instance, is an expected part of mutuality.

8. *Yielding*. This word suggests giving way under pressure, most often with hopes that it will be temporary. As an alternative to surrender it is suggestive more of an attitude than a course of action. To be yielding is to be pliable and flexible, two qualities that often have great spiritual benefits. There is even a power that exists in yielding, as one might find in the exercise of Taijichuan (Tai Chi), the Taoist martial art/exercise where the yin of receptive yielding energy quickly evolves into the yang of a grounded forcefulness.

9. *Letting go*. This is the expression suggested by Matthew Fox, in his book *Breakthrough* (pp. 221ff), as a replacement for the word detachment, which he feels carries too much negative ascetical baggage with it. It carries the sense of releasing something from a grasp or hold. In that sense it is similar to the meaning behind kenosis. It does have the advantage over several other expressions in that it is a neutral action. It has the further benefit of expressing an active willing. Because I am the one choosing to let go, there is no sense of being forced or having to submit to something against my will. Its own neutrality, however, does not give it the forcefulness of some of the other expressions I have suggested.

Perhaps you have found a word in the above list that attracts you more than the word "surrender." If so, I suggest by all means that you use it. Or perhaps it is better to let the context determine what best conveys our fundamental spiritual experience. Still I find surrender as good as any of our choices, and so if only for the sake of consistency I will continue to use that word to convey the experience that in the final analysis probably does not have any adequate expression.

Surrender in Conversion and Paradox

In a previous book I spent a great deal of time exploring the life process that we call conversion. I looked at conversion in its biblical roots and how the understanding of conversion has developed through the Christian experience. I also explored the connections that exist between a theology of conversion and the psychological and spiritual dynamics of the enneagram, especially through understanding the addictive nature that is present in the incompleteness of the human person. In presenting conversion as a transformation process I suggested that surrender plays a crucial role, a foundational role. As I have in this book, I called surrender the fundamental spiritual experience.

Without surrender there can be no conversion. Conversion in the theological sense is not simply a change. It is not like taking off one kind of hat and putting another on. The type of change that conversion suggests is one where life is experienced as substantially different. Life as previously experienced is no longer seen as fruitful or, sometimes, even possible. The traditional language in which conversion is presented is that of death and rebirth—the dying of the old self, primarily seen as egocentric and delusional, and the rebirth of a new self, which is stronger, freer, more trusting, and more open. This kind of conversion is seen as transformative. But this new life is only possible when I can surrender the old life. Without surrender nothing is transformed, nothing is new.

> If surrender is the act of "letting go," the experience of conversion can be understood as the hinge on which that act swings—it is the turning point, the turning from "denial" as a way of seeing things to acceptance of the reality revealed in surrender. The self-centeredness that undermines spirituality is rooted in a self-deception that reflects a false relationship with reality, and that false relationship begins with distorted seeing, with some kind of false understanding about the nature of reality and our relationship with it. (Kurtz and Ketcham, *The Spirituality of Imperfection*, pp. 168-169)

Surrender happens in the clear moment of grace, when God's life bursts into our experiences and asks us to choose between what we now have and what the promise of transformation holds out to us. Surrender makes relationship with God possible, for that relationship can only happen when we freely respond to grace's invitation. Surrender, then, acts as a door or portal through which I must pass in order to allow conversion to bring me to the graced experience of God, of myself, and of others. It acts as a trigger that releases the power of grace. At the same time it is a gentle act of hospitality, welcoming the Spirit as guest into the heart.

Paradox, like conversion, is transformative. As I have presented paradox, living with its mystery allows a new reality to be called forth in the reconciliation of opposites. Just as surrender provides the breakthrough point in the conversion process, the point where transformation happens, so it plays that same role in the transformation of paradox. Surrender again functions as the door or portal through which oppositional forces pass into paradoxical power. The door remains closed until I choose to open it. I surrender my categorical extremism, my indifference, or my compromising spirit, and I step through into a new perception of reality.

Surrender, then, plays a similar role in both kinds of experience, the opportunity to at once take action toward life and yet to be receptive to grace. This can only be experienced as a present reality; in surrender there is no past or future. I might celebrate past choices or lament my lost opportunities; I might make preparations for decisions that I know lie ahead, but I cannot know surrender in any other way than as something that can only happen now. We can speak, therefore, of the act of surrender as an experience of conscious living. To the extent I truly surrender, I let go into freedom. However, at least when it comes to conversion, I cannot be sure that just because I have done it once, I will act the same way the next time. Each moment of surrender must be freely recommitted. While habitually living in consciousness will enhance our choices of surrender, we cannot say that it ever becomes totally automatic.

If surrender lies at the heart of both paradox and conversion, are they interchangeable? Are they two expressions of the same thing? No, the two are different. While both experiences are transformative, they lie at somewhat different levels. Transforming consciousness, the term I present to indicate the more or less habitual awareness of paradox in life, is a holistic perceptual state. As such it enhances my understanding of reality. It allows me to see reality as graced and mysterious. We might say it is a pathway that brings me to the gate of conversion. While I can see and experience reality transformed, it is still only an invitation to then become a new creation. Transforming consciousness gives me motive for conversion, yet I am still called forth to that deeper surrender.

While paradox is not conversion, however, we could say that every conversion is in some way paradoxical. If we speak of conversion as life coming from death, as new life from old, then we acknowledge that there is no categorical way to fully understand conversion. While this is more or less true theoretically, it is definitely true experientially. To have undergone conversion is to see the world differently, and the old categories do not apply. However, conversion is fragile and can slip away from us if not nourished. Transforming consciousness can give us the awareness of life that we need to continue the conversion process, not to believe we have done enough or that our journey is ended. Paradox understands that the end is only the beginning.

ENDNOTES

1. Told in more complete form in Idries Shah, *Tales of the Dervishes,* pp. 75-76.
2. While surrender is probably by far a more problematic word, a similar linguistic conflict could be found to exist around another important word that lies at the heart of this book, and that is transformation. What is transformation in its essence? Is it something new that I become, or is it really something I always was but am only now discovering? If it is new, then is there no continuity to the person I was before? If it was always there, and my growth has simply been a matter of uncovering it, then how can it truly be seen as something lying on another plane of grace? It is my understanding (in keeping with the paradoxical nature of reality) that both are true. I rely upon the book as a whole to make this clear, and I leave any further reflections on this paradox to the reader's discretion.
3. Marie Dennis, Cynthia Moe-Lobeda, Joseph Nangle, and Stewart Taylor.

IV

Paradox
Then and Now

An awareness of paradox has probably been part of the spiritual quest of humanity from the very beginning, a constant companion on the journey of the human spirit. It has always been present because paradox is intricately woven into our encounter with experience at every level. Humans have always struggled to resolve the contradictions and oppositions they have met in the world. This is true of the simplest daily realities; it is all the more true when our human quest urges us to explore the edges of our understanding and the frontiers of the infinite.

The need to deal with paradox has been a part of the spiritual journey in both the East and the West. In one sense we could say that the East has been less hesitant to meet it head on. We can find a strong sense of paradox in a number of Eastern religions, perhaps the most notable being Taoism and Zen Buddhism. In Zen, for instance, the practitioner is intent upon breaking through to the enlightened experience known as *satori*. It is an experience, or really a permanent state, that defies all conceptualization. Zen is a spirituality without formal doctrines or creeds, and the student is not led through intellectual study or speculative thought. Instead, the masters of Zen have developed methods that attempt to bring their disciples directly to enlightenment. Frequently these methods involve the use of paradox, as for instance in the assigning of a koan, an illogical statement that is designed to frustrate the thinking process and prepare the student for a directly intuited experience of reality.

Perhaps even more than Zen, Taoism has found its very roots in paradox. There is essentially a paradox that lies at the heart of the Taoist understanding of reality. This is seen clearly in the symbol that represents the Taoist perception of what that reality is like, the circular yin and yang. The Tao, which is most frequently translated as the Way, is both total reality and how that reality is and moves and changes and manifests itself. It is characterized by the two movements of yin and yang, two polar opposites that continuously unfold one into the other, and in so doing become one. Traditionally yang represents the active, creative, male element and yin the receptive, grounded, female force. Their dynamic interaction forms the basis for understanding life, the world, and human experience in Taoist culture. It also provides the basis for understanding spirituality. It is a spirituality, as one might expect, with a profound sense of paradox. We read in the *Tao Te Ching* (p. 59) attributed to Lao Tzu:

> The ways that can be walked are not the eternal Way;
> The names that can be named are not the eternal name.
> The nameless is the origin of the myriad creatures;
> The named is the mother of the myriad creatures.
>
> Therefore, always be without desire
> in order to observe its wondrous subtleties;
> Always have desire
> so that you may observe its manifestations.
>
> Both of these derive from the same source;
> They have different names but the same designation.
>
> Mystery of mysteries,
> The gate of all wonders!

This underlying oneness expressed in the Tao is characteristic of Eastern spirituality in general. It developed first in India with Hinduism. In the Hindu understanding all that we see around us, all the events, all the multiplicity of things, are different manifestations of one ultimate reality. This reality Hinduism calls Brahman. All things come from Brahman and all things return there. Ultimately for the Hindu there is nothing other than Brahman. This basic monistic understanding can be seen as a fundamental principle throughout Eastern spirituality, although the different spiritualities express it in different ways. The underlying principle of oneness is perhaps the greatest difference between the thought of East and West. It also means that to some degree East and West have formed different perceptions of paradox. In the East the elements of opposition tend to be absorbed into the oneness of things and lose their identity there. As we shall see, the West has generally developed a somewhat different understanding.

In one sense the paradoxical nature of Eastern spirituality is better known and has probably been more thoroughly explored. The West has generally shied away from paradox—not from acknowledging it but from systematically exploring it. Probably one of the reasons for this is that the West has been so successful and productive, technologically and economically. Paradox threatens our concepts of productivity and success. It threatens our understanding of measurability and usefulness. But more than anything else, a sense of paradox threatens our desire for control. So it has remained on the edges of Western thought, but it has not been absent. Perhaps it has not been "mainstream," but its voice has never gone away.

The first Western thinker to thematically address the experience of opposition was Heraclitus of Ephesus around the dawn of the fifth century BC. In his philosophical framework, which is striking in its similarities to Eastern thought, all of reality is in flux, constantly changing, constantly becoming something new. Fire is the basic element of reality, and fire never remains static. Change occurs because of the interplay of opposites moving in continuous cycles. There was for Heraclitus, however, a basic unity underneath all of the opposition, a transcending unity he called the Logos, which was a principle of universal order.

Shortly after the time of Heraclitus came another philosopher, Zeno of Elea, a disciple of Parmenides. Zeno was the first to actually construct formal paradoxes, which he used in a polemical way to disprove the philosophical positions of his opponents. Generally they were for Zeno an attempt to discredit a total reliance on the senses.

At the same time that these and the other classic Greek philosophers were formulating the foundations of what would become the mainstream of Western philosophical thought, the Hebrew Scriptures were also taking shape. While paradoxical structure is not predominant in the writings of the Old Testament,[1] there are some examples of reversal, the kind of oppositional language we found to be so prevalent in the gospels. Hannah's canticle (1 Sam 2:1–11) is an example of this. Perhaps the closest thing to a direct statement of paradox in the Hebrew Scriptures is in the Book of Ecclesiastes. "For everything there is a season," the author writes, "and a time for every matter under heaven." (Eccl 3:1) There follows an extensive list of "seasonal" opposites, from birth and death to war and peace. The author concludes that God "has made everything suitable for its time...yet they cannot find out what God has done from the beginning to the end." (vs. 11)

Paradox in Christian Spirituality and Theology

Certainly not the mainstream of Christian philosophical or theological expression, paradox nonetheless surfaces periodically throughout the Christian era to make a dramatic impact, particularly upon spiritual literature.

In Pseudo-Dionysius, an anonymous writer of the sixth century, we find a type of spiritual writing that has become known as apophatic spirituality. God is ultimately unknowable by our usual reasoning processes because God transcends them. We can say that God possesses all attributes of reality, but strictly speaking does not possess any of them because of this transcendence. We can come to possess a profound knowledge of God, however, through a process of not knowing. This negative method of unknowing achieves a level of knowing beyond understanding. Pseudo-Dionysius was an often quoted source for many Christian spiritual writers and theologians of the Middle Ages. His influence on later apophatic writers, like the author of *The Cloud of Unknowing* and John of the Cross, was of primary importance. He also exerted a strong influence on the number of Christian writers who expressed themselves through the medium of paradox. We find in the writings of Pseudo-Dionysius, particularly in this language of knowing by not knowing, the sense that paradoxical construction is perhaps the most appropriate means we have of attempting to express the human experience of the divine. This focusing on the ways of seeing God as paradox can be seen in the writings of both Bonaventure and Eckhart. Through most of the tradition of Christian spiritual writing following Pseudo-Dionysius, where paradox was present, it came to be seen as an instrument more for exploring our encounter with God than for understanding the dilemmas of human existence. Today, while not denying the former understanding, paradox is more and more seen as a means for Westerners to explore the human mystery as well.

Bonaventure of Bagnoregio, a Franciscan theologian and spiritual writer of the thirteenth century, in the line of Pseudo-Dionysius, found paradoxical structure an important way of expressing the mystery of God. The presence of God has emanated throughout creation, and there are traces of God to be seen everywhere. Bonaventure's writings are understood by Ewert Cousins through the expression "a coincidence of opposites," a term first used by Nicholas of Cusa. Cousins sees the coincidence of opposites as "the single unifying structure in all the dimensions of his thought" (*Bonaventure and the Coincidence of Opposites*, p. 9). We find it first in his emphasis on the Trinitarian construct, and we find it just as much in his reflection on the person and role of Christ. Christ is the medium in which all opposites coincide, the locus where the vast differences between the divine and the human are reconciled. Highly influenced by the Franciscan movement he joined, and especially by Francis of Assisi, its founder, Bonaventure saw Christ as the center of everything, both historically and metaphysically.

In a poetic passage from *The Soul's Journey into God* (the *Itinerarium*), Bonaventure proclaims:

For if an image is an expressed likeness,
when our mind contemplates
in Christ the Son of God,
who is the image of the invisible God by nature, our humanity
so wonderfully exalted, so ineffably united,
when at the same time it sees united
the first and the last,
the highest and the lowest,
the circumference and the center,
the Alpha and the Omega,
the caused and the cause,
the Creator and the creature,
that is, the book written within and without,
it now reaches something perfect.

(Cousins, *Bonaventure: The Soul's Journey into God*, pp.108-109).

At first glance we would not expect to find much common ground between Bonaventure and Meister Eckhart. Eckhart, the bulk of whose writing was produced in the first quarter of the fourteenth century, was a Dominican friar, a member of the same order as Thomas Aquinas, frequently perceived as a theological adversary of Bonaventure. He was greatly influenced by Aquinas as well as by the writings of Bernard of Clairvaux. However, he was also highly influenced by Neoplatonism, a common source he shares with Bonaventure. Like Bonaventure, who served as minister general of his order, Eckhart held responsible positions in the Dominicans, serving for a time as minister provincial. Bonaventure, however, went on to be named a cardinal and ended his days in high ecclesiastical esteem, while Eckhart's avant-garde temperament led him to increasing difficulty within the Church's structure. Eventually, although Eckhart maintained his allegiance to the Church, some of his works were declared heretical, and he died before he could complete his defense.

That these two men should find a common ground in paradoxical structure is probably every bit as much the result of their own religious experience as it was their intellectual background. It was the ineffable and boundless Mystery they both met and lived in that led them to the recognition that human reasoning could not grasp the fullness of the divine. There were, however, some major differences in the language they each chose to articulate their experiences. Bonaventure, writing out of the Franciscan school and influenced greatly by Augustine, tended to speak of what the human heart was most seeking through the language of love. Eckhart, on the other hand, out of his Dominican background, perceived this deepest seeking as a Wisdom of the Heart, a true knowledge of God.[2] For Eckhart knowledge meant union with God, which is part of our human destiny, and in fact at some level something we already possess. But this knowledge of God was not something that could be facilely held in the human mind. According to Cyprian Smith in *The Way of Paradox: Spiritual Life as Taught by Meister Eckhart* (pp. 22-23), Eckhart saw "the Reality of God as something that can be grasped only within the tension and clash of opposites. This tension has to be experienced in our daily life; this is the practice of detachment. But it also has to be experienced in our thinking and talking about God; and this involves paradox."

Much more so than Bonaventure, Meister Eckhart's use of paradox seems to have been a purposeful structuring of conceptual opposition. Bonaventure spoke occasionally of God in oppositional language because he felt that it most clearly articulated the God who was met in love and the pursuit of the Good. Eckhart used oppositional concepts, on the other hand, more systematically to introduce the God who could not be so easily met. God becomes at once more pervasive but less tangible, vast in scope yet present in the depths of every soul. Matthew Fox terms this tendency in Eckhart toward paradox dialectical consciousness, which is radically different from the kind of dualistic thinking we usually live in.

> There is required a dialectical consciousness to grasp the cataphatic God on the one hand and the apophatic God on the other. Dialectical consciousness is presumed when Eckhart says that "height and depth are the same thing," as well as when he says that "God is in all creatures insofar as they have being, and yet he is above them." Thus God's inness is in dialectical tension with the divine beyondness. Grace and nature work

dialectically in God's plan for us. "Do not consider anxiously whether God works with nature or above nature. Both nature and grace are his." He draws lessons of everyday living from a dialectical model when he says that people ought to "eat with perfect propriety who would be just as ready to fast." Thus fasting and eating are not dualistically opposed, but dialectically related. Hatred and love are related dialectically, Eckhart observes. "The very hatred of evil is itself the love of good or of God. It is one habit, one act." (Fox, *Breakthrough*, p. 197).

Therefore, just as we can speak of paradox within God, there is a kind of paradox within each person who is pursuing this unitive knowledge of God, for at once each of us shares an affinity with God and yet can only perceive God as other. In his *Commentary on Exodus* (#112), Eckhart writes:

> You should know that nothing is as dissimilar as the Creator and any creature. In the second place, nothing is as similar as the Creator and any creature. And in the third place, nothing is as equally dissimilar and similar to anything else as God and the creature are dissimilar and similar in the same degree. (McGinn, *Meister Eckhart*, p. 81)

Nicholas of Cusa, writing in the middle of the fifteenth century, was greatly influenced by Eckhart, as well as by Pseudo-Dionysius. In one sense Nicholas took the paradoxical construction that Eckhart had so frequently used, gave it a methodology, and put a name to it. He doesn't use the word paradox, but is the first to use the expression "coincidence of opposites"(*coincidentia oppositorum*) or "coincidence of contradictions"(*coincidentia contradictoriorum*). His method is mathematical in origin, and flows out of a logic that was meant to show that all our knowledge is ignorance.

> Because, O Lord, You are the End that delimits all things, You are an End of which there is no end; and thus You are an End without an end—i.e., an Infinite End. This [fact] escapes all reasoning, for it implies a contradiction. There, when I assert the existence of the Infinite, I admit that darkness is light, that ignorance is knowledge, and that the impossible is the necessary. (Hopkins, *Nicholas of Cusa's Dialectical Mysticism*, p. 181)

This quote is taken from Nicholas's *Vision of God*, a series of medita-tions that is perhaps the clearest expression of his coincidence of oppo-sites. It was written for a monastic community and sent to them accom-panied by an icon. The face on the icon was omnivoyant, that is, giv-ing the impression that the eyes of the image are upon the beholder no matter from which angle it is viewed. The monks were asked to gaze upon the icon whenever the book was read in chapter. Nicholas meant the Vision of God, therefore, to represent both our vision of God and God's vision of us.

Dialectical thinking is not necessarily paradoxical. Georg W. F. Hegel developed a method of dialectics through his study of the Idealism of Kant and the other eighteenth- and nineteenth-century idealists. His primary intention was to reconcile what he considered to be the most fundamental duality, that which lies between subject and object. This duality was resolved for him in Absolute Mind. At this highest level of the Hegelian ideal we might recognize something of a transforming nature to this method. However, the general thrust of Hegel's dialectical method did not presume transformation in the sense I am suggesting here.

In Hegel's dialectical method of thesis-antithesis-synthesis we find a development through opposition. The antithesis is the nega-tion of the thesis; the synthesis is the negation of the negation, which itself becomes a new thesis. Hegel stressed the dynamic impulse generated by the opposition. In the synthesis he resolved his under-standing of opposition, but he did not really address paradox, for as it appears in historical and social development the dialectical method unfolds systematically. It is not transformative. It resolves itself, and does not require any additional impetus. This accounts for how easily the basic structures of dialectical method were adapted to Marx's dialectical materialism, the basis for socialist theory. Hegel's structure is an attempt to reach for unity, but it does not give us a true means whereby we can live with mystery.

On the other hand, another nineteenth-century thinker, Søren Kierkegaard, did develop an influential philosophical and theological world view with paradox at its heart. Kierkegaard attacked Hegel's theories as intellectually dishonest, and to some degree formulated his own philosophy in reaction to them. He created a highly elaborate understanding of paradox, seeing it as lying on two different levels. First, there was paradox that existed at the natural level, for instance, in the contradictory task of simultaneously upholding both freedom and transcendence. Real freedom is arrived at by making an ethical choice, which comes with the acceptance of law and responsibility. But at the same time freedom is held in check by a transcendent power over which the individual has no control.

Secondly, Kierkegaard also posited an absolute paradox, which he found to reside in the person of Christ. The demands of the Christian faith placed such a burden on freedom and the truth of subjectivity as to be absurd. At the same time the Christian faith became the highest existential truth for it led the individual to a truth beyond subjective freedom. Kierkegaard is generally credited as the most significant forerunner of existentialism. His impact on the thought of philosophers such as Sartre and Heidegger was enormous. Kierkegaard's ideas were also influential on developing Protestant thought in the twentieth century, especially with theologians such as Barth and Tillich.

With the advent of existentialism in the twentieth century we might say that paradox had once again found a home in the dilemma of the human situation. With the upheaval of two world wars in Europe, the growing realization of the impact of the Holocaust, the unrelenting anxiety of the nuclear threat, and later the struggle that American society went through in the Vietnam era and thereafter, Western culture in the last century came face to face with the existentialist's angst. The effects of the accumulation of all this can be seen in the West practically anywhere we turn, from the growing dissolution of religious structure to the self-destructive tendencies of the drug culture to the sacrifice of the human spirit upon the altars of corporate greed and its effects upon the poor. Spiritual writers could no longer approach God in the dispassionate manner of the Scholastics. Instead they sought throughout the twentieth century to find ways of touching God while carrying the weight of our own human suffering.

Perhaps no spiritual writer of the twentieth century was more characteristic of this search than the Trappist monk Thomas Merton.

We might think that Merton would be secretly pleased at the suggestion that he as much as anyone could represent the spiritual struggle of this age, for he fought hard for the chance to express from behind his cloistered walls his own questioning spirit and to give voice to his loyalties as well as his roguish delinquencies in his pursuit of God. Merton embodied the angst of the twentieth-century spiritual pilgrim, as well as the conviction, the devotion, and the vulnerability that accompanied it. Not only did Merton use the language of paradox extensively in his writings, he moreover embraced the thought patterns of paradox in his understanding of God, the world, and himself. It is not surprising that Merton could so thoroughly weave a sense of paradox into his writings, for he saw himself as the embodiment of a paradoxical world view. Consider this quote of Merton, taken from his preface to the *Merton Reader* (p. 16).

> I have had to accept the fact that my life is almost totally paradoxical. I have also had to learn gradually to get along without apologizing for the fact, even to myself....It is in the paradox itself, the paradox which was and still is the source of insecurity, that I have come to find the greatest security. I have become convinced that the very contradictions of my life are in some way signs of God's mercy to me: if only because someone so complicated and so prone to confusion and self-defeat could hardly survive for long without special mercy. And since this in no way depends on the approval of others, the awareness of it is a kind of liberation.
>
> Consequently I think I can accept the situation with simplicity. Paradoxically, I have found peace because I have always been dissatisfied. My moments of depression and despair turn out to be renewals, new beginnings.

The liberation that Merton spoke of allowed him to look at the world like few writers before him. While he sought a solitude with God, he realized that he would never be able to isolate God, for God always kept pulling him back into the world he had left. While he sought to flee society, he found it facing him at every turn, and moreover in the meeting he discovered that he had been given a prophetic word to speak to it. He came to recognize that he could freely mingle the sacred and the profane because for him the two were continuously interacting until their distinction was no longer important. Social issues like war and civil rights were just as much religious and spiritual issues. He recognized that East and West both spoke a truth, and the chasm between them, the unwillingness to hear what the other said, could be bridged if both sides could get beyond their fear.

If Merton's world was paradoxical, it is because it flowed from his belief that at the root of this earthly existence there is a paradox in the makeup of each human person. He called this oppositional reality the false self and the true self. The false self was the superficial "I," the "I" that is met on the surface of life. "It is our 'individuality' and our 'empirical self' but it is not truly the hidden and mysterious person in whom we subsist before the eyes of God." (*New Seeds of Contemplation*, p. 7). That "hidden person"was the true self, but for the most part the true self remained hidden even from itself. It is not that Merton was being particularly original here. He was in effect doing no more than paraphrasing the gospel passages of saving life and losing life that we find in Matthew 16:24–26 and its parallels. He was, however, also presenting to his world of the mid-twentieth century that its experience could find expression in terms that made the gospel come alive.

> To say I was born in sin is to say I came into the world with a false self. I was born in a mask. I came into existence under a sign of contradiction, being someone that I was never intended to be and therefore a denial of what I am supposed to be. And thus I came into existence and nonexistence at the same time because from the very start I was something that I was not. (*New Seeds of Contemplation*, pp. 33-34)

In *Merton's Palace of Nowhere* (p. 17), James Finley sees this true-self/false-self polarity as Merton's articulation of the paradox that revolves around the question of human identity.

> Merton leads us along the journey to God in which the self that begins the journey is not the self that arrives. The self that begins is the self that we thought ourselves to be. It is this self that dies along the way until in the end "no one" is left. This "no one" is our true self. It is the self that stands prior to all that

is this or that. It is the self in God, the self bigger than death yet born of death. It is the self the Father forever loves.

Merton's conviction that this self that is "no one" is the true identity loved by God shows us why he was able to reach out so effectively to the East. It was as if he felt that he had come to the point where he recognized that his own tradition and that of Eastern spirituality had reached common ground. The Christian mystic and the Eastern mystic had found in the paradox of human identity the key to the greater paradox of how this "no one" comes to be found even as it is lost in the fullness of Mystery.

Other Western Developments

The Christian tradition was not the only Western tradition that was evolving a line of thought that furthered the development of a sense of paradox. In the Islamic tradition, particularly within the orders of Sufism, there was a mysticism developing that had a high regard for paradoxical thinking. The essential paradox for Sufism lay between wisdom and ignorance. While many intellectuals and scholars might consider themselves to be wise, the Sufis would maintain, their wisdom is really ignorance because their knowledge is misdirected. On the other hand, the follower of Sufism, who might seem to be an "idiot" by the standards of ordinary judgment, is the real person of knowledge. The knowledge of the Sufi, received under particular conditions and with special effort, can bring the initiate to a higher working of the mind.

Unlike other branches of Islam, the Sufi tradition developed along esoteric lines. Not everyone was in a state of mind to receive the teaching or to profit from it, so admission into a Sufi order was tightly controlled. Nazir el Kazwini is credited with this rather cryptic and paradoxical account of the qualifications necessary for admission:

If you read, if you practice, you may qualify for a Sufi circle. If you only read, you will not. If you think you have had experiences upon which you can build, you may not qualify.

Words alone do not communicate: there must be something prepared, of which the words are a hint.

Practice alone does not perfect humanity. Man needs the contact of the truth, initially in a form which will help him.

What is suitable and unexceptionable for one time and place is generally limited, unsuitable or a hindrance in another time and place. This is true in the search and also in many fields of ordinary life. (Shah, *Wisdom of the Idiots,* p. 107).

Sufi teachers were known for using enigmatic stories as tools for passing on their wisdom. The Sufi teaching story is said to contain many levels of meaning, not all of which are known to the ordinary hearer. The following is a short story that might strike us as having a ring similar to Merton's true and false self:

Shibli was asked: "Who guided you in the Path?"

He said: "A dog. One day I saw him, almost dead with thirst, standing by the water's edge.

"Every time he looked at his reflection in the water he was frightened, and withdrew, because he thought it was another dog.

"Finally, such was his necessity, he cast away fear and leapt into the water; at which the 'other dog' vanished.

"The dog found that the obstacle, which was himself, the barrier between him and what he sought, melted away.

"In this same way my own obstacle vanished, when I knew that it was what I took to be my own self. And my Way was first shown to me by the behavior of—a dog."

(Shah, *The Way of the Sufi,* p. 185)

Not surprisingly, because of its esotericism, the mysterious ways of the Sufi were not widely known in the mainstream of Western European thought. Today their teachings are more readily available, but, as the Sufis themselves might say, availability of information should not be confused with possession of wisdom.

It is presumed to be a particular circle of Sufism that had the most powerful influence on the teachings of George Ivanovich Gurdjieff (1870–1949), an Armenian seeker whose extensive travels through the Middle East and the Orient in the early years of this century led him to establish himself as a teacher and master of the spiritual life. In the years prior to the Russian revolution he collected around himself a circle of students in Moscow and St. Petersburg where he taught them principles of what he called "the Work." When the revolution began in Russia he fled from there and eventually made his way to Paris, where he continued and expanded his teaching. Gurdjieff's Work was generally focused on how to bring about a permanent state of conscious living within the individual. It was his belief that, quite to the contrary, the vast majority of humanity lived in a state of unconsciousness, which was like a sleep where life was experienced primarily at an automatic or mechanical level. Much of what humans do, even much of what seem to be "free choices," Gurdjieff taught, arises from lives of highly conditioned responses. Gurdjieff taught the use of many techniques and exercises to enable people to wake up, to break out of their patterned existence.

One of Gurdjieff's teachings built upon what he called the Law of Three or the Law of Trinity, which he believed to be the fundamental law of creation. Through it he developed a sophisticated yet concise theory of paradox. While he did not refer to it by that term, his presentation of the Law of Three basically saw every event that came forth as a reconciliation of stated dualities. These dualities are universal; they are part of the cosmic order. They are of course also inherent in human nature. Peter Ouspensky, in *In Search of the Miraculous*, quotes Gurdjieff as saying:

> Man, in the normal state natural to him, is taken as a duality. He consists entirely of dualities or "pairs of opposites." All man's sensations, impressions, feelings, thoughts, are divided into positive and negative, useful and harmful, necessary and unnecessary, good and bad, pleasant and unpleasant. The work of centers proceeds under the sign of this division. Thoughts oppose feelings. Moving impulses oppose instinctive craving for quiet. This is the duality in which proceed all the perceptions, all the reactions, the whole life of man. (p. 281)

Yet for Gurdjieff this state of duality is only an apparent one. The reality is that there are not two but three forces. He called the apparent dualities Affirming and Denying, or first and second force, but there is also a third force, which he termed Neutralizing. Every event and manifestation has to have all three forces present to be truly creative. The presence of duality is really a human misperception due to the present state of human consciousness. Gurdjieff maintained that we are "blind" to the third force. Again he is quoted by Ouspensky:

> The first force may be called active or positive; the second, passive or negative; the third neutralizing. But these are merely names, for in reality all three forces are equally active and appear as active, passive, and neutralizing, only at their meeting points, that is to say, only in relation to one another at a given moment. (p. 77)

Because of the esoteric nature of his teaching, it is practically impossible to pinpoint the sources of Gurdjieff's thought. Was it really Sufi in origin? How much did Gurdjieff himself add to these ideas? Because of his own reticence to speak about his sources, it is difficult to say.

A very different development of paradox in the twentieth century can be seen in the work of Carl G. Jung. Jung was a contemporary of Gurdjieff, born in 1875. He was a physician, a scholar, and a psychiatrist. As a young psychoanalyst he had developed a close relationship with Sigmund Freud, but he had a very public break with Freud and launched his study of psychology in its own directions. Jung's interest in symbol and myth led him into extensive studies of esoteric material such as alchemy and the occult. His numerous writings have had a powerful impact not only upon the psychological community but also in the fields of theology, sociology, and other social sciences. He has spawned several generations of disciples and students who have had significant influence upon psychology, sociology, anthropology, and religion in their own right. Jung's impact on the understanding of the human mind seems only to be increasing.

Carl Jung's psychological theories could be summed up in terms of the human quest for wholeness. This wholeness of personality takes place for Jung in the psyche, which is made up of consciousness and unconsciousness in continuously shifting roles. The organization of the psyche runs on energy, and represents a closed system where this energy constantly moves from one aspect to another. The shifting from consciousness to the unconscious takes place through the process of compensation. The compensatory and complementary nature of the psyche is most important for Jung since he imagines it as consisting of innumerable oppositional pairings which to some degree offset each other. While consciousness is dominant, the unconscious remains primarily dark and unknown. These roles could shift, however, as for instance in an individual's dreams, when the unconscious becomes the dominant mode. Whatever can be recognized in a person's conscious attitude can also be found in a compensatory nature as an opposite attitude residing in the unconscious. Jung, for instance, developed the concepts of anima and animus as the unconscious correlates of the attitudes found in our conscious (biological) sexual personality.

Another way in which Jung contrasts consciousness and unconsciousness is through the archetype known as the shadow. In consciousness the ego acts as a kind of monitor or gatekeeper that performs the function of focusing the psyche's attention. It also tends to keep consciousness intent on the ideal, sometimes unrealistically so, as for instance when we downplay our failures and emphasize our successes. The shadow, which resides in the unconscious, becomes the receptacle for what the conscious ego ignores, or perhaps refuses to deal with. Robert Bly speaks of the shadow as an invisible bag each of us drags behind us. He suggests, "We spend our lives until we're twenty deciding what parts of ourselves to put into the bag, and we spend the rest of our lives trying to get them out again." (*Meeting the Shadow*, p. 7).

Consciousness grows through the development of four functions, sensation, intuition, thinking, and feeling, and two attitudes, introversion and extroversion. Again these functions and attitudes are paired with each other and exist in compensatory tension. The more an individual develops sensation as a predominant and conscious mode of perception, the more intuition remains undeveloped within the unconscious realm of the psyche. When an individual develops a dominant attitude of extroversion in consciousness, the unconscious would tend to express itself through the attitude of introversion.

Jung realized that the individual could never be whole, could never achieve what he called individuation, as long as this shifting from one aspect of the personality to its opposite continued. June Singer, writing in *Boundaries of the Soul* (p. 350), tells us that "In his later work he was devoted to the possibility of bringing together the opposites, to finding the harmony both within and without that is consonant with seeing the person as a whole, instead of as a collection of parts and pieces." The way this harmony would have to be achieved was to find some way of bringing both consciousness and the unconscious together, first into dialogue and then into balance and integration. This, however, was not a simple task. Jung found that there was frequently resistance on the part of both the ego and the unconscious. It was only after an extensive process of inner openness that both consciousness and the unconscious were brought together in what Jung called the transcendent function.

> The shifting to and fro of arguments and affects represents the transcendent function of opposites. The confrontation of the two positions generates a tension charged with energy and creates a living, third thing…a movement out of the suspension between opposites, a living birth that leads to a new level of being, a new situation. The transcendent function manifests itself as a quality of cojoined opposites. (*The Portable Jung*, p. 298)

The expression of human individuation and wholeness is something that impacts the person at every level. It manifests itself consciously and also at the various levels of the unconscious. Jung did not think of the unconscious as one simple reality. Beyond the store of our personal memories, desires, and perceptions that have made their way into what he called the personal unconscious was another vast subconscious space he referred to as the collective unconscious. This term refers to Jung's belief that the human psyche is not simply a collection of information made available to us out of our own unique experiences. We also inherit some degree of psychic content from the wider store of universal human experience. Archetypes such as the *anima/animus,* and the shadow are available to us not because of our own individual invention, but because they have in some way been passed on to us.

The archetypes of the collective unconscious are instrumental in the exploration of our own experience, and they are necessary for us to understand one another and the human experience as a whole. It was Jung's belief that this common understanding was woven together in the process of creating myth. Myths are not fables created solely for entertainment, but instead are rich and deeply symbolic representations of universal human meaning. They aid the process whereby consciousness and the unconscious come together. They are the way entire cultures hold themselves together and enrich them-selves with meaning. Myths are invariably the faith statements of their creators, for they tell the stories and unfold the symbols that profess their deepest understandings of life, death, experience, knowledge, and mystery. This is true of the religious myths of ancient peoples and just as much true for our own contemporary cultures.

Myth has always been important in dealing with paradox. It is in the field of myth that life's contradictions have struggled with each other in endless battle, and finally, when all would seem hopelessly unresolved, sought each other out in reconciliation and transforma-tion. Mythic structure provides the way in which humans have sought to articulate what otherwise could not be spoken, to view what was otherwise invisible.

Jung found in the studies of ancient people truths that are still valu-able for us in today's world, which is why he felt the understanding of myth, legend, and ancient symbolism held the secrets to unlocking our contemporary psyches. The contradictions that we struggle with in life are not new, even if in some cases our knowledge has given us new ways of perceiving this struggle. We are old and new at the same time. Our ancient wisdom must be available to us even as we reach beyond the frontiers of present knowledge into what is still unknown. The ongoing paradox of reality is nowhere more apparent than in the most recent discoveries of physical science.

The Paradoxical Nature of Contemporary Science

Initially science and religion were closely related fields of study, but the two began to go separate ways during the Renaissance when Western theology could not keep abreast of the rapid developments in the scientific community. There is no clearer testimony to this than the Church's condemnation of Galileo for asserting that the earth revolved around the sun. The relationship was almost totally severed during and after the Enlightenment. Even though scientists such as Sir Isaac Newton were deeply faith-filled people, the mathematics and science that they created led to perceptions of our world that seemed to create ever-widening gaps between the scientific community and traditional theology.

In the twentieth century much has changed on the part of both of these branches of human knowledge and investigation. Theology, with major advances in biblical scholarship and a deep commitment to human development and social change, has in recent decades found science a much more friendly ally in its mission to the world and in its ongoing understanding of human nature. But the changes in the theological world pale before the major changes in the world view of science. A century ago science stood on the brink of discoveries that would so drastically change its perspective on physics, chemistry, biology, astronomy, and medicine as to be unimaginable. Today science knows immensely more about our cosmos than ever before, but paradoxically seems to understand it less. As it sought to delve deeply into the universe's problems, science also discovered its mysteries which lay hidden beneath the surface. The dialogue between science and theology now lies open at the point where the two, at least in some quarters, are listening to each other with a respect that has not existed for centuries.

We need only reflect on contemporary physics, which of all the fields of science seems to many people to be farthest from the world view of theology. Physics, the word the ancient Greeks gave to their quest for the essential nature of things, developed through most of human history alongside other disciplines such as philosophy, religion, and mathematics. In the seventeenth century, using as a springboard the philosophical dualism of René Descartes, which allowed scientists to totally separate mind from matter, physics began to view the physical world around us in a very mechanistic way. This was seen particularly in the work of Isaac Newton, who laid the groundwork for a fundamental approach to physics that was unquestioned for the next two centuries. Newton presumed that reality existed in a three-dimensional space that was always stable and unchangeable. Time was a separate reality that flowed from past to future and had no connection with the material world. In the midst of space was matter, which consisted of solid particles and was essentially passive unless acted upon by outside forces such as gravity. These forces were recognizable and measurable.

While this world view was already cracking at the end of the nineteenth century, the first few decades of the twentieth century saw Newtonian physics crumble under two significant scientific advancements. The first was Albert Einstein's theory of relativity, and the second was the related but distinct development of quantum mechanics. In Einstein's theory of relativity, space as a three-dimensional reality is not seen as a separate entity from time. Instead, space and time are connected to form a four-dimensional continuum. There is no universal flow of time. Time is perceived differently by different observers depending on their velocities relative to what they are observing. Measurements of space and time are therefore no longer absolute, but relative.

Einstein found this relativity to be determined through the constant of the speed of light. It was through this constant that Einstein was able to propose that mass itself be identified as a particular form of energy. This dual realization that all that exists can be understood as disparate forms of energy, and that time and space could no longer be seen as "constants," required science to reevaluate some of its basic presuppositions of how our world is structured.

While Einstein was developing and refining his theories, a second major development was taking place within physics. An international group of physicists, including Niels Bohr and Werner Heisenburg, joined efforts and began to unlock some of the secrets of subatomic particles. What they discovered challenged everything they had previously believed about the structure of the universe. Fritjof Capra writes in *The Tao of Physics*:

> Every time the physicists asked nature a question in an atomic experiment, nature answered with a paradox, and the more they tried to clarify the situation, the sharper the paradoxes became. It took them a long time to accept the fact that these

paradoxes belong to the intrinsic structure of atomic physics, and to realize that they arise whenever one attempts to describe atomic events in the traditional terms of physics. (p. 66)

Scientists had previously arrived at the conclusion that heat radiation was not emitted continuously but appeared in forms of "energy packets," which were referred to as quanta. Einstein postulated that light and all other electromagnetic radiation could appear as both waves and quantum packets. Physicists now refer to these light packets as photons. They are massless particles that act in a way similar to other particles. They also have wave properties, however, which seems to be a contradiction, since waves and particles follow different laws of physics that had been thought to be incompatible. When looking for a particle, for instance, we would look for it in a particular location, but a wave does not have location. Instead, it is spread out over space. Quantum physics has since discovered that this same kind of particle/wave paradox found in photons holds true for the makeup of all other subatomic particles as well. This includes electrons and protons, the attracting electrical charges that are responsible for the formation of all molecules, and thus for all of physical reality as we know it.

How, physicists asked, can matter consist of particles, localized points in space, and at the same time appear as waves, energy dispersed over a finite volume? To attempt to answer this paradox, Niels Bohr proposed the principle of complementarity. A wave packet must include potential for both forms that matter can take, particle and wave. They must be two complementary descriptions of the same reality, each being correct in part but needing the other to have the full description of the atomic reality.

Part of the problem in the particle/wave paradox was clarified in the principle of uncertainty proposed by Werner Heisenburg. As seen through the complementary nature of the particle/wave, matter contains certain pairings of properties, such as the pairing of momentum and location, or energy and time, or spin and angular position. Heisenburg's principle maintains that these pairings of waves and particles cannot be studied simultaneously. We can measure the position of a particle, or we can study the momentum of the wave, but we cannot do both at the same time. In fact, the more we know about one side of the pairing, the less we know about the other. In the extreme, if we are absolutely certain of a particle's location, we can know nothing at all about its momentum. In other words, the nature of this particle/wave as a whole can never be known with certainty. This is not a question of human ignorance. The properties of the pairings must always elude any measurement we hope to arrive at. Making precise predictions simply is not possible.

Relativity and quantum mechanics have left us with some very unusual conclusions about what reality is like. From the point of view of contemporary physics, "things" no longer exist; matter is simply dense concentrations of energy, like passing clouds in the atmosphere. All the "hard" matter that we perceive around us is primarily empty. Everything is made up mostly of space. Even the atoms that make up the stuff of our existence are 99.999% empty. But, paradoxically, emptiness is not really empty. Space is filled with fields, invisible conditions that have the potential of creating a force. We have the scientific means to identify only two types of fields, electromagnetic and gravitational, but there is no reason to believe that these are all there are.

The world of Descartes and Newton seems to be lost in the dust. This does not mean, however, that Newton's physics was wrong, only that it was limited. It was and still is useful within a certain spectrum of experiences. What is wrong is to presume that this spectrum of observable experience is all there is.

> Quantum theory has…demolished the classical concepts of solid objects and of strictly deterministic laws of nature. At the subatomic level, the solid material objects of classical physics dissolve into wave-like patterns of probabilities, and these patterns, ultimately, do not represent probabilities of things, but rather probabilities of interconnections. (Capra, *The Tao of Physics*, p. 68)

In fact, in today's physics it is the interconnections that become primary. The subatomic world is perceived as a web of interconnecting relationships. Electrons, photons, protons, and neutrons all exist in patterns of relationship. Now they are wave, now particle, changing as they respond to each other, to the environment, and to their observer. In perhaps one of the most far-reaching discoveries of contemporary physics, scientific objectivity itself has been brought into question. Quantum matter develops a relationship with the observer and changes to meet the expectations of the observation. When scientists set up an experiment to study particles, the atoms behave like particles. When an experiment is established to study waves, the atoms appear as waves. It is almost as if the atoms themselves anticipate what is expected of them. At the subatomic level nothing can be observed without the observer's interfering in the observation. This situation has raised questions about the very nature of relationship, not only at the subatomic level but throughout the entire chain of existence.

While developments in relativity and quantum mechanics have occupied center stage in twentieth-century physics, they have not been the only areas where revolutionary advancement has taken place. In recent years a great deal of interest has appeared in connection with what is called chaos theory. We know what the word "chaos" means, a total and complete lack of order. Chaos theory in physics identifies as chaotic any system where it is not possible to know what the system will do next. When it is in chaos, a system acts in a random and unpredictable way. Scientists have discovered that, while a system in chaos is unpredictable, it still has boundaries.

Through the use of recordings on a computer screen, the chaotic movement of a particular system has been shown to create a pattern or shape that is held together through what physicists have termed a strange attractor. According to Margaret J. Wheatley, writing in *Leadership and the New Science*, "A strange attractor is a basin of attraction, an area displayed in computer generated space that the system is magnetically drawn into, pulling the system into a visible shape." (pp. 122-123) What is so astonishing is that a chaotic system will never exceed the bounds of its strange attractor. There is, in other words, an order that exists alongside the disorder.

Chaos theory has presented us with a formidable paradox. In the Bible, order and disorder are the first things dealt with in creation, and in a simplistic theological framework it is generally felt that one is good and one is bad. But in science, and in the complexities of pastoral experience, order and disorder take on a dynamic tension. Margaret Wheatley states:

> Throughout the universe, then, order exists within disorder and disorder within order. We have always thought that disorder was the absence of the true state of order, even as we constructed the word: dis-order. But is chaos an irregularity, or is order just a brief moment seized from disorder? Linear thinking demands that we see things as separate states: One needs to be normal, the other exceptional. Yet there is a way to see this ballet of chaos and order, of change and stability, as two complementary aspects of the process of growth, neither of which is primary. (pp. 122-123)

While we cannot fully comprehend the dance of order and chaos, we can at least make sense of their interaction through our growing awareness of something called systems theory. Systems theory works on the presumption that the dynamic tension between the whole and its parts is in place and is functioning in recognizable ways. The whole is not simply the addition of autonomous parts. The whole, the system itself, is seen as being organic; in other words, the system has a life of its own. As with all life, self-organization and autonomy are seen as being paramount in the functioning of any system and in the course its development takes. In every dynamic system, relationship is seen as the basic reality of that system's life. This can be seen if the system we are speaking of is on the level of cells, or if the system in question is that of a family, a parish, a religious community, or when we view society itself as a system. Some scientists speculate that the earth itself is a living, organic system (the Gaia Hypothesis).

Systems continuously renew themselves in an effort to preserve themselves. This means that systems are frequently in a process of change. From the observer's point of view (which we now realize is in some way part of the system), that change can sometimes look like growth and sometimes like dissipation. But we have seen that disorder does not necessarily indicate something totally negative. Wheatley says that it could be "part of the process by which the system let go of its present form so that it could reemerge in a form better suited to the demands of the present environment." (p. 19)

And just as a system maintains the total interconnectedness of the relationships of all its parts, so do systems relate to each other in continuously increasing complexity. Fritjof Capra, in *Belonging to the Universe*, sees something paradoxical in the tension that this creates.

> Now if you look at this from the systems point of view, from the point of view of living systems, you realize that since all living systems are embedded in larger systems, they have this dual nature that Arthur Koestler called a Janus nature. On the one hand, a living system is an integrated whole with its own individuality, and it has the tendency to assert itself and to preserve that individuality. As part of the larger whole, it needs to integrate itself into that larger whole. It's very important to realize that those are opposite and contradictory tendencies. We need a dynamic balance between them, and that's essential for physical and mental health. (p. 74)

In the midst of this realization that life as we experience it forms an ever-increasing complexity of systems, Capra and others have proposed that we need a new paradigm for how to understand reality. Relativity, quantum mechanics, chaos theory, and the other advances in our understanding of the physical world point to a reshaping that is already taking place, not just in science but in every dimension of our experiences. He suggests that while traditional science understood reality as a building, where it was important to isolate and identify the "building blocks" upon which the structure rested, we must now perceive reality as a network of interconnected relationships.

> Now we are moving to the metaphor of knowledge as a network rather than a building, a web where everything is interconnected. There is no up and down; there are no hierarchies; nothing is more fundamental than anything else. (p. 133)

This would suggest that the quest for basic principles or fundamental models as a means of explaining reality will only be successful up to a certain point. Any model or paradigm is arrived at by taking into consideration a limited number of aspects of reality, and from the vantage point of those aspects the model is helpful. But those aspects are interconnected to others that presume a different approach. From this point of view, another paradigm might be more helpful in understanding that perspective, and in fact the previous model might be misleading. We arrive at a paradigm that presumes the coexistence of many other paradigms, and this is intriguing with regard to integration, reconciliation, and holistic spirituality.

It would seem to have relevance for the paradigm of paradox itself. While this book attempts to make a case for the importance of what I am calling transforming consciousness, the awareness of paradox and its integration into life, as the fundamental principle for understanding spirituality and life, we could also say that in some way this is not true. Paradox could be seen as merely one vantage point from which we can understand the complexity of our spiritual interconnections. Perhaps, much like a subatomic particle, we find paradox when we look for it, and only then discover that indeed the rules apply.

ENDNOTES

1. This could be due to the more concrete and immediate nature of the Hebrew religious experience. Edmund Keller believes that the concept of religion was bound up in an understanding of compact and bargaining, which did not lend itself to paradoxical thought. See: Edmund B. Keller, *Some Paradoxes of Paul*, New York: Philosophical Library, 1974, p. 26.

V

A Look at Spiritual Dichotomies

A Story: The Table

Once there was a woman who had a finely crafted antique mahogany table. It had hand-carved legs and a deeply polished finish. It could seat six comfortably, but it could be pulled apart at the middle, where inserts allowed for additional guests. For many years it had been the admiration of all her friends. When she died, the woman willed the table to her two daughters. Each received ownership of half of the table. The whole family thought this strange, but recognized that the woman loved the two daughters equally and could not bear to show favoritism to one over the other.

Predictably, the table soon became a source of tension between the two daughters. Each deeply resented the other's ownership. Finally the bitterness and contention became so great that they pulled the mahogany table apart at the middle, and each had her half hauled off to her own home.

Now one daughter was a scholar, and she found a number of old books in her library which she used as a support for the end of her half of the table that had no legs. The other daughter had always had a great interest in gardening. She found a few old garden tools she did not need as a prop for her half of the table. When friends and family came to visit one or the other, they would see the half-table displayed in a prominent position. They did not think the props made for a very attractive appearance, but they generally felt that each sister had found her own unique expression of self in the matter. Their respective guests seemed rather amused at the fuss the two sisters made over the table, but there was also an air of sadness at seeing something so beautiful divided up and defaced. Usually their friends felt that the less said about it the better.

In such a condition the table halves sat for many years. Each woman felt that she should be the sole owner of the entire table, and would not allow her monument to her grievance to be moved or undone for any reason. Those who knew the two women were most saddened by the gulf that had been created between the two. Before, they had been very close and had shared many things as they were growing up. They had supported each other, and the one had even chosen her sister to be the godmother of her oldest daughter. The ongoing situation greatly distressed this daughter, for while she loved her mother, she also had a great affection for her aunt. She lived with a tremendous ache in seeing what had become of their relationship.

And so the strain of the relationship continued for years. The daughter grew up and left home to begin her own life. One day she met a young man and soon they fell in love. The two made plans to get married, and contacted their families to prepare for a wedding. When she and her mother sat down to work on the details for the wedding, the daughter could see that the strained relationship between her mother and her aunt loomed as a threat to the whole celebration. The young woman thought about the situation and decided that she needed to head off any further family tragedy.

She went to her mother and aunt separately and said to each, "You know how much I love you, and you know that I am aware of your care and affection for me. I ask you, then, for one favor, that you let me pick out the wedding gift that you will give me. I will tell you what the gift is at lunch next Tuesday." She did not, however, reveal to either of the sisters that the other had been invited as well. Since both loved and trusted the girl, they each agreed to her unusual request.

When the time for the Tuesday lunch arrived, both women met the girl at the designated restaurant. When each realized the other had been invited as well, an atmosphere of hostility settled over the room. But the girl said to them, "You are two of the most important people in my life, and I love you more than anything. I know you feel the same for me. I know you each want to do something special for me for my wedding. But there is really only one thing that I want from each of you—the half of my grandmother's table that each of you owns."

Their surprise at her request left the two sisters speechless. Then it dawned on them what she was really asking for, and they both saw the reality of their situation for the first time. They had allowed the very object their mother had intended to keep them always together to be the occasion for driving them apart. And they also saw in that same instant that, because of their mutual love for this young woman, what had separated them would ultimately become the clearest sign of their reconciliation and forgiveness.

They both immediately agreed to fulfill the girl's request, and during that lunch renewed their bonds of love and tenderness for one another.

Paradox and Spiritual Experience

Much like the women in the story, we have a tendency to take what was meant to be one and split it in two. The human mind, left to its ordinary level of functioning, cannot seem to recognize the inherent oneness of what appear to be opposites. This is no less true of "spiritual" things than it is of so many other apparent opposites in life. Often against our better judgment and usually contrary to our best interest, when it comes to exploring the spiritual life we tend to divide up our experiences and place them in opposition to each other.

Humanity's track record on dealing with issues of religion and faith has tended to look much like the unfortunate experience with the fine mahogany table in our story. The classical spiritual dichotomies presented in this chapter are among the oldest and most durable of spiritual experiences. However, over the course of the human journey, to varying degrees they have tended to become problematic. They have been the source of contention and misunderstanding, hatred and judgment. To the extent they have been perceived as problems, we have sought solutions. But as paradoxes they have nothing to solve. I hope, then, that viewing these issues as paradoxes rather than contradictions will give rise to some new understanding of them. As paradoxes we can affirm their transformative nature without feeling we must judge or negate the elements of the dichotomies.

We have long recognized that life presents itself in the form of innumerable opposites. We recall that in the book of Ecclesiastes the author looks at many of our ordinary experiences and recognizes how they tend to be dichotomized (Eccl 3:1–11). He contents himself with reflecting on the time-oriented nature of life's contradictions. Time seems to allow for one extreme to give way to the other. Nothing lasts forever; nor, we hear elsewhere in Ecclesiastes, is anything truly novel (Eccl 1:9). But for all the variation that time offers, the way one moment allows for something different than another, we are not content to live with the problems of life's dualities. Often the opposites of life pull at us in one and the same moment. It seems that a single experience could be one way or its opposite. Sometimes it is only a matter of perspective.

We could simply acknowledge this as part of life's mystery and get on with "more pressing things," but this rarely satisfies our human desire to truly understand life. Our minds seem to rebel at the thought that apparently two opposite or even contradictory aspects of one reality could be present at one and the same time. In their book *The Spirituality of Imperfection*, Ernest Kurtz and Katherine Ketcham express this mental dilemma in this way:

> We tend to like our reality divided into neat and distinct parts, seeing it as either one or the other: either black or white, good or bad, answer or question, problem or solution. But the vision offered by the spirituality of imperfection cautions against that tendency, pointing out that the demand for an absolutely certain truth—the quest for a single, unalterable answer to our

spiritual question—involves the kind of "playing God" that denies and ultimately destroys our human reality. Precisely because we are not either-or, not one-or-the-other, paradox and ambiguity reside at the heart of the human condition and therefore at the heart of all spirituality. For we are both: both saint and sinner, both "good" and "bad," both less and more than "merely" human. In some strange (and not-so-strange) ways, our failures are our successes, our suffering is our joy, and our imperfections prove to be the very source of our longing for perfection. (p. 38)

This realization that we are both/and and not either/or is difficult to come to experientially and even harder to maintain consistently through our life journey. We keep slipping back to embracing one side or the other. Of course, when we do that we end up centering our beliefs on only one of two extremes. It is almost a foregone conclusion that there will be others who will feel led to take the opposite position. Most often then, for almost every question, there are people on either side of an issue ready to formulate the statement "I am right, because you are wrong." Down through the centuries this has led to untold amounts of hatred and violence. (Often this has been especially true within religiously oriented groups.) The only alternative has always seemed to be "I'm not right." We have found it especially hard to live for long with this option.

Not all of our either/or posturing has led to physical violence, but still the tendency to gravitate toward extremes has plagued our human journey. This is true of even the most profound spiritual experiences. The spiritual issues I mention in this chapter are concerned with some of our most important ways of realizing the nature of God and of our human response to God's self-revelation. Still they have frequently been the focus of much contention and misunderstanding among religious or spiritual people.

The following issues are not contradictions; they are paradoxes. This means they create the potential for transformation within us if we are willing to surrender to their mystery. Some might not present much difficulty in our attempt to accept them as paradoxical. With others we might feel a resistance to giving up our right or wrong position. It is good to notice any such resistance, and consider it in relation to surrender as the fundamental spiritual experience.

Other, Yet in Our Midst

The first paradox embraces immanence and transcendence. This paradox considers how God chooses to engage in self-revelation and self-communication. Transcendence indicates the perception that God is very different from us. The divine is experienced as Other. The more transcendent, the more totally other God appears—unlike us in all aspects, beyond us. In transcendence revelation is a totally gratuitous act of God, for without self-revelation a transcendent God could never be known. In total transcendence the human mind would be unable to comprehend God at all. In a similar manner, communion with God would lie beyond sensual experience. In fact, throughout the literature of transcendence it is frequently stated that communion with such a mysterious God might even be dangerous. "Woe is me!" Isaiah cries out in the midst of his inaugural prophetic vision. "I am lost, for I am a man of unclean lips, and I live among a people of unclean lips; yet my eyes have seen the King, the Lord of hosts!" (Is 6:5)

Opposite transcendence lies immanence. Immanence indicates that God is present and recognizable in the midst of human experience. In immanence the revelation of God is manifested close at hand and the experience of God is literally at our fingertips or even closer. God is desirous of communication, which itself becomes the motive for creation. This communication can be found through the natural world, within human relationship, and perhaps most dynamically in our own self-awareness.

The paradoxical nature of God is understood most clearly from these two issues. Every experience of God in some way flows out of and through our sense of God's immanence or transcendence. This is because these qualities address the question of how God is known at all. In their extreme, that is, in the absence of the opposite, transcendence and immanence almost have the effect of denying God's existence. If God is absolutely other, for instance, how have we come to know anything about God to begin with? If we have no common ground with God, wouldn't it be like ships passing in the night, at least from our experience? Does not revelation itself, even as a totally gratuitous gift, suggest some sort of possible meeting ground? If, on the other hand, God is in our midst fully revealed, then why do we continue to struggle with the encounter? Why does anyone doubt? Why is there even such a thing as mystery? Furthermore, if God is absolutely immanent, then why would we even wish to distinguish God from nature, or from humanity, or from ourselves? Would I be God? Or is a purely immanent God merely a projection of my mind? Or is there a difference?

Moving from the two extreme poles, however, we find there is a great deal of room for variation and difference of emphasis in how we understand God. Every religion, every spiritual path, indeed every individual comes to some general conclusions on how to perceive God on this spectrum. Some religions tend to emphasize God's otherness, some God's closeness. Depending on their experience, their upbringing, and their religious education, all individuals too, whether they are aware of it thematically or not, perceive God from somewhere along this continuum. This is true whether they are believers, nonbelievers, or agnostics. For instance, in his book *A Brief History of Time*, physicist Stephen Hawking concludes by questioning whether God is really necessary at all for the running of our universe. The idea of God that Hawking works from, however, is so extremely transcendent that it is not surprising there is no practical role left for this kind of God to perform.

Our perspective on transcendence and immanence can change. Because the experience of the divine is vital and dynamic, we should not expect our perception of God to remain static. Sometimes this change can happen as the result of a dramatic experience of God manifested from one pole or the other. Usually, however, this kind of shifting occurs gradually over a period of time. This change of perception, of course, is most likely to happen within an individual's experience rather than that of an entire group. Such powerful theophanies as experienced by the Israelites at Sinai or by the early disciples in the Upper Room at Pentecost are possible but rare. We would expect much more frequent occurrences on an individual basis.

Because the Incarnation is one of its central beliefs, Christianity has found the paradox of transcendence and immanence to be at the heart of its self-definition. Jesus, at once Eternal Word and fully human, becomes the definitive manifestation of the convergence of transcendence and immanence. That Christianity places its belief in the Incarnation at all is itself the clearest indication that God's immanence is central to its message. Jesus' continuing presence with the Church in the sacraments and through the Mystical Body demonstrates Christianity's belief that God permeates the world. And yet, as he always has, Jesus continues to remain mysterious. The encounter with the risen Christ is hidden and ineffable, as the gospels themselves suggest. The Christian mystics and spiritual writers down through the ages, while acknowledging the immanence we find in God Incarnate, still maintain the most profound sense of God's transcendence. David Steindl-Rast expresses this by quoting Pseudo-Dionysius: "At the end of all our knowing, we shall know God as the unknown." But Steindl-Rast also goes on to note: "He doesn't say, 'Oh, don't bother, you will never know God.' We shall indeed know God, but we shall know God as the unknown." (Capra and Rast, *Belonging to the Universe*, p. 102)

The rich array of Christian mystics attests to how well Christianity has integrated this particular paradox of immanence and transcendence into its faith life. It is no doubt because of Jesus that his followers have been able to accomplish this. Early on, the Christian Church faced a number of theological challenges around the person of Christ and the meaning that should be attached to him. These came in the form of assertions, some denying Christ's divinity, some his humanity. The Church was able to affirm both, leaving ample room for a God both permeating and other. While this paradox might be the most important of all those discussed here, it is probably the one that has caused the least difficulty for the Western mind.[1]

God's Communication

The second spiritual paradox we will look at is related to the paradox of transcendence and immanence. It is not, however, directly addressed as frequently. Like the previous paradox, it also explores some of the deeper implication of God's nature, particularly God's desire to communicate. The paradox of immediacy and mediation has had a surprising (although sometimes hidden) impact on every religion and every spiritual pursuit. We can pose the primary question of immediacy and mediation in the following way: how does God essentially communicate with the individual? Is it more likely through an immediate or direct communication with each person, or does God choose to use some form of mediation, whether persons, places, or things?

Another way of asking the question is this: is God what I can experience directly, or do I need to rely on some intermediary? Taking the view of direct experience would generally, though not always, indicate a tendency toward God's immanence. If God permeates creation, then the divine presence would more likely be expected to be direct and immediate. Espousing the need for an intermediary might for the most part be connected with a view toward transcendence. A God who is Other would more likely be expected to choose to communicate through some form of mediation. This is not, however, simply a more refined statement of the last paradox, for God's transcendence can still be direct and, on the other hand, divine immanence can also at times be mediated.

Immediacy tends to support just what the word indicates, the possibility of an immediate and direct contact with the divine. This could simply be through the immediate perception of God in nature, in others, or in myself; or it could be through something more profound (and by the way, more transcendent) such as mystical experience. Mediation, on the other hand, can be manifested in a wide variety of forms, such as religious laws, sacraments, rituals, priesthoods, scriptures, sacred places, sacred teachings, gurus, healers, or prescribed meditation practices. While mediation generally presumes that God is so transcendent that the individual needs some go-between, something that can transmit divine communication, it can also be based on the presumption of some degree of human ignorance. Mediation is necessary, in other words, because we do not know how to make God's communication available to us.

Practically all religious and spiritual traditions are structured to some degree on mediation. At the same time, practically all maintain the belief in some aspect of immediacy. However, each presents itself to its adherents as somewhere on the spectrum between the two extremes. Immediacy as an extreme is more likely the domain of the free thinker, while more mainline religions, not surprisingly, tend to be suspicious of unstructured spirituality. Ironically, some religions or spiritual cults, while maintaining a public stance of immediacy, and in turn disparaging certain forms of mediation such as liturgy and other public religious practices, are themselves highly mediated in terms of the importance they place on their own spiritual teachings or devotion to their masters or gurus.

The paradox of mediation and immediacy treats what Christianity understands as grace. The question is concerned with how grace comes to the individual. To what degree is God's grace directly available to each person? The various Christian denominations differ a great deal in how they seek to integrate this paradox, their positions corresponding generally to where they are perceived on the spectrum of high church/low church (high church having relatively more liturgy and more elaborate ritual). Liturgical structure, different sacramental forms, and ritual community prayer are normal ways in which grace is understood to be mediated. This is, however, only a rough guideline. Some low churches, for instance, place a very high value on the mediating role of sacred scripture. Beyond whatever forms of mediation a particular denomination maintains, however, the reality is that every congregation is made up of individuals who will ultimately answer their own questions of immediacy and mediation.

It is again worth commenting on the paradoxical nature of Jesus as he appears in the gospels. There he seems to be ambiguous in regard to mediation. While he is accused of undermining the Law, and in fact appears to preach against some of its precepts (such as Sabbath observance), he maintains that he upholds the Law completely. It would at least seem that Jesus does not presume the Law has the same mediating role that his detractors ascribe to it. Or again, while setting extremely high standards for discipleship, he does not seem to treat discipleship as an office that is necessary in order to mediate the access to divine power. When the disciples find someone not of their number using his name to expel demons, Jesus does not try to stop the person. Quite the contrary, he suggests, "Whoever is not against us is for us." (Mk 9:40) Nor does he seem to be particularly concerned about prescribed liturgical cult. He says to the Samaritan woman, "Woman, believe me, the hour is coming when you will worship the Father neither on this mountain nor in Jerusalem....But the hour is coming, and is now here, when the true worshippers will worship the Father in spirit and truth." (Jn 4:21,23)

Still, the gospels leave us with one clear impression. As Jesus is portrayed in all four gospels, he presents himself as the one necessary mediator between God and humanity. "I am the way, and the truth, and the life," he says. "No one comes to the Father except through me." (Jn 14:6) "All things have been handed over to me by my Father; and no one knows the Son except the Father, and no one knows the Father except the Son and anyone to whom the Son chooses to reveal him." (Mt 11:27) In fact, this role of mediation is consistent with how Jesus is presented throughout the entire New Testament. There is no clearer expression of this than in the Letter to the Hebrews, where Jesus assumes the role of eternal high priest.

> In the days of his flesh, Jesus offered up prayers and supplications, with loud cries and tears, to the one who was able to save him from death, and he was heard because of his reverent submission. Although he was a Son, he learned obedience through what he suffered; and having been made perfect, he became the source of eternal salvation for all who obey him, having been designated by God a high priest according to the order of Melchizedek. (Heb 5:7–10)

This means that Christianity always presumes some degree of mediation, because no matter what we do, grace is always mediated by Christ. In Christian theology humans receive the offer of God's life and communion through the mediating role of Jesus. Paradoxically, however, because Jesus is also God, there is no grace that can be received from Christ that is not immediate as well. Once again, in Christian theology we can recognize in Christ the transforming point of the two extremes.

The Paradox of the Self

The question of mediation and immediacy, the two modes of grace's availability, could lead to the more basic question of how the individual is to be understood in the first place. The next spiritual paradox is centered around the individual self. In a sense, it could be seen as several paradoxes tied up around one focus, the focus of human identity and how it is understood. This paradox of the self places in contrast the different understandings of certain aspects of Western and Eastern thought.

We might formulate our questions this way: how is individual identity to be understood? Is it a reality of existence or, in the final analysis, is it an illusion of the mind? Is there really such a thing as the person, a unique human entity? I identify myself as "me," but who or what am I really? Furthermore, is the spiritual desire of the individual self, the desire to continue on the spiritual quest in order that it might be led to find its true fulfillment, a legitimate spiritual venture, or is true spiritual freedom really to be found in nothingness, the disappearance of the self or its absorption into the All?

In the East the spiritual goal of the self is more that of disappearance. At its teleological point, the point of its completion, the individual self will be absorbed back into Brahman, the One, the All. Until that time it is caught in *samsara*, the unending cycle of individual existences or reincarnations. The individual's separate existence presents an illusion of importance with its experiential mixtures of success and failure, hope and disillusionment, joy and suffering, but all this is just an appearance. What is happening to the individual is simply the playing out of karma, which is the accumulated lot of past existences as well as the work he or she must now undertake. In some Eastern thought (like Buddhism), a way out of the endless cycle is offered through enlightenment. This could be seen as leading to a state of bliss, nirvana, but this is perceived quite differently from the Western understanding of heaven or paradise.

Contrary to this goal of absorption and disappearance, in the West individuality has generally been seen as something to be perfected or fulfilled. The self is not to be lost in a formless whole, but, quite the contrary, it is to come to a sharper definition. There is a reason behind what happens to the individual in the course of life. No actions are unimportant, and all help to bring the individual into clearer focus, for better or worse. For most in the West the individual's point of completion is perceived as some form of afterlife. "Truly I tell you," Jesus says to the good thief, "today you will be with me in paradise." (Lk 23:43) And whatever Westerners understand this paradise or heaven to be, they expect that it will bring with it the awareness of who they truly are, as well as who others are in this most heightened and perfected form of existence. Even Westerners who do not believe in an afterlife still tend to see the journey of this life as a quest for individual fulfillment.

For the general Western mind there is a struggle with an idea like reincarnation because it is not clear how individuality can survive such multiple existences. In something like the Hindu concept of samsara, the unique identity of the individual—termed the soul, the spirit, or the true self—would seem to be lost. Instead, individual identity is perceived in the West as something to be developed and in some way perfected in the one life that the self is given. However, the survival of a true personal identity is not so important in the East, which sees individual manifestation as ultimately an illusion. Anthony de Mello tells the Eastern story of the salt doll that travels across a continent to the sea. Mystified by this vast reality, the salt doll asks, "Who are you?" The sea replies, "Come in and see." The salt doll enters in, and just before it completely dissolves, exclaims, "Now I know what I am!" (*The Song of the Bird*, p. 98)

For the Eastern mind the appearance of individual identity is only a temporary occurrence, but even Westerners can see how fragile the self truly is. We know how quickly we can lose our sense of individuality. There are any number of ways we can lose the self negatively, as for instance when we give ourselves over to an ideology. The Nazi officer who claims, "I was only following orders" has lost a sense of who he truly is. We can lose ourselves in mass hysteria, in "group think," in social conformity. We can lose the self in work, in the performance of a role, in addiction, or in codependency. But the loss of self is not simply a negative experience. Some of the most rewarding and transforming human experiences are "selfless." The heroic offering of one's life for another and other forms of extreme sacrifice have always been recognized in the West as an extraordinary act of placing ultimate principles before the self. In a very ordinary sense, we surrender something of our individuality simply in pursuit of the common good.

All this has generally been seen as representing another kind of paradox of the self, one that I have already addressed in a couple of places. In the West we have explained the difference between the loss of self and selflessness as the distinction between the false and the true self, or between ego and essence. I mentioned that Jesus spoke of such a distinction (Lk 9:24 and parallels). I have also mentioned that many others—like Thomas Merton, for instance—have sought to understand our individuality in this way. Is there some kind of a key in this understanding that can help bridge the gap between the Eastern and the Western self? It seems Merton thought so, for he became deeply involved in the East/West dialogue toward the end of his life.

Coming to a transformative understanding of the paradox of the self is one of the most difficult tasks to be accomplished in the human project. There is much on the line in terms of culture, history, and ethnicity even beyond the theological issues. Certainly there are many efforts being made to find a mutual understanding between the Eastern and Western mind. Perhaps Merton stands as a symbol of the bridge that is needed in order to develop an appreciation of the both/and nature of the self. In my own way of thinking, I suspect that exploring the primary importance of surrender in our lives can further a constructive dialogue. When we surrender the self we also come to realize that the self survives, and is transformed in the process.

Going Out and Going In

If the paradox of immanence and transcendence is the most profound of paradoxes, and the various paradoxes of the self are perhaps the closest to our life experiences, it would have to be said that the next paradox we will look at has attracted the most attention in spiritual literature down through the ages. I call this the paradox of going out and going in, which is a more encompassing image for what has traditionally been termed action and contemplation. These are generally Western terms, although they roughly correspond to some of the ideas behind the Taoist yang and yin. The two movements of the Tao are meant to be elements of universal dimension, however. They represent principles of activity and receptivity, but they go beyond that to take on cosmic proportions. In the West, on the other hand, action and contemplation have generally been understood to be limited to particular modes of human life and the experiences that flow from them.

When I speak of going out I mean such aspects of life as forming and living in community, involvement with parish or church life, the deepening of relationships, participation in social involvement, active social ministry, compassionate and just action beyond oneself, involvement in ecological issues, and generally anything that brings our faith to the marketplace. Going in implies all the dimensions of life that involve us in what is called "development of the inner life." These include experiences like solitude, meditation and prayer, the development of aesthetic appreciation, the pursuit of wisdom and knowledge through study and reflection, the development of imagination and inner creativity, and everything that fosters the contemplative life. From this more expansive view, it is easy to see that we are not only talking about choosing an active or contemplative lifestyle. There is no concrete vocational calling that will not have a blending of the going-in and going-out elements.

When viewed from the vantage point of the classical literature of spiritual theology, this understanding of the going in/going out paradox seems like a major innovation. Through much of Christian spiritual literature the dichotomy of contemplation and action was more narrowly understood. Much of this is because, by and large, the writing itself was predominantly coming from one side of the dichotomy. Until recently—that is, more or less prior to this past century—spiritual literature in the West was to a great extent the domain of Catholic religious life. The average Christian, trying to earn a living in the preindustrial world, had little time to be writing or even reading spiritual books. For one thing, most Christians did not know how to read. Education was the prerogative of the rich or the religious, and the means of education was generally held in the hands of the churches.

At first the monks and nuns, and gradually later on those religious of less monastic congregations, had the opportunity to reflect on prayer, virtue, and the like, and then record their reflections for those to whom they were offering spiritual direction.

The outcome of this general situation can be seen in the example of the Mary and Martha literature. Medieval spiritual theology developed the story of Mary and Martha, found in chapter ten of Luke's gospel, along the line of thought that was easiest to understand from their own experiences. In the gospel account Martha asks Jesus to instruct Mary to help her with her tasks of hospitality. Jesus' response is to indicate that Martha is concerned and anxious over many things (which any host or hostess could appreciate), but Mary's pursuit of the one thing that the moment offered, the opportunity to be present to Jesus, took precedence. From the view of medieval religious life, however, Jesus was not instructing Martha to take full advantage of how God's grace appears in the present, but to affirm Mary's embrace of prayer and the contemplative life. This was so even though the passage actually has nothing directly to say about prayer. Jesus was understood to be recognizing contemplative life as the "better part" rather than immersion in the secular life of the average Christian. This was an interpretation very supportive of the many monastic writers who saw this passage from the perspective of their own contemplative lifestyle.

The problem is that in our contemporary Western society we seem to have made a 180-degree turn from the classical position. Our modern world, far from seeing a life of contemplation as the "better part," now tends to question if there is any valid place at all for developing a spiritual life. Frequently contemporary monastics are asked in so many words how they can even justify their existence. From our high-rolling economic world view, such spiritual elements as solitude, prayer, and spiritual reading seem rather quaint and archaic. Why develop habits of reflection that might only drain precious time better spent accessing information from the superhighways of cyberspace? Why give time to an inner life when time seems to be the essential ingredient necessary for that elusive financial success we so desperately seek?

Of course, this is not a totally fair picture of our contemporary culture. We are also a culture with a deep spiritual hunger and a desire for balance and wholeness. The problem is that many people do not know how to attain what they intuitively long for and know they need. Even though they lacked formal education, our ancestors had a spiritual birthright that to a great extent has been lost to us. Most Westerners today are growing up without deep roots in the traditions of faith and spirituality, roots that the generations before us possessed. We are turning to anything that seems to offer us some spiritual consolation. Some of it is good and solid; much of it is a loose patchwork of untested combinations of the old and new. A great deal of it lacks the very balance and wholeness that the going-in/going-out paradox offers as its richest fruit.

There are a few principles concerning this paradox that it would be helpful to keep in mind. First of all, we need to recognize that a contemplative life is quite different from a contemplative lifestyle. The majority of Christians will never be called to "leave the world,"as the classical language referred to it. But everyone is called to contemplation. By that I mean something more specific than affirming that we are all to develop the going-in side of life. That is true enough, but I specifically mean that we need to develop habits and methodologies around prayer and meditation. I will have more to say about this in a later chapter, however.

Second, if we are all to be contemplative, we are also all to be active. Here, in fact, I do mean that we need to find ways of developing both the going-in and going-out aspects of life. If our contemporary world longs for something more, it is because it intuitively recognizes that there is a more that exists. We can come to wholeness and balance; this dimension of life is offered to all. One word of warning, however: wholeness and balance are fruits of paradox, and not of compromise. That means we arrive at them through the transforming process of surrendering. The elements of life that comprise the going in and the going out are not feats to be mastered but powers to be integrated. It is not simply a matter of "finding time" to do a little from both lists. Action and contemplation, used in the broadest sense of the word, find us. We are found in faith and called forth by grace. We surrender to the mystery of wholeness, and then allow it to take us where we never expected.

Expressing the Spirit

The paradox of going in/going out deals with what we do; our next paradox focuses on how we choose to do it. In other words, the question of religious temperament is concerned with the ways we embody our spiritual beliefs or how we present them to ourselves and to the world. In recent years our spiritual "language" has used the words Apollonian and Dionysian to express the two poles of religious temperament. These two terms are based on the archetypal images of two Greek gods. Apollo was the god of the sun, and Dionysus the god of wine. Their cults of worship in the ancient world were very different, and this difference has flowed over into the understanding of our own spiritual expression. The Apollonian view of spirituality stresses a religious temperament that is measured, reasoned, and controlled, pursuing the religious spirit through the golden mean, and extolling a life of moderation.

Dionysian expression, on the other hand, is primarily one of excess. The ordinary limits of life are set aside. Emotion and passion are given free rein; reason is bracketed out. In Dionysian expression the pursuit of ecstasy is acclaimed. The movements of the spirit are painted in vivid colors, and they don't stay within the lines. The ethereal Apollonian melody of violins gives way to the wild enthusiasm of the drums. However, to say that Dionysian expression is one of excess is really to measure expression by Apollonian standards. It is perhaps truer to say that Dionysian expression originates from different centers of control. While Apollonian expression arises from our more analytical center, the Dionysian temperament is more emotional and instinctual in origin. By Dionysian standards Apollonian temperament is excessively heady.

This should alert us to a primary realization necessary in dealing with this paradox. When it comes to religious temperament, it is very easy to judge one pole from an extreme position at the other end of the dichotomy. I do not mean the judgment of evaluating the appropriateness or effectiveness of the opposite expression; I mean judging it in terms of good and bad. It has always been easy to look askance at how other people express their beliefs. But on the Apollonian/Dionysian spectrum, our differences of expression are brought into extreme focus.

The area of religion and spirituality that is most dramatically influenced by Apollonian/Dionysian tension lies in liturgical expression. Because liturgy and ritual are holistic experiences—that is, because by their nature they bring into focus a dimension of balance between our heads, our hearts, and our bodies in some kind of group expression of faith—our common worship must always take them into account. It is not hard to imagine what Apollonian ritual is like. It is calm and reasonable, well-ordered and systematic. In the Christian context it would focus on understanding the Word of God and drawing spiritual sustenance from reception of the sacraments. Dionysian ritual is enthusiastic and charismatic. There is less attention to our watches and more attention to our emotions, and, most importantly, these emotions are physically expressed. Word and sacrament are there, but interaction with them is much less intellectual.

Our contemporary Christian culture has ample examples of both kinds of liturgical expressions. It is safe to say that most mainline churches in America that have their roots in European culture have adapted themselves quite comfortably to an Apollonian approach to religion. Congregations that have drawn strongly from other cultures, particularly of African or Hispanic background, or from some Pentecostal influences, have been freer to develop more Dionysian elements in their worship. All of this is only to indicate tendencies, however, for there is usually some blending of the poles of expression.

In suggesting, however, that there is some mixture of the two elements in American religious experiences, I am not saying that it is a blend of even proportions. It is probably safe to say that in mainline religion there is a general mistrust of religions or cults that become too Dionysian in emphasis. Some of this has probably always been true—even back to the original Dionysian cult of ancient Greece, the bacchanal (in the Roman pantheon the god Dionysus became Bacchus). Certainly throughout European history Dionysian cult has always remained on the fringes, and more frequently in the shadows, of mainline spiritual expression.

This tendency has not been totally without basis in experience. When the head is subjugated to the heart's passions or the body's impulses, most people of our culture feel too much in danger of losing control. When this happens in a dimension of life as powerful as spirituality, the risks can be great. Think, for instance, of the results of mixing spirituality with drugs. The two have had a long tradition together. Some shamanistic religions have used forms of psychedelic drugs in their religious ceremonies for centuries in order to induce ecstasy. Apollonian religion feels very uneasy with such practices, if only because of the tremendous harm that drugs have had culturally upon our society.

The Apollonian approach, however, can become too restrictive even of much safer forms of Dionysian expression. Some people feel very threatened by anything that would ask them to step out of their Apollonian comfort zone, even for a moment. In many places, for instance, such things as liturgical dance or any type of creative movement can send shock waves through a congregation gathered for worship. Some are suspicious of exercises such as active imagination, or guided imagery, or anything where the head does not seem to have absolute control. This mistrust is most often based on the unfounded assumption that the cognitive head is somehow less susceptible to delusion.

When dealing with the Apollonian/Dionysian tension we need to remember that we are concerned with paradox. From the basic principles of this book, that means we are interested in how we might bring both poles to some transformation. That is a very different project than calling for the "wise governance" of Apollo over Dionysus. To find a fruitful balance between the two is going to require some timely surrender where surrender is necessary. Western society has paid a high price for its enslavement to Apollo. A case could be made, for instance, that the high degree of addiction to alcohol, drugs, and so many other things in our society is itself in large part a shadow reaction to Apollonian repression. My head cannot be truly free if my heart and my body remain captive.

The Availability of Wisdom

The final paradox I wish to deal with in this chapter is concerned with how spiritual knowledge and instruction are preserved and transmitted. This is the paradox that is expressed in the tension between exoteric and esoteric religion. At first glance it would seem that this paradox deals almost totally with the values of openness or hiddenness. What we find, however, is that the mind-set that each pole represents has tremendous impact on a number of elements within particular spiritual traditions.

Exoteric religion presumes that revelation is a public phenomenon. God has spoken, and all has been made known. The question is what one intends to do about this. This has implications on at least two fronts, that of the adherents to the revelation and that of those who do not yet believe. In exoteric religion, faith is to some degree a matter of publicly accepting the given body of beliefs. Christianity is one of a number of good examples of exoteric religion. Christianity has its creeds and its doctrines, and these are well known. It is presumed that people identifying themselves as Christian are making some kind of public statement, no matter how indirect, about their faith.

The other major impact of the exoteric on religion concerns how the religious belief is passed on. Exotericism understands that revealed knowledge is meant to be transmitted in an open and active way. This gives the religion to some degree a missionary spirit. In more insistent forms the exoteric religion can be blatantly proselytizing. The archetypal image we could use here is the apostle. The apostle is one who is commissioned to go forth and proclaim the faith, calling others to join. Most major world religions are primarily exoteric. Most religions have some degree of missionary zeal, or at least a public openness to bringing others into their faith.

In esoteric religion, while some truths of the faith are widely known, the full knowledge of the revealed truth is reserved for those who, for whatever reason, are deemed ready to possess it. Instead of the apostle, it is the spiritual master who is the archetypal image. The master is the one who possesses the spiritual wisdom to transmit the belief and to recognize those who might be ready to profit from the teaching. Usually there is a clear period of initiation when the prospective believer is gradually brought into the full understanding of the faith. This could be a time of some testing. Once this initiation is over, the adherent may or may not make a public pronouncement of belief, but the full revelation is never publicly expressed.

It is not that esoteric religions do not want new members. It is rather that they are very guarded about how their faith is received. This is usually because of the belief that the faith could be easily tainted or diluted. Esoteric religion is therefore noticeably less missionary, and substantially more secretive. This is often based on a rather pessimistic view of humanity. The average person is not yet prepared to receive the full teaching, often because of an inherent ignorance or even depravity. Interestingly enough, exoteric religion can also have a pessimistic view of humanity, but there it becomes one more incentive for urgency in spreading the faith.

Even though they lie at opposite poles, both the exoteric and the esoteric have an extremely high regard for truth and revelation. This respect for truth becomes the motivating element in both approaches. It is because the faith is so precious that exoteric religions feel their beliefs must be spread universally. Not to do so would have the effect of depriving the world of its means of salvation. The regard esotericism has for the truth is the very reason that it is not shared. It is guarded as a treasure against external perversion.

Proponents of either form are quick to point out the drawbacks of the other. Members of exoteric religions can take on faith as a public show or for the sake of social conformity. While adhering to the external structures of the spirituality, their values might be largely superficial. Their faith might become so watered down as to raise the question of whether they are spiritual disciples at all. They might even end by doing great harm to the religion through scandal or hypocrisy. On the other hand, the secretive nature of esotericism has left it open to the charge of elitism. It can be easy, in fact, for members of esoteric religions to become arrogant and judgmental in regard to others not of the faith. Also, because of the tendency of unbalanced cults and sects to frequently exhibit esoteric traits, esotericism has often been charged with abuses such as brainwashing and extremism.

The two poles are not mutually exclusive, and can be found even within the same religion. We need only look at the religion of Islam, for instance. As an example of exoteric religion, the Islamic mainstream would be quite fitting. The Koran is available for anyone to read, and Islamic missionary zeal is well known. The branch of Islam known as Sufism, however, has very clear traits of esotericism. While Sufism has frequently been held suspect by other branches of Islam down through the centuries, it has remained in existence within the Muslim world and has continued to prosper.

As I mentioned earlier, Christianity is by and large an exoteric religion, calling for public profession of faith and missionary in nature. It would be natural to presume, then, that Jesus was also predominantly exoteric in nature. The gospels strongly suggest otherwise, however. We find in his teachings that Jesus attempted to instill within his disciples models that embraced both exotericism and esotericism.

There is clearly present in the gospels a call to spread the Good News universally. Matthew's gospel ends with a familiar call for missionary zeal. "Go therefore and make disciples of all nations, baptizing them in the name of the Father and of the Son and of the Holy Spirit." (Mt 28:19) Of course, it could be said that these words might more accurately reflect the early Church's experience rather than actual words spoken by Jesus. Still, the thrust of the gospels indicates that Jesus presented his teachings to all. He was by all accounts a very public figure. He preached in the open. He performed miracles for all to see. At his arrest and trial, all the gospels place upon the lips of Jesus statements regarding the open manner of his preaching. (See, for instance, Jn 18:20–21 and Mk 14:48–49 and parallels.) Moreover, even in the midst of his ministry Jesus sends his disciples out to proclaim the Reign of God. There is an urgency about the Reign and the need to make this Good News available that has all the familiar markings of exoteric spirituality.

On the other hand, Jesus is also presented as having a strong leaning toward the esoteric. While we do not often think of it in this way, to dismiss this tendency is to read the gospels with a clear bias. Jesus singled out some of his disciples for special training, and from that group still others were selected. It is clear from many passages that Jesus did not expect all people to understand his message at the same level. Regarding his teaching in parables, Matthew records Jesus as saying, "To you it has been given to know the secrets of the kingdom of heaven, but to them it has not been given. For to those who have, more will be given, and they will have an abundance; but from those who have nothing, even what they have will be taken away." (Mt 13:11–12) Nor does he expect that all will respond with the same enthusiasm. His ideas of renunciation of all possessions and attachments by his disciples seems to be adequate indication that Jesus saw varying degrees of commitment. He says in regard to his rejection by the spiritual leaders of his own people, "For many are called, but few are chosen." (Mt 22:14)

Again, it is my belief that none of this indicates contradiction in Jesus, but his paradoxical nature instead. If we can see in Jesus the transforming of the esoteric and the exoteric, it seems to lie in how he understands the nature of his message. Jesus is not esoteric in the sense that he feels his teaching must be guarded in any way. This is true even though to preach the word is to surrender it to the unpredictable. The extravagance of the sowing of the seed in the well-known parable is adequate indication of what Jesus knows must befall his word (Mk 4:3–9 and parallels). It falls everywhere, but it does not take root everywhere; still it must go out in all directions. Jesus is esoteric, however, in terms of his message's fruitfulness. Those who have ears to hear will be the ones who finally hear. The word itself establishes the criteria for the chosen. Jesus' teaching is hidden, but hidden only from those whose disposition places them in a position of blindness. The word of God costs nothing, but to have it I must pay the highest price.

ENDNOTES

1. The perennial challenge to Christianity's embrace of the transcendence/immanence paradox has come from various historical schools of gnostic thought. In creating two conflictual principles of Good and Evil (Spirit and Matter), Gnosticism has placed what we would understand

as God (the Good/Spirit principle) in about as extreme a transcendent position as possible. God cannot be immanent if the material world is defined as evil. While Christian theology has always denied the gnostic position in theory, the practice of gnostic spirituality has surfaced again and again throughout history, and continues to show itself in the contemporary world in certain spiritual attitudes that deny the goodness of creation or of the human body.

VI

Virtuous Reality

The title that I have assigned to this chapter is, of course, meant to be a play on words. Virtual reality is a current source of fascination in the world of high technology. There is, however, a vast difference between virtual reality and virtuous reality. The word virtual carries the connotation that, no matter how high the technology, and no matter how close the simulation, the experience will still fall somewhat short of the real. The virtual can only approximate its object. High tech or not, our world too frequently lives in virtual reality. We approximate our experiences. We fall into routines and patterns that leave us performing mindless actions. We pursue happiness, or pleasure, or quality of life, but our pursuits more often than not end up sounding tinny when we were really seeking the solid tone of gold.

To me virtuous reality is not an approximation. On the contrary, virtuous reality is what is truly real. In his book *Jesus' Plan for a New World*, the Real is the word Richard Rohr uses to describe the Reign of God. Virtuous reality is what is needed to help us encounter that Reign in our everyday lives, and what we need to make that Reign a deeper reality for the world we reside in. To me virtuous reality implies the epitome of what reality is all about. It does not leave us empty, looking for the next experience. It says we have experienced life to the full.

This perspective on reality does ask us, however, to do some refurbishing of the word virtue. I once belonged to a faith-sharing group. It was made up of a cross-section of individuals, men and women, with different religious backgrounds. One evening a man in the group was speaking about his religious upbringing. He said that when he was growing up he was always taught to be virtuous, and now he had come to realize that virtue was the biggest trap he could have fallen into. This threw me for a moment. What did he mean by this? I began to listen closely to what he was intending when he used that word. As he continued, I began to realize that what he had understood virtue to be was a list of dos and don'ts. If I do this, I will be considered by others to be virtuous; if I do that, I will be considered wicked or bad or fearful or lazy. What he had discovered was that following his list closely had not necessarily made him a better person, but it had taken away his freedom.

We have been used to equating virtue with morality or ethical standards. To be virtuous is to behave. The stereotype of the virtuous person is one who always acts out of high principles. Yet some individuals do very nasty things in the name of their principles. Others whose behavior gives very little evidence of being directed by principle still have a human dignity that cannot be denied them. Either way, virtue is not the behavioral code we wear on our sleeves so that others might approve of us. Nor is virtue the name we give to our culturally sanctioned efforts at chastity. Frequently in the past, the word was almost synonymous with sexual purity. When it was said that someone had lost his or her virtue, everyone knew what that was supposed to mean. In this sense, virtue is something like a new dress or a new suit. When you first get it, it is clean. Whether it stays clean is up to you. Virtue is then seen by many as what you have, but what you then could lose.

The reality is quite the opposite. Virtue is not something that is simply handed to us. It is something that is acquired with a great deal of discipline and consciousness. It doesn't have much to do with morality, at least in the sense of objective ethical standards laid out by somebody else. It has to do with an inner moral strength that each individual is invited to possess but might not achieve. When we do encounter real virtue in ourselves, it does not take away our freedom, but it gives us, perhaps for the first time in our lives, an understanding of what it is to be truly free.

What is virtue then? How might it be defined? In its original Latin meaning, *virtus* was understood to mean excellence, capacity, and worth. Traditionally in moral theology, virtue was understood as a habitual disposition that directed a person to some specific goodness in one's action. It was the way in which our human power of free choice was modified so that we would be ready to act in a specific direction. Theology named and understood a number of virtues, existing in different classifications depending on the degree to which they were directly provided by God or the result of human will and action.

I would suggest, however, that virtue is not just a disposition, nor is it a habitual activity, if by habitual we mean something that is done automatically. That could be seen as a major difference between virtue and something that is frequently spoken of in a similar way, character. Character is frequently seen as something good and lasting in a person, but it can also point to a deeply imbedded quality that the individual has little power to regulate. When we wish to defend or rationalize our actions, we say, "That's just who I am; it's my character." Instead, virtue is essentially a present strength and a manifestation of a particular way of acting.

I would like to suggest that virtue be understood as related to activity because it is always concrete. It is never content to remain in the ideal, merely in the head. In fact, virtue that is only in the ideal is no virtue at all. The words "I love you" can be hollowly repeated until, in exasperation, the recipient cries out: "Shut up, and prove it!" Love and every other virtue must be manifested in action, or its existence can be rightly called into question. The world progresses through virtuous action, not through verbal idealism. The Reign of God, if we wish to understand it as the Real, or if we wish to see it as the mysterious pervasive presence of God, or however we image it, is furthered through virtuous action. And conversely, every virtuous act in some way makes the Reign manifest.

If virtue is always concrete, it is also conscious. That means we don't just fall into virtuous action. There are many things that we do or that happen to us that have unforeseen positive benefits. We have all experienced them, and we have a number of names for them. We call them luck, or chance, or fate, or serendipity, or divine intervention. But none of them are virtue, for virtue only comes with free choice. Virtue, unlike character, has the quality of doing what I set out to do, certainly not solely on my own power, but with my own conscious intention. Consciousness, however, is not the same as cognition; it is not necessarily thinking my way through an action. Take driving, for example. We are the best drivers we can be when we are driving consciously, but cognitive drivers, who for instance might try to think their way through rush-hour traffic on the expressway, can be a hazard on the road. In time virtue can become practiced and even spontaneous, but at its heart it involves the making of a conscious decision as to how one wants to live. Consciousness has a number of levels; any of those levels can potentially be the source of virtuous reality.

Every virtue, therefore, presents itself as a life strength. It must always be concretized in action, and it is always a conscious choice at some level. Finally, it also has some degree of surrender to it. In chapter three I referred to surrender as the fundamental spiritual experience, and I described it in terms of consciousness, similar to how I have just presented virtue. The two are closely connected. It is conscious surrender that allows virtue to become concrete. Idealized virtue is something we have not yet given up; we are still holding on to it like a treasure. Perhaps we are afraid to act; perhaps we are too proud, or too lazy. Whatever the barrier, we have not yet surrendered our antiseptic ideal to the grime of reality. Hence real virtue eludes us. When we do let go of our hesitation, virtuous reality bursts upon the scene, for our benefit and the benefit of others. It is like the servants we hear about in the parable of the talents (Mt 25:14–30; Lk 19:12–27). The one who acts with what has been received is rewarded, not the one who tentatively maintains what was given without risk or investment. It is the act of surrender that makes real virtue the greatest freedom.

As we look at the paradox built into several virtues, we will be able to see the surrender and freedom that are present in each.

Scripture lists a number of qualities that have come down to us as virtues—qualities such as temperance, prudence, justice, courage, patience, and truth, to name a few. Other sources present their own lists. The enneagram system names nine specific virtues, some of those already listed and others, such as serenity, equanimity, detachment, and innocence. There are many virtues. I would like to suggest as a basic dictum, however, that each virtue has a paradoxical dimension within it. That is to say, when we find the manifestation of these conscious strengths in our experiences, it has been the result of our cooperation with a grace that has transformed some polar opposites. To explain this a bit further, I would like to look at a few virtues. For the sake of space, I am choosing to limit my comments here to only three of them, which are usually called the theological virtues—faith, hope, and love. But prior to addressing these virtues, I want to set a context by briefly exploring something called trust.

The Fundamental Nature of Trust

There is no attitude more basic than trust. How we choose to live our lives, and what we perceive our lives to be in the first place, will depend as much on our ability to trust as on anything else. Erik Erikson chose to identify the crisis between trust and mistrust as the first and most important issue with which we humans have to deal.[1] We either resolve this crisis by seeing the world as a trusting place in which to be and ourselves as trustworthy, or we will live in the world as strangers, suspicious of everything around us and doubting our own value. Trust is basic to everything we do, and so it is not surprising that we can expect to recognize the presence of trust in each virtue.

While trust itself might be placed on some lists of virtues, I am choosing not to speak of it as such. At least trust is not a virtue in the same sense as faith, hope, love, or many others are. Instead, I prefer to identify trust as a spiritual attitude. In fact, trust is the fundamental spiritual attitude, just as much as I have called surrender the fundamental spiritual experience. The relationship between trust and surrender is very close. Trust is the attitude we always find at the heart of surrender. To let go of something requires a necessary level of trust, or

I simply will not be able to do it. Likewise, surrender forms the basic structure of trust. The universal experience of letting go in the face of tremendous uncertainty (whether that be leaving mother's side, going off to school, or making a lifelong commitment) and then discovering that I have somehow survived the ordeal is the necessary human experience upon which a positive attitude of trust rests and grows. Surrender and trust are both essential and are mutually supportive.

Trust, I am suggesting, like surrender and everything else transformative, is paradoxical. As such, it can be presented to us through two elements that are in some way polar opposites, and a third element that represents a transformation of the other two. Let me suggest the following paradoxical triad regarding the attitude of trust that I first mentioned in my previous book, *Conversion & the Enneagram* (p. 200):

- First, the best things in life are free.
- Second, everything in life has a price.
- These are experienced in transformation: the best things in life are free at a terrible price.

When we look at our first statement, it appears to be itself a statement of trust, but it is not. Instead it is an attitude of what could be called optimism, taking a hopeful view of life, looking on the bright side. It was the motif of a classic song, and it is true. The things we prize most dearly have no pricetag. They cannot be bought, even if we would want to try to purchase them. Furthermore, a strong case might be made that, at least compared to its negation, optimism probably has a better chance of resulting in a happier life. However, in itself it is no indication of trust. Sometimes, in fact, an overly optimistic attitude masks a deeply entrenched mistrust that is being denied. Furthermore, when optimism is carried too far, it ends in irresponsibility, which is not particularly transforming. To truly believe that life gives us things freely, even in the face of much evidence to the contrary, not only sets us up for grave disappointment, but it puts us in the position of living life at the expense of others.

Our opposite statement—everything in life has a price—initially does not look much like a statement dealing with trust at all. This is a pessimistic pronouncement. It views life as always demanding something from us, and it gives us a clear feeling that nothing about life is going to come easy. This negation, however, is born of the longing for trust, even if the pessimist feels that trust seems permanently out of reach. It also carries with it the important concept of value. Things that are free are of no value. To assign them a price makes them more valuable, as our mercantile culture clearly understands. Pessimism, however, when it is carried to its extreme, becomes fatalism. From this position the price that life extracts will ultimately doom us. Due to the ravages of the twentieth century our culture has taken on a substantial aspect of fatalism. "Life is one damn thing after another, and then you die," the saying goes. Here the price of life is too much; I am no longer willing to pay it. The irony of fatalism, then, is that it too becomes free of cost, and ends up looking very much like irresponsibility.

Our transforming statement is, of course, a paradox. Linguistically, it is merely a combination of the other terms, but in reality it is nothing that can be derived by simply mixing the two. How can the good things of life be both free and costly? And yet we instinctively know they are. Knowing this truth and learning to act out of it, however, are two different things. Trust is not a matter of cognitive knowledge. But in fact trust is what is generated when I come to an awareness born of the experience that life is both free and costly at the same time. I am free to be spontaneous and vulnerable, responsible and risking. I am also willing to give payment to life, to know my limits, to carry my load, and to help bear the burdens of others.

Trust is primarily threefold—trust of self, trust of the world around me, and trust of God. It begins with a complex interaction between myself and my world, which can be understood as everything that is not me. Gradually through my life experiences, through the freedoms I take, through the prices I pay, and through the surrenders I make, I begin to see my world and myself transformed by trust. I do not run to optimism and deny my fear. I do not cling to pessimism for self-protection. And in the process of coming to trust the world and myself, I slowly begin to trust God. It is important to note that I do not begin with trust of God; it is something I must learn. Perhaps that is one of the reasons why each of us is here, to learn how to truly trust God.

And maybe there is a clue here to this crazy paradoxical reality we live in. The process of taking freedoms, paying prices, and undergoing surrenders is not nearly as easy as it sounds. Many of us spend a lifetime learning how to do this gracefully. All of us have known the hard lessons of the freedoms that ended in enslavement, the high prices we paid for what turned out to be illusions, and the surrenders we could have made but didn't, choosing instead to merely give up. Many of us have used the language of trusting in God to cover our spiritual failures, but it has not been a true trusting because we have not taken the time to learn the lessons. Even our national currency says we trust in God, but it stands as a memorial that the lessons have not been learned. When we have learned them, then perhaps we will recognize what trust of God is and what it has always been.

Trust is the attitude that opens us to the availability of all the virtues. As I stated above, there are many virtues. They are all important, and they are all freeing. Some virtues hold a key to opening other virtues and other kinds of transforming experiences. In some way all virtues are connected. There are, however, some virtues that have traditionally been seen as being the most important. They are recognized as being necessary for all of us, the pillars upon which the others are based. These virtues—faith, hope, and love—are indispensable strengths for living the spiritual life. Traditionally they have been called the theological virtues because they are seen as being generated from God and placed within the person. I would like to suggest that each of these virtues is paradoxical, probably in many different ways not expressed here. Let us explore briefly a little of their paradoxical nature.

Faith

Every book of scripture is in some way a testament to faith. In the Old Testament it is primarily understood as remaining faithful to the covenant, the special relationship God formed with the Jewish people. In the New Testament faith in God is directly tied in various ways to faith in Jesus. Each of the New Testament authors looks a little differently at this faith. For Paul, faith is a gift given to us through Christ. It is only through this gift that we can stand justified before God. In Mark faith is coupled with conversion and is our response to the manifestation of the Reign's presence in the person of Jesus. In John's gospel, the noun faith is never used. Instead faith becomes a verb, an act of believing. It is at the center of our life with God. We are called to belief in and through Jesus. "But to all who received him, who believed in his name, he gave power to become children of God, who were born, not of blood or of the will of the flesh or of the will of man, but of God." (Jn 1:12–13)

What is interesting is that all the times faith is spoken of in the New Testament, whether as a noun or a verb, we are also being called to the attitude of trust, for the same word in Greek, *pistis*, designates both English concepts. This clearly shows the close connection between the two. While faith and trust are the same word in Greek, however, I feel there is a very important benefit that comes with our English separation of them. While trust is an essential attitude for the fullness of human life, faith is more properly an action, or, as many Protestant theologians have pointed out, a decision. Once again, a true virtue must be concrete. Faith more than anything runs the risk of simply remaining in the head. Christianity at the beginning of the twenty-first century is filled with many "believers" for whom faith offers little real impact on how they live out their daily lives. Real faith calls forth action and asks each person to radically restructure life.

Yet for all its concreteness, faith is not certitude. The radical decisions we make about how we are to live, the heroic actions we feel called to perform, and the prophetic stances we undertake are all done in the face of Mystery. With faith there is always doubt. This is true even though we would wish it otherwise. There is nowhere we can go to escape this doubt. It cannot be squelched through food, or drink, or drugs. It cannot be outgrown or outlasted. It cannot be successfully sublimated or repressed. Even our prayer to God does not protect us from its presence, as Thomas Merton points out:

> Let no one hope to find in contemplation an escape from conflict, from anguish or from doubt. On the contrary, the deep, inexpressible certitude of the contemplative experience awakens a tragic anguish and opens many questions in the depths of the heart like wounds that cannot stop bleeding. For every gain

in deep certitude there is a corresponding growth of superficial "doubt." This doubt is by no means opposed to genuine faith, but it mercilessly examines and questions the spurious "faith" of everyday life, the human faith which is nothing but the passive acceptance of conventional opinion. This false "faith" which is what we often live by and which we even come to confuse with our "religion" is subjected to inexorable questioning.

(New Seeds of Contemplation, p. 12)

As Merton recognizes, faith and doubt are not opposites. In the midst of our experiences of doubt we might wonder if we have suffered a loss of faith, but doubt is not really the absence of faith. Nor is faith what holds doubt in tension. If we were to make a paradoxical triad concerning faith as we did above with trust, we would not place faith over and against doubt. Instead, faith would be the reconciling and transforming element of the triad. This remains true for all the virtues.

What I am going to suggest really opposes doubt is desire. Just as doubt fixes its eyes on an object, so is desire essentially a gazing upon something we wish to possess. Our paradoxical triad regarding faith would then appear in this manner:

• Desire for the eternal and transcendent leads to a longing for what we feel is beyond us (which might still be deep within us).

• Doubt lying with our uncertainty over the immeasurable or unprovable, but really born of our own fragile mortality, builds a resistance within us.

• The transformation: a conscious surrendering of both desire and doubt leads to the decision of faith in a God of mystery.

Desire and doubt can live within a person in stagnant opposition for years. This can be seen at a strictly human level in unrequited love. If my deep desire for the beloved is balanced off by my doubts about my own lovability, I remain inactive, unable to let go of the beloved and unable to risk the rejection I believe will surely come if I try to initiate a meeting. The same thing is true at the deepest levels of reality. A person can struggle for years with the "God question." It is the stance of many agnostics. Such an individual is unable to get beyond the doubts about God, but still cannot let go of the deep desiring for something beyond mundane reality. This tension drags on endlessly, always remaining short of the power that comes with a true faith decision.

Desire and doubt, however, are both necessary for faith. It might not be hard for us to imagine the role that desire plays in coming to faith. Desire is, in a sense, what keeps us going. Much as in our example of human love, desire holds us before the beloved and pulls us forward. Doubt, on the other hand, might seem more problematic to us. But ironically the one who claims to believe without a doubt is the one whose faith is most suspect. This person is really clinging to control, not to faith. It is the illusion of certitude. Much like the *psanky*, the highly decorated eggs we see at Easter time in the Eastern and Orthodox Christian traditions, it presents an attractive veneer, but it is precariously thin and delicate. It is just this illusion of certitude that doubt corrects. Doubt keeps us spiritually honest. Such honesty is an important prerequisite to surrender, for real surrender is impossible in the midst of self-deception.

For faith to come forth, both desire and doubt must be transcended. It is understandable that doubt would need to be transcended (not eliminated), for we have seen over and over again individuals whose clinging to doubt has kept them from a true faith decision. It is harder to see why desire must also be transcended. Would not desire continue to fuel the fires of faith? Yet if we continue to cling to desire, we reach an impasse we do not at first expect. Desire can, if you will, hold faith captive if it is not transformed. It would present us with a "faith" that always needs to be affirmed. The mystics, however, are clear that faith is not always affirming; sometimes it is dark. Transforming desire is part of the surrendering of faith. In the deep experience of mystical faith, one must even give up the desire for God.

Hope

The apostle Paul claims that we are saved by faith, but he also says that hope is part of that process. And hope, Paul tells us, is dark. "For in hope we were saved. Now hope that is seen is not hope. For who hopes for what is seen? But if we hope for what we do not see, we wait for it with patience." (Rom 8:24–25) This should make logical sense to us. If something is in our possession, we do not still hope to get it. Yet we do not often think of hope as a dark reality. Instead, we more frequently rush to the stance of optimism and attempt to recognize hope as being essentially light-filled. When someone is in the pit of gloom, we frequently tell them, "Snap out of it; try to be hopeful. Things are bound to get better." This light/dark contrast is only one aspect of the oppositional elements we find in the virtue of hope.

"Try to be hopeful." The statement indicates some kind of belief that hope can be manufactured by sheer willpower. Or it suggests that somehow hope is a state of mind. From this point of view, the virtue hope becomes an autosuggestion, a self-hypnosis, and would seem to indicate that it is open to trance-like qualities. There is something of a paradox here, to be sure. If hope is seen as a power of the mind toward self-suggestion, entering into a trance-like hopefulness is also an abdication of the mind's power. It would be a choice, as it were, toward self-deception. Yet this would not be the virtue of hope.

Hope can also become confused with anticipation. "I hope to make a career change next year," one might say. Anticipation can have several meanings. It could indicate to look forward to, as it does in the above statement; or it could carry the sense to forestall; or finally it could mean to act ahead of time. All of these seem to be very positive qualities. In fact, it would be possible to formulate a kind of spirituality of anticipation based on these understandings of the word. Anticipation as a spiritual reality then would:

- look forward to what God is about to do.

- forestall evil by taking appropriate measures.

- act ahead of time to uncover God's presence in the here and now.

These qualities seem to indicate good things. It would do well for the Christian to anticipate what God will do in the world and in one's own life. Acting against evil would also be a good positive action, as would playing a role in uncovering God's presence in a given situation. But we must also recognize that in simple anticipation all these actions are open to deterioration. Looking forward to what God is about to do, we can begin to see God making miraculous interventions at inappropriate or mundane opportunities. This is technically known as *deus ex machina*. People who thus anticipate God's actions in this manner always seem to be privy to their own brand of unique revelations, which nevertheless for some reason often seem to place many demands on other people. Or in forestalling evil by taking appropriate measures, a laudable quality in itself, we can assume the heroic role even when such a role might be contrived or self-serving. Often we forestall evil as we see it, and where we see it, and with the full extent of our righteous anger. Or in acting ahead of time to uncover God's presence in the here and now we can become frivolous and manipulative with God. God comes to be looked upon as a supporter of my group, my team, and my plan, with everything that happens to me offered as a proof of God's blessing.

The ironic thing is that all these "hopeful" forms of anticipation could easily be pointing to a deeply concealed stance of mistrust toward myself or reality. If I am always proclaiming my belief that God is making special revelations to me, or uniquely blessing my actions, or using me as a private sword of righteousness, I might actually be overcompensating for unconscious feelings of hopelessness. I might really feel quite insecure in my relationship with God, and the "marvelous deeds" that I see visited upon me can be my own self-made brand of reassurance.

So anticipation in a spiritual sense is a double-edged sword, possessing both positive and negative aspects. Yet, by the very nature of the word, it is still a statement of affirmation. If anticipation is to be considered an affirming statement toward hope, then what would lie in opposition to it? We could possibly call it apprehension, but perhaps to maintain the overall nature of the extreme in paradoxical structure, we might also want to call it dread. Dread contains the same three elements that anticipation possesses, so we could again formulate a spirituality of dread, even though we don't particularly like to reflect on it any more than we have to. As with anticipation, it would:

- look forward to what God is about to do.

• forestall evil by taking necessary measures.

• act ahead of time to uncover God's presence in the here and now.

When dread looks forward to what God is about to do, it sees judgment and retribution. One hopes to be on the right side of that judgment. In this way dread has always been seen as a motivator for a kind of repentance, even though traditionally this has been known as "imperfect contrition." When it seeks to forestall what it believes to be evil, dread does not tend to the heroic stance, as does anticipation, but instead it seeks to play it safe and cover all the bases. We could call this the "third servant mentality," named after the last servant of the parable in Matthew 25 (vs. 24–30) who buried the master's money rather than taking the risk involved with investing it. Again, safety can be a powerful motivator, even if it leaves us somewhat unsatisfied or, in the case of the servant in the parable, cast out into the darkness. Finally, when dread acts ahead of time, it may claim to be seeking God's presence, but it is more likely trying to uncover all the pitfalls possible in the proposed courses of action. It is interesting to note that dread can be just as mistrusting as anticipation is, but it is a bit more honest about it.

So if anticipation offers us an affirming statement about hope, dread or apprehension can supply us with a negating statement. But of course neither of these is truly the virtue of hope. Once more hope is found in the transformation of the two poles. Our paradoxical triad regarding hope would therefore look something like this:

• Anticipation, which could be born of optimism in relation to what we expect of God, but could also deteriorate into an overly sanguine manner that seeks to mask mistrust.

• Apprehension, which gravitates toward dread that seeks self-protection from the insecurities of life and from my own uncertainties about God.

• Transforming hope: letting go of our need to anticipate happy outcomes or to dwell in dread or apprehension, we allow an attitude of trust to transform both into hope that relies upon an assurance of God that is not tied to expectations or results.

The real virtue of hope has the same qualities that we have already mentioned. It looks forward to what God is about to do, and it forestalls evil by taking appropriate measures, and it also acts ahead of time to uncover God's presence in the here and now. In hope, however, these qualities all possess a freedom that was not present before. The essential fact of hope is that it transforms both anticipation and dread by bringing to them the presence of trust and surrender. Hope can live with the reality of anticipation and dread, because they are a part of human life. But it cannot do so without trust.

We can see that trust and hope have a very close relationship to each other. In many circles, hope and trust are seen as synonyms. I believe, however, that the relationship between hope and trust can be seen in the same way as the connection between faith and trust. There is an important benefit that comes with our separation of hope and trust. While trust is the fundamental spiritual attitude, hope as a virtue manifests itself in concrete action. Trust, therefore, places us in an open stance to the future; hope, on the other hand, allows us to act gracefully from that position.

Love

Despite its few letters, love is a very big word in our language. It is used in innumerable contexts by people who mean very different things by it. Love is the energy that holds the world together, just as it can very easily drive apart in very hurtful ways those who have found new loves to which they cling. It is seen by some as the motive for the greatest philanthropy and altruism, while others would see it as an act of sheer libido and animal instinct. It is a word used to explain the actions of mystics and contemplatives as well as the characters who inhabit afternoon soap operas. The word no doubt carries too much meaning; that is probably the main reason we have so many problems with it.

Among the countless understandings of love is the one that recognizes it as a virtue. To see love as a virtue is very different from regarding love as a feeling or emotion. The feeling of love is frequently bound up in the movements of passion, in the drive to conquer, and in the need to be satisfied. As a feeling, love can be very intense, but then it can fade over time. The feeling of love can quickly turn to hate or indifference. No doubt, love's capacity as an emotion to be here today and gone tomorrow itself has paradoxical dimensions that could be explored, but that would be beyond our present scope. Instead I want to explore the paradoxical nature of the virtue of love. That means focusing on love as an action.

Love in action is a very noble thing, and not surprisingly its dialectical elements have a certain nobility in themselves. Probably a number of oppositional statements about love could be offered, but in focusing on this action-oriented love, I want to explore one particular pairing that has great impact on how we live out the spiritual life, which of course means how we function in our day-to-day existence. Many of the problems that we encounter when we seek to manifest love arise from the conflicts that we experience between compassion and truth.

Compassion and truth, like love, are both big words. They do not strike us as being particularly opposed to each other. They do become oppositional, however, when it seems to us that acting with compassion is going to have the result of denying the truth of a situation, while speaking truthfully will be harsh and hurtful. It is my experience that the opposition that lies between truth and compassion has been the cause of a vast number of problems. They are problems that arise at all levels, including the personal, relational, familial, communal, and societal. They are among the most difficult problems to resolve.

Here, then, is my proposed triad for the paradoxical virtue of love:

• Affirming with compassion: the ability to accept giftedness, to share pain, and to long for the fulfillment of oneself or another.

• Proclaiming with truth: the ability to recognize an experience and act toward it with total honesty in regard to self, another, or an event.

• Love in action: an action of surrender toward compassion and truth.

A few things need to be said about this triad. First, it needs to be stressed that compassion and truth are both very good qualities.

Really, they are both virtues in themselves. It is just that neither of them, in itself, is the same as love. I find it interesting that both truth and compassion are qualities that can be held without intimacy. Truth can be maintained in cold objectivity, while one can have compassion on strangers and faceless crowds. It seems to me, on the other hand, that the real action of love is always in some way an intimate thing.

There also needs to be some explanation as to why truth is seen as a force in the triad that seems to negate compassion. It is not that truth is a negative thing at all. Indeed, truth as a virtue itself possesses a transforming power. But situationally, when opposed to a course of action determined to be one of compassion, truth plays the devil's advocate. "You want to do what? Don't you see what's really going on here? Can't you see that this stands against what we believe? Don't you see that it's just a band-aid solution? Can't you recognize that you're being manipulated?" In such a role, truth acts as the negating energy to affirming compassion. It is true, however, that in other situations the tables are reversed, and truth becomes the proposed affirmation while compassion takes on a negating role. In either case, however, the dynamics involved remain essentially the same.

In my previous book I mentioned the tension that lies between these two forces. Some of what I said then bears repeating.

> Love is always embodied in some way in truth and compassion. We are constantly being called to seek both at all times. If our love lacks either of these qualities, we run a great risk of manufacturing something else and merely calling it love. If, for instance, my love does not possess truth, I am in danger of sliding into manipulation and the co-dependent mode we sometimes call enabling. If, on the other hand, my love lacks compassion, I can fall into perfectionism, judgmentalism, and violence. These can appear in very subtle forms, and can be extremely hard to find and root out.
>
> The Christian call, from the preaching of Jesus onward, has been to seek compassion. If we as individuals and as a community of faith have failed in our efforts to be disciples of Jesus, it is

predominantly here. There are many reasons for this....However, one major reason for our failure to be compassionate is fear. It is most often our feelings of radical mistrust and insecurity that cause us to withhold mercy from our sister or brother. Moreover, the feelings of a lack of worth and mistrust of self can keep us from showing ourselves care and compassion.

...Not all of life's experiences are easily discerned, and sometimes it is difficult to know how to balance truth and compassion in the course of our life's circumstances. In many ways the withholding of one can pass as the possession of the other. In the name of compassion I can live for years in a relationship that is self-destructive and dysfunctional. In the name of truth tremendous harm has been done to countless people within the faith community whose life circumstances do not quite match the Church's "standards." We must recognize that, as followers of Jesus, we are called to embrace both truth and compassion, and that it is possible to do both. We must also recognize that it is likely we will often fail. Sometimes in our frailty we may have to come down on one side or the other. It seems to me that, as disciples of Jesus, if we had to choose, we would want to err on the side of compassion. While avoiding manipulation, Jesus always did the compassionate thing. If in doubt we also seek to do the compassionate thing, we will, at least at a trust level, be choosing to stand with Jesus. (pp. 214-15)

The ability to appropriately embrace both compassion and truth in each situation is the manifestation of the virtue of love. As can be seen in the transforming statement of our triad, it is an action that will always imply some sort of surrendering. Surrendering, however, does not mean giving up on something. To arrive at love, it is not that I must give up either a part of my compassion or my truth. Neither one is meant to be sacrificed on the altar of love. Instead, they are both meant to be transformed. What is really surrendered is most often my own intransigent world view, which holds defiantly to past conditioning. When I find myself saying, "No, it has to look like this," that is the time I need to take stock in where my investment truly lies.

While truth and compassion are not given up in arriving at love, it might well be that one or the other will have to be put on hold for the moment. Love requires that both be maintained, but sometimes, because it is a process, the virtue asks that my actions proceed from one while the other is held in reserve for the time being. For instance, an addict's family members who choose what is called "tough love," the speaking of truth, as the best way to deal with a deteriorating situation have not given up compassion for the person. They have merely discerned that at this moment love looks truthful. They instinctively know, however, that the day will come when love must look compassionate, or else all the truth that is now spoken will turn into bitterness for all involved.

The ability to live consciously and consistently in the virtue of love, or that of faith, hope, or any other virtue, is not easy. Many failed attempts will occur, even on a daily basis. We cannot afford to hold ourselves to impossible standards of perfectionism when we are truly seeking to live out the spiritual life. We need to exercise a little compassion on ourselves, and quite frequently at that. But our abilities to live out of virtuous reality can be enhanced. Perhaps it is frequently difficult to be a hero, but we can still seek a certain mastery in our responses to life's everyday events.

Putting Virtue into Practice

Understood as an activity, there are two ways of practicing virtue. One way is spontaneously, and the other is through a planned course of action. Of the two the first is by far the better, and in fact is necessary if virtuous reality is to be an integrated aspect of life. To act spontaneously from virtue is to act consciously in the present moment. This is a key to transforming consciousness. The transformation of paradox happens only in the now moment. Surrender is possible only as a present reality. It is like the bridesmaids waiting for the groom to arrive in the parable of Matthew 25:1–13. When he comes I am either ready or not; I either go into the wedding or I don't. Perhaps it's not my last chance to go to a wedding, but if I am not prepared I have certainly missed this one.

Of course, it is not much help to tell myself that I have to act consciously. Even if I am cognitively convinced of the benefits of conscious living, that does not mean that I am in a position to live that way. To live consciously has a few other requirements. The willingness to surrender is a prerequisite, but I have already addressed that sufficiently in chapter three. Living my life prayerfully from a centered existence is also necessary. I will address that in the next chapter. I also want to examine discernment there, which is another important element in conscious living. But all of these are enhanced by a quality that we could call awareness.

Awareness, we could say, is a positive outcome of conditioning, although it needn't be confined to conditioning. Usually, those spiritual writers who advocate conscious living are opposed to conditioned behavior, because conditioning is generally inversely proportionate to freedom and grace. It is, for instance, the conditioning of childhood that can become one of the biggest barriers to living a holy and whole life. In that sense I am also opposed to conditioning. Much conditioning, however, is rather innocent. For instance, we do not often stop to consider what we do in the morning to prepare for the coming day. While it could be most beneficial to live that first half-hour of our day in consciousness, most of us just follow a normal routine. The washing and shaving and grooming that each of us does has probably developed into a pattern over a long period of time. To follow that pattern really does us no harm, as long as it is not compulsive, and it effectively saves our conscious energies for other things.

Awareness is born of such conditioning. For instance, a small child is playing around an open flame and gets burned. The pain and panic register. This is reinforced in the child with subsequent accidents. Gradually the child becomes aware of the dangers that can exist in being careless around fire. The child does not really have to think this through; it is known and remembered at the level of conditioning. Later in life the person can still start campfires and light candles, but there is a healthy respect for the power of fire. This awareness is not just in unconscious conditioning. It is an awareness that has also become in some way conscious. We do not go from place to place consciously looking for open fires, but when we are around a fire we know how to make conscious choices to act appropriately.

We can bring this same kind of conscious awareness to virtuous reality. With the right kind of awareness my actions of love, or faith, or hope can be greatly facilitated. I can know how to act gracefully with faith when in a given moment I find my mind filled with doubts, or with love when I am torn between my desire to be compassionate and my sense of the reality of the situation. This kind of awareness, coupled with prayerful centeredness, discernment, and the willingness to surrender, allows me the opportunity to take full advantage of the transforming grace of this moment. While the choice that I make is no guarantee of the choice that will be asked of me in the next moment, my increasing awareness of virtuous reality does build a growing openness to a course of direction. In this sense, then, we can talk of the virtues as dispositions. They are, however, conscious dispositions, for even with heightened awareness, they are actions I must choose to do.

Yet how does one go about strengthening awareness? This is where the second way of putting virtue into practice becomes important, for we can grow in awareness through a planned course of action. The traditional word for such a plan is called asceticism. The word has a bad connotation in many quarters. We can possibly remember many aberrations connected to the ascetical practices of the past. Frequently in an earlier time actions were taken in the name of some kind of spiritual merit that was really unconnected with anything else in our lives. The presumption was that the sheer fact of performing these actions would benefit us, perhaps through a kind of heavenly record keeping, or at least they would in themselves raise us to a new height of spiritual heroism. This kind of asceticism smacked of salvation by our works alone, but this was lost in the overall system of piety that supported it and gave it a kind of consistency. We therefore need to redefine asceticism to salvage it as a beneficial spiritual practice.

When I was a child my religious education cautioned about the dangers of putting myself in the occasion of sin. There were many situations, I was told, that for many compelling reasons were blatant invitations to temptation. Asceticism, on the other hand, implies to me a desire to place myself in an occasion of grace. In other words, there are some situations that for very concrete reasons might offer themselves as fertile ground to exercise the practice of a particular virtue. Have I found that fear is a big barrier to my response to grace? There are certain common situations that I know will call forth courage within me. Have I discovered a tendency to make myself the center of attention? I can imagine everyday situations that will offer me the opportunity to practice humility. To place myself in these situations and then consciously choose to act differently from my automatic response is a very basic form of asceticism.

The difference between this sort of action and the old asceticism can be seen in a couple of areas. First of all, these actions are not per se negative. They are not undertaken to be some kind of mortification of the flesh. Some actions that fall within my planned course of practicing virtue are quite fun and enjoyable. Perhaps as a workaholic, for instance, I need the asceticism of a movie or even an entire day off. Perhaps if I am compulsively rigid in my diet, I need to experience the joys of an occasional ice cream sundae. The asceticism I have in mind is not negative, but it is difficult. It asks us to move into new territory.

Second, the actions of this new asceticism are directed actions. They are done for a very particular purpose. They are simple actions, limited in scope, that are meant to stretch the parameters of my life, to get me out of the comfort zone of conditioned behavior. As such they are to be understood qualitatively. In the old asceticism, actions were more seen as being quantitative or cumulative. The actions of this new asceticism are not "stored up" for us. They are not laid away for the future, but are directed to the present. They are therefore concrete and immediate.

This brings us to a third difference between the old and the new asceticism, and that is concerning the matter of results. The old asceticism had few tangible results. The actions were understood as meritorious, but their benefits were focused somewhere else, quite possibly beyond this life. This does not mean that the ascetical practices I am suggesting are bereft of ultimate meaning. Quite the contrary, any such benefits would hold just as true for this new asceticism, but in addition these actions have very tangible results in our present lives. The results are not like keeping a scorecard of how well I am doing. It is much more the nature of seeing the richness of my life expanding and deepening. It has to do with recognizing a growing balance and flexibility within me, a greater capacity to gracefully meet the demands of everyday living.

Another expression for this kind of asceticism could be found in the word discipline. The process of practicing the virtues through planned action could be termed discipline toward transformation. While we often balk at harsh discipline, we realize how important in the long run a healthy discipline is for fruitful living. In his book *The Road Less Traveled*, M. Scott Peck offers a very high estimation of the importance of discipline. "Discipline is the basic set of tools we require to solve life's problems. Without discipline we can solve nothing. With only some discipline we can solve only some problems. With total discipline we can solve all problems." (p. 15-16) While his point is well taken, his evaluation of discipline is a bit higher than I would choose to go. Discipline is indeed necessary to deal effectively with life's problems, but it is my sense that there are some problems of life that are simply not in our power to solve. There are some problems in life, in fact, whose paradoxical nature makes finding a solution next to impossible. Perhaps they do not need to be solved in the first place; perhaps they need to be transformed.

ENDNOTES

1. See, for instance, Erik H. Erikson, *Identity: Youth and Crisis*, pp. 96-97.

VII

Prayer and Discernment

A Story: The Quest of the Lady in Blue

Once upon a time there was a fair lady and she was dressed all in blue. She wore a light blue gown trimmed in deep blue velvet. She had on her head a silver tiara that was set with precious blue sapphires. She rode in a blue carriage, with a driver in a blue uniform, and pulled by two white horses with blue bridles. She was seeking the great castle that had been built at the very center of a fabulous kingdom, in response to an invitation she had received.

She had never seen the castle, but she knew of it by reputation. She had heard of its great wealth, and she had heard that anyone invited there would find tremendous happiness within its walls. She desperately wanted to get to the castle, but, never having made this trip before, she was not sure exactly of the itinerary she would have to follow.

It seemed that she had journeyed many days, perhaps weeks, before she finally came near to her destination. The castle was easy to see even at a distance, for it had been built upon the very top of a high mountain. It was truly majestic. Its walls were thick and strong and well-fortified. Its towers were innumerable, and from far off its commanding presence could be felt throughout the region. But even from this distance the lady could see that there was no direct way to approach its gates. There were, instead, many paths that seemed to go off in diverse directions. These paths could all be distinguished from one another. Some appeared to be rugged, some crooked; some were very steep, some overgrown. But none of them seemed to go directly to the castle. The lady was not sure what she should do next.

As her carriage approached the base of the mountain, where many of the paths seemed to intersect, the lady in blue saw some other figures standing about. Drawing closer, she saw that one of the figures was another lady who had alighted from the carriage in which she had been traveling. She was dressed all in red. She was talking to a wizened old man who stood along the roadside. It seemed likely that the lady in red was also seeking the castle and had stopped to ask directions of the bent-over figure. The lady in blue then saw the old man clearly point down a very crooked and winding road. By the time she had reached the spot, the lady in red had again entered her carriage, and it had pulled away along the path the old man had indicated.

From her carriage the lady in blue greeted the old man and stepped out onto the dust of the road. She asked him if he knew how she might get to the castle far above them. The old man studied her for a time in silence, and then he pointed up a rugged and steep climb that rose off roughly in the opposite direction from the one on which the lady in red had proceeded.

"That is the road you will want to take," he said in a gruff voice.

"What about that winding road?" asked the lady, indicating the one the other carriage had taken.

"That road will not take you to the castle," said the old man.

"But the other carriage took it just now."

The old man remained silent and grim. He gave her no indication that he had any understanding of her concern, and the lady began to distrust him. He had not hesitated to point out that path to her predecessor. Was he trying to throw her off for some reason? Perhaps he had been bribed. It was unlikely the other woman was not also going to the castle, so for some reason this old man did not want her to follow the lady in red. She would foil his plan, however, she said to herself. And later she would report his deception when she arrived at the castle.

She got back into her carriage and told her driver to proceed along the crooked road taken by the lady in red. They set out without so much as another word to the old man. The road wound this way and that. It was indeed a very crooked trail, with innumerable blind turns. After a very long time, however, she seemed to be drawing no nearer to the castle. Finally the carriage took a very sharp turn to the right and the lady discovered that she had come upon a crossroad where the same old man stood. He looked at her as her carriage pulled to a stop, but she could see no expression on his face.

"How did you get here?" she asked, in an accusatory tone.

"I am in the same place I have always been," he said. "You have simply come back to where you started."

"But where is the lady in red?" she asked.

"I imagine that by now she has arrived at the castle. The road you took was her path, not yours. You must take your own. Otherwise you will never reach the castle."

The lady in blue turned and looked once again at the rugged road the old man had originally pointed out. Her own doubts and uncertainties had needlessly added to her journey. But the castle was still within her sight. Profusely apologizing to the old man, she again set her mind to proceed toward her goal.

Prayer

"I feel I need some help with my prayer." Every spiritual director or retreat director has heard this statement on the lips of directees again and again. We have in turn spoken it to our own directors. While each of us walks our own path of prayer alone, if we are humble enough and trusting enough we recognize that there is help to be obtained. Many have walked a similar path before us, and we can benefit from their experiences.

There is no aspect of spirituality more written about and reflected upon than prayer. It is considered by most to be the centerpiece of the spiritual life, and countless books on the subject are available in spiritual libraries. More are published each year. Some people feel that our spiritual agenda itself is basically one of learning how to pray, and many even equate prayer with spirituality. However, that does both prayer and spirituality a disservice. It asks prayer to carry too much weight, and it too narrowly understands what spirituality is to be. While prayer is very important in our journey toward God, we must recognize that it is only a part of spirituality.

I would like to suggest that spirituality be understood in as broad a manner as possible. This is because it encompasses our entire life. Our spirituality must be recognized as the process of taking in all the events and experiences that happen in life, perceiving them in the context of faith commitment, and then acting upon them in light of that faith context. This understanding of spirituality means that everything we do has an impact on our spiritual life, because everything we do can be understood, acted upon, and transformed through faith.

In this broad context, prayer cannot be seen as synonymous with spirituality, for prayer has a much narrower focus. Prayer is understood to be an attempt with some degree of consciousness (at least in desire and intention) to encounter God in mutual presence. The heart of prayer, therefore, is an encounter between two subjects, God and myself. It is a conscious attempt to recognize a presence, an indwelling. Prayer is therefore a relational reality. It is the mutual presence, subject to subject, that is at the heart of prayer. No matter what else we say about prayer, we cannot forget the indwelling relationship that must be at its core. It is very easy to be sidetracked and forget the heart of prayer. We can become concerned about aspects of prayer, blowing them out of proportion, and forget its relational heart.

I have said that prayer is to some degree a conscious activity. This implies that it could also be in some way an unconscious experience. We do well to realize that every prayer touches us at both a conscious and an unconscious level. Prayer must at least be conscious in desire and intention. I must want to pray and attempt to pray. God, however, is not waiting for our intention. There are many wonderful things that happen to us in the spiritual life, and many come without our seeking them. We receive many graces as pure gift, and we realize that it was not our intention, or even our desire, to receive them. They are grace, but they are not prayer. Perhaps upon reception I discover a desire to encounter the Giver who lavished them upon me. That is where prayer truly starts.

Yet, who but God fully understands prayer? Even as a beginner in prayer, when I am more completely reliant upon words, thoughts, and feelings, could I say that this is all there is to prayer? Certainly not. First of all, there is God's part of the indwelling, for it is a relationship. But even beyond this, I am not fully aware of what I myself bring to this encounter. Is my spirit lifted in prayer? Is my soul deepened? Much of what happens to me is hidden in consciously inaccessible places within. Later, when my prayer has deepened and simplified, perhaps it has become almost totally hidden to me. Without words, without thoughts, without feelings, perhaps all that is left is desire and intention. Yet, consciousness must still cling to that. Prayer is neither totally conscious nor unconscious, but a paradoxical blending of both.

I have been saying that prayer is an attempt to encounter Another; it is a relational reality. As such, it has a different intention than the kind of meditative practices that have the express purpose of getting us in touch with our deepest levels of being or that seek to enhance our relaxation. Coming to know another is quite different from getting to know myself. In other words, we are not intended to be the focus of our own prayer. When we encounter another, even in our everyday life, we are always meeting someone who remains partially unknown to us. There is always a dimension of mystery involved in relationship. But it is still the other person we intend to meet. Perhaps when we were adolescents we had relationships that were little more than mirror images of our own undiscovered self, but as adults we recognize that relating to others means so much more than our own identity formation. So it is with prayer. Our intention remains focused on the Other we are encountering as we learn to surrender ourselves in prayer.

Yet, in some way the opposite is also true. First of all, while prayer is not identical with meditation and relaxation practices, many of the techniques that are at our disposal in prayer are the very same as those used in meditative practices. This is particularly true of techniques that involve breathing, imagination, and various forms of centering. Using these kinds of meditation practices will facilitate our prayer as they enhance our openness to the encounter with Mystery. Of course, their use also allows us the opportunity to experience the other benefits of meditation as well. We do learn to relax and become more centered; we do come in touch with deeper and deeper levels of being.

In reality, prayer and meditation are a mysterious paradoxical blend. Is getting in touch with our deepest being an altogether different experience than encountering the mystery of God? If meditation changes my view of myself and my world, can God be absent from that practice? In discovering God, how can I not discover who I really am? How can I not see the world in terms of universal connection and oneness? There is an incarnational principle at work in every prayer and in every meditation sitting. I discover that God and I blend, while still remaining distinct. I discover that I am at one with all that is, and this is a graced reality.

An aspect of prayer that receives too little attention is that of solitude. Solitude is both a requirement of prayer and one of its chief benefits. Solitude builds on the fact that prayer has dimensions. Among other things it is made up of space and time. But to fully understand this, we have to first open ourselves to the experience of solitude itself. In Mark's gospel one of the very first things we discover about this Jesus who is the Christ is that he is a seeker of solitude. (Mk 1:12–13) The Spirit drives Jesus into solitude in order that he might understand his call. As with Jesus, the Spirit urges me to spend time by myself. I need to do this so that I might get to know both myself and God.

This time of solitude can be a frightening experience, and we have always found very creative ways to avoid it as long as possible. To enter into solitude will require that I, like Jesus, explore the wild beasts and the angels that inhabit my inner desert. I must come to terms with both the negative and the positive aspects of myself. I cannot fully understand myself, my life, or God, if I give myself no time and space for the encounter. When I take the necessary time and space I need, I find that it opens me to a greater awareness of how these dimensions are filled with the mysterious presence of God.

Prayer is perhaps the simplest thing we can do in the world. All that is necessary is to keep focused on the presence to God. In the final analysis there are no rules to prayer, even though we will be offered many if we are of a rule-oriented mind to seek them. Yet, while it is simple, prayer always leads us directly into paradox. The truth is that prayer is one of the most paradoxical things in which life involves us. It seems to me, for instance, that most problems dealing with prayer that people bring up in spiritual direction arise from one thing. Most of us are trying to find or create a prayer that is manageable. The first and most general paradox we need to accept is that while the structure of our prayer is totally under our control, the reality of our prayer is never manageable. This is a difficult lesson for the Western mind to learn, because we have been convinced that manageability of the structural context of our lives is one of the highest goals we can achieve. It is a sign of maturity, success, and productivity. It is something for which we are rewarded. And we want desperately to be rewarded in prayer. So while prayer is the simplest thing in the world, we continue to struggle with it.

My attitude toward prayer is essential. If I approach it with apprehension, self-judgment, or perfectionism, prayer will become one of the biggest burdens that life asks me to carry. If I feel that it is something by which I must please God, God will in turn become parental to me and I will always be working for an "A"on my report card. If I pray with the attitude that it is something at which I must succeed, prayer will become a project and I will begin to keep progress charts toward sainthood. Instead of all this, my prayer will be more fruitful if it consists of attitudes such as openness, reverence, and attentiveness. These attitudes have no payoff other than mutual presence. They are all summed up in the word "trust," that fundamental attitude so important to transforming consciousness. My depth of prayer and its transformative power will correspond to my trust of God.

Prayer is indeed a simple thing, yet we find as many contradictions in prayer as anywhere in life. However, people presume that they shouldn't be there. As with most other dimensions of life, we think that our "problems will be solved" if we could just eliminate the contradictions. In reality our prayer calls out, not for problem solving, but for transforming consciousness. The question is not how can I find the answers to my prayer difficulties, but how can I recognize the presence of paradox in my prayer and allow it to nurture my transformation? The variety of paradoxes in prayer is quite extensive. There are a number of paradoxes around the structure of prayer, which include paradoxes of time and space, and other paradoxes that deal with the nature and experience of prayer.

Some of the structural paradoxes connected with prayer have been discussed in chapter five, in the context of the spiritual dichotomies. One of these dichotomies, the paradox of going out and going in, of action and contemplation, is relevant to how we go about structuring prayer. Each of us seeks to balance these two spiritual needs. In chapter five I mentioned that our present culture has overemphasized activity. I said that we need to develop habits and methodologies around prayer and meditation. Of course, this is done fruitfully only when our call to action is also recognized.

We can also recall the Apollonian/Dionysian tension that was discussed in chapter five. It applies nowhere more than in our prayer life. This tension represents a structural paradox in prayer that deals with discipline and spontaneity. Every prayer life needs discipline. Even the most spontaneous among us (and sometimes especially the most spontaneous) need a well-ordered life of prayer. Yet some think that by structuring and ordering their prayer, they can succeed in managing it. We cannot manage our prayer through discipline. Rigidly holding to set times, places, and postures will not bring us spiritual freedom, nor will it necessarily hasten mutual presence. On the other hand, prayer that seeks to embrace total spontaneity has great risks. It can end up being something else entirely, or at least it can remain unfocused and dissipated.

When we speak of structuring prayer, we are speaking about issues of time and space. Human beings understand time in two ways. One way is to understand time in linear progression through memory and intention. This kind of time in Greek is called *chronos*. It is where we get our English word chronology. Here time has a past, a present, and a future. This time is measurable through our relative perception of reality in minutes, days, years, and so on. Time, however, is also understood existentially as a current moment. In Greek this is called *kairos*. This kind of time cannot be measured; it can only be experienced. The two different kinds of time exist in tension. Both present us with a different sense of value. Our society longs for kairos, which it superficially equates with experience and calls the pursuit of happiness. Ironically, society has lost its connection with kairos, and so it lives in a permanent state of dissatisfaction. The result is that, while extolling kairos, it really ends up overemphasizing chronos. We live in a world that is overly planned, where every moment is accounted for. Even our free time is planned. Otherwise we feel we might "miss something."

In spirituality both chronos and kairos are important. For instance, the way in which we understand our faith development is chronological. When a spiritual director asks a directee to speak about his journey of prayer, or to tell how God has been encountered through her life cycle, the question is asking for some type of chronological perspective. We celebrate anniversaries of important life events, both secular and religious. The reason dates are kept in spiritual journals is that chronological time has meaning in the spiritual life. But prayer itself is primarily existential; it is involved essentially in kairos time. It is like the servant in Scripture who is waiting for the master's return. (Lk 12:35–38) Prayer is experienced in the present, and no matter how intense the prayer is, it cannot really be held on to. The time of prayer is really no time. It is a time that is timeless. We need to honor chronos in our prayer, to be aware of how God has led us in the prayer journey, but we will always need to know its relative importance. In our encounter with the Other, every moment is fresh and new, and only that moment matters.

Prayer also asks us to consider a paradox of space. We could speak of this as a tension between our sense of holy ground and what James Finley called "the palace of nowhere." There has always been a natural human gravitation to holy places. We see this in the archaeological remains of the most ancient of people. Each of us has felt the kind of awesome reverence that comes over us when we are silently present in a chapel, overlooking a mountain vista, or alone in a desert place. We feel the need to structure our holy places with icons, candles, religious art, and crucifixes, making them places of beauty and devotion. But despite all this, in prayer there really is no place to go. Ancient Israel understood this. Throughout its history there were some who felt that God could not be confined to a temple or to any place of worship. We ourselves know that at that deepest point of prayer we come into a place that is no place. It is space without space just as kairos is time without time. Then we discover that all the spatial structure we have added is nothing more than an aid, one that falls away when it is no longer needed.

These structural paradoxes of prayer, however, are relatively simple compared to those that deal with the nature of the prayer experience itself. We might think again, for instance, of the structural tension between spontaneity and discipline. Why, after all, would some people feel they want or need discipline and order in prayer? What comes with successful management? The answer is accomplishment. We want to feel that we are getting somewhere in prayer. We have heard preachers urge us to make greater progress in the spiritual life. Perhaps some have prayed at the beginning of the spiritual exercises or a hermitage experience to have a successful retreat. And yet success and accomplishment are about as far away from prayer as one can get. I am fond of challenging groups to consider that prayer is actually useless. There is nothing to accomplish, and nothing we can accomplish. Some quarters of our highly pragmatic (and frequently agnostic) culture are quick to point out that prayer seems to have little practical use. When our beliefs are thus challenged, we often feel defensive and wish to justify our actions. We try to convince people of the usefulness of prayer. No doubt there are ways in which prayer is pragmatically defensible, but its uselessness also needs to stand as a prophetic witness. When I come to prayer, I do not need to do anything. Success is not part of the quotient.

Perhaps the best-known paradox in regard to prayer experience lies in the difference between consolation and desolation. Consolation is the experience of receiving a kind of spiritual unction or blessing as the apparent result of our prayer. It is what could be

called a feel-good experience. Particularly those who are only beginning the prayer journey can greatly desire consolations from God.
Desolation, on the other hand, is the feeling of dryness or emptiness,
or even a feeling that has certain depression-like qualities connected
to it. When desolations first come, many feel that they have started to
do something wrong in prayer, or perhaps that they have sinned in
some way. They question themselves, and they long for a return to
some kind of consolation. Those further along the journey know that
consolations and desolations come and go. They understand that
feelings are not a true barometer of the spiritual life. The mutual presence with God that we seek in prayer lies deeper than emotion.

Related in some way to the above, but more enduring as an individual's overall mode of prayer, is the paradox between what is
called cataphatic and apophatic prayer. These terms come from
Greek expressions that indicate something positive and something
negative. Cataphatic prayer designates a general inclination toward
prayer that is characterized by praise, vivid imagery, and an affirming tenor in one's language and expression of prayer. Apophatic
prayer, on the other hand, tends to be a wordless and imageless kind
of prayer. It is sometimes referred to as the negative way. Frequently
they represent two styles of prayer experience that to some degree
are responsive to the particular temperament of the individual.

It would seem there are some people, in other words, who are
more inclined to one or the other way of praying. Great mystics, such
as Francis of Assisi and Thérèse of Lisieux, had a style of spirituality
that was generally cataphatic in its approach to God, while equally
mystical was the decidedly apophatic approach of John of the Cross
and Meister Eckhart. Yet because prayer is relational, because it
involves the mysterious relationship with God, to some degree we
can also speak of being led for a time into cataphatic or apophatic
prayer. Most people who faithfully walk the journey of prayer will
probably find elements of both approaches in their experience. Or
perhaps they will find one approach predominates at one phase of
life, while another emerges later. The paradox beneath them remains,
however. God is both knowable and unknowable at the same time.

There is a danger, however, in even identifying such distinctions in prayer. Even when we say that they are paradoxical, and therefore can be present at one and the same time, our linear minds have a great penchant for clinging to the particular nature of things. The result is that such distinctions cause us to begin to evaluate and then to judge our prayer. We judge it, however, as we frequently judge our lives, based on our expectations. We have in our heads what we think our prayer should look like, and critique our experiences accordingly. Yet these mental expectations cause us great difficulties, because we use an ideal that does not exist anywhere but in our minds. Actual prayer experience is too nuanced and subtle to match our mental picture, and God's own activity is too unpredictable. But when we begin judging, we never consider this. Our prayer seems to be always falling short. It never seems to pass muster. It occurs to us that our prayer is seldom "as it should be," and our efforts at prayer are never "enough." Instead of judgment, we need discernment. But if this is true of prayer, it is all the more true of our life experiences in general.

Discernment

Discernment deals with a much larger question than simply what is going on in my prayer. Discernment deals with the sense of what is actually going on in my life. It attempts to recognize the presence and activity of God in the experiences of life that are open to me. It also asks me to evaluate my own choices, decisions, and actions in light of that presence. It is, therefore, a major spiritual issue in its own right, and its importance is often underestimated.

Traditionally it has been called discernment of spirits, which was understood to involve the individual in the attempt to sense movements of life that are either good or bad. In the Ignatian Spiritual Exercises the language of consolation and desolation is used to distinguish in which of two general life movements the individual presently dwells—one, the movement of Christian faith, or the other, the movement of sin and dissipation.[1] In our process of discernment, however, we can frequently recognize that the movements of life are not always easily distinguished as either good or bad, healthy or unhealthy, growthful or diminishing. It is possible that at times my discernment will be relatively simple, but often the complexity of life will not easily line up one way or the other. There are innumerable variables surrounding the choices we are called to make in life, and many of them reflect life's paradoxical nature. Discernment is frequently not a question of good and bad directions, but more often of how the Spirit of God works through conflicting values. Sometimes the values are generally positive; sometimes negative. Most often the values present in a given situation are varying shades of gray. There might be a large number of values at stake in some circumstances. We might not even be able to identify all of them. The quest for certitude around our discernment is often a chimera.

Then again, discernment is frequently absent from our spiritual process altogether. It is sometimes considered important only when we are in the process of choosing a major life direction, or making an important decision. But then, following our decision, when life seems to come back to "normal," discernment is put back on the shelf until the next retreat or the next crisis. In reality, discernment needs to be a pervasive presence in our lives. Discernment should be involved in the moment-by-moment journey of life. Each moment carries great significance with it. No moment is inconsequential. If spirituality is my life lived in faith, and every dimension of my life has a faith context, then discernment is the ongoing process by which I discover that context and make my choices accordingly.

I have frequently heard it said that the most important criterion of discernment is peace. While this can be true, it can also be just as true that peace can be a self-deception. It is important for us to be aware of our source of peace. There are a large number of experiences that can go by the name of peace. Is what I call peace really the desire for noninvolvement? Is it appeasement? An avoidance of conflict? Real peace can be an excellent source of discernment, but real peace takes into account the paradoxical nature of life, and is an outcome of transforming consciousness. The peacefulness that I arrive at through self-deception is never sufficient, and in fact is misleading. If I have lulled myself into a false peace, it means I will feel, or at least pretend to feel, self-satisfied, but this kind of satisfaction will be a strong barrier to a true willingness to surrender.

In my previous book I suggested that fruitfulness was a much more solid criterion for discernment. Our sense of discipleship, our response to faith in all its aspects, calls us to act toward what is most fruitful for the Reign of God. Does a particular action further this Reign? Do the choices that are open to me have the likely possibility of bearing fruit? Is there one choice that offers the best opportunity for manifesting the most fruitfulness?

> It is important to remember that fruitfulness is not to be equated with productivity, success, acceptance, progress, or a lack of conflict. In itself, fruitfulness is not measured by "what I want," "what you need," or "what will fulfill me as a person." Fruitfulness is not necessarily an element of what is needed for my happiness or a situation's peaceful resolution, although it might come to be. Fruitfulness is solely intent on what furthers the Reign of God at this moment. As such it is possible that the fruit of an experience will vary from moment to moment, even in very similar circumstances. This is all the more reason why our discernment must be conscious.
>
> (*Conversion and the Enneagram,* p. 204)

The fantasy of peace, on the other hand, can frequently live in automatic habitual behavior with great comfort. It is likely to favor the status quo, or to follow the path of least resistance. There is also a desire for easy answers. False peace tends to close its ears to difficult questions. This is significant, because a real process of discernment involves me with a plethora of difficult questions. Questions are very helpful for conscious discernment. Most often the seeking of questions is far more important than getting answers. Answers tend to stop processes. Once I have an answer I am satisfied with, I no longer need to look further. On the other hand, questions keep the spiritual processes of my life open. I have to explore further, go deeper, and thereby make connections that I had not seen before. There are some spiritual questions that are practically universal in their appearance, and always significant in their meaning. Our discernment will likely lead us to explore the following questions at one time or another.

What is my awareness of who I am? What is my understanding of my own identity? Does my life seem to be a consistent whole? Do I understand who I am only in terms of what I do? Do I go through life playing a series of roles or fulfilling some unspoken expectations? Have I given myself enough time and space to discover who I truly am underneath the roles?

What keeps me from owning the experiences of my life? Am I comfortable with the person I have become through my life journey? Are there memories that give shape to the past that I feel I have not yet integrated? Are there inner blocks that I just cannot seem to get beyond? What kind of things have happened to me that stand as a block to accepting the events and circumstances of my life? Many of these questions are also relevant to the process of healing, to be discussed in the next chapter.

What is the stamp of God's activity on my life? Can I find meaning in the person I have become through my faith context? How has God been at work in the events of my life that have led to this moment? How am I being called to be sacramental, a human sign instilled with the presence of the Spirit? Can I recognize the presence of a divine intimation that speaks to me through my actions and calls me to recognize meaning beyond their face value?

What choices are being laid out before me now? Are they choices that are calling me to be proactive or reactive? How will my choices reflect the fruitfulness of the Reign? Are there areas in life that appear to offer me no choices? Are there other ways that I can understand them that allow me more creativity?

Where is the challenge of growth for me now? What are the resistances in my life that I am coming to recognize? What are the conscious actions I will have to undertake to counterbalance these resistances? Are there challenges I am taking on merely in order to prove something to myself? How am I presently experiencing the ongoing challenge to surrender the resistances that are keeping me from transformation?

Most of these questions, and many others besides, will involve me in various forms of tangible paradox within my life. While we might not always consciously recognize them as paradoxes, they create oppositional choices that are constantly coming into focus. This in turn leads to a further set of discernment questions. Where am I currently finding elements of opposition in my life, areas that I seem to be stuck in, or perplexed by? What are the affirming forces in each of these areas, the forces that usually represent that aspect I am "holding out for"? What are the denying forces in each area, the forces for which I likely need to reach a new level of appreciation? Where are the forces that can represent a movement in the direction toward transformation? What am I being called to surrender in order that this transformation might come about? True choice always involves me in surrender, because with every real choice something is going to die. I say yes to something, and surrender all the other options, at least for the present, and possibly forever. But I do this with the realization that in transformation all the previous choices look different, and that includes the path I have chosen to take.

In the midst of seeking a deeper exploration of all these questions, discernment does not leave us isolated. There are many aids that are available to us in a complete process of discernment. We must recognize the presence of the Spirit within the Church as the first and primary power given to us. It is present to us first of all through Scripture, the Word of God, which remains the objective norm of faithful action for the Christian. It is also present to us in what is called the apostolic tradition. Before a single word of the New Testament was written, there was a living, discerning community of believers who were making life choices out of their understanding of the paschal mystery, the death and resurrection of Christ, and witnessing to their faith in the risen Christ on a daily basis. This apostolic tradition in conjunction with Scripture has been regarded as normative in the Catholic Church, and the two form the basic sources of its teaching. Catholics also recognize the teaching Church, especially papal and episcopal teaching, as an essential way in which our understanding of Scripture and the apostolic tradition has been handed down through the ages.

When seeking aid in discernment, we also need to recognize the presence of another important aspect of the Church, and that is, of course, its present living members manifested communally and individually. Jesus said in Matthew 18:20, "For where two or three are gathered in my name, I am there among them." The Christian call is a call to community in faith. This itself has been manifested in countless ways in the Church's experience down through the centuries. In regard to discernment, in recent days it often takes the form of small informal groups whose members openly reflect with one another on the movements of their lives and invite each other's deeper sharing of their faith. Such faith-sharing groups can have many different contexts. Sometimes these groups exist within parishes or congregations. Sometimes they cross parochial or even denominational lines. With proper structure and leadership, they can be of great help in aiding their members in deeper exploration of their spiritual lives.

Such groups could generally be called spiritual friending groups. The idea of seeking out spiritual friends is by no means new, but today it is receiving renewed interest. This is enhanced by the realization settling on the Christian population that everyone is called to the deepest holiness in Christ. Christian discipleship is not subject to a class system. Each person is uniquely touched by God's Spirit, and each person is called to the deepest transformation in Christ. Spiritual friends support us in this realization, and encourage us to continue the journey in faith.

From one vantage point spiritual direction could be considered a form of spiritual friendship. In another sense, however, it is a professional relationship that is expressly structured around the need for discernment in the spiritual life. The spiritual director is a friend in the sense of being someone who seeks the best interests of the directee, but the director is also aware of the importance of remaining objective in regard to what the directee is presenting of her or his life. Spiritual direction is becoming more and more popular within the Christian community, and rightfully so, for it serves an increasingly growing need within the Church. Today spiritual direction exists across denominational lines, and its impact continues to grow with training centers, professional organizations, and a wealth of published material supporting those who offer their services as directors.

Spiritual direction needs to understand paradox. One of the most important tasks of the director is to help one's directees make their way through the numerous transitions inevitably found on the spiritual journey. In that journey there will be crossroads and dead ends, new beginnings and terminations, revelatory flashes of insight and glaring blind spots, and in each of these there will be an abundance of apparent contradictions that will need to be sorted out and worked through. The director must be able to offer the directee encouragement in the midst of decisions, honesty in the call to conversion, and support in the face of mystery. The director will also need to raise many questions for consideration. Again, it is the willingness to explore these questions, and not the expectation of immediate answers, that is likely to produce the most fruit in the direction relationship. In my own experience as a spiritual director I have found an understanding of the dynamics of paradox to be irreplaceable in helping directees make sense of the many intricate pathways that make up the process of their lives.

While spiritual direction and all the other aids to discernment are extremely helpful, however, none of them can do the actual discernment. Nor can anyone ultimately make my life choices in my place. At times I might try to give my responsibility away, and I might even find someone who is willing to take it for a while. The results will not be beneficial. Or I might think that all I need to do is follow someone else's life plan, like the lady in blue in the chapter's opening story. But another's journey will not be the same as mine. In the end, the choice of how I will respond to God's transforming Spirit in this present moment of my life, and in the next moment, and in the one following, is only mine to make. Any other expectation I might have is self-delusional.

The paradoxical virtue of discernment is called obedience. The root of this word means to listen. Many people might have a negative reaction to this word because it often has the connotation of being asked to listen to someone who is in charge. In other words, obedience is one of our loaded authority words. It is therefore helpful to remember that, when it comes to my discernment, there are only two persons in charge, the Spirit and me. In different ways I must learn to listen to both. This implies that the listening involved is exercised with a surrendering heart. Obedience is paradoxical because, if I am truly listening, I will hear many voices that speak to me. Some will almost certainly be contradictory. Many of the aids to discernment that I have mentioned above will present us from time to time with insights that have paradoxical aspects. This should not surprise us or discourage us. If all of the voices that presented themselves to us were in consistent agreement, discernment would be superfluous and unnecessary.

It is helpful to realize that a complete process of discernment involves being obedient, that is, attending with a listening heart to both outer and inner voices. All of the outer voices that we listen to in our discernment, including Scripture, tradition, community, and direction, are complemented and balanced by a number of inner voices that are also available to us. Sometimes there is a tendency to forget the inner voices and solely rely on what the outer voices are "telling me I should do." This is at best irresponsible, and at worst dangerous. Our inner voices are no less graced than those outside of us.

As an inner voice, our prayer is of special importance in discernment. To imagine I can bring discernment to my life outside a context of prayer is like imagining I can listen to a violin concerto at a football game. Another important voice from within is the powerful inner conviction we call conscience. While discernment is frequently more complex than choosing between right and wrong, there are often strong elements of right and wrong present. When they are, they cannot be disregarded. An informed and mature conscience is essential to spiritual growth. There are also many other inner voices—intuition and sensation, emotion and reason, and a number of others. But the truth is that our inner voices are frequently just as contradictory as the outer ones. It is of great help to discover ways of working with our inner voices that can bring clarity and eventually transformation to the issues of our lives. Dream work is one powerful tool available to us that can be a tremendous aid in discernment, if we are willing to trust its processes.

Dream Work

The sense that dreams are significant for charting the course of life is probably as old as human consciousness itself. Dreams have been considered to be everything from magical and sacred in their own right all the way to meaningless or even diabolical. Our human understanding of dreaming, it seems, is almost as paradoxical as dreams themselves. Generally, dreaming is the term we use to identify everything that happens to us in our "night life," so it is not entirely clear that we can speak about dreams in any absolute fashion to begin with. Perhaps to say "I had a strange dream last night" indicates a number of possible experiences. These experiences might be meaningful to us in different ways.

Asking questions about the meaningfulness of dreams raises a larger question about spirituality itself. It is an area I have already addressed, but it is worth elaborating on a little. What do I understand this thing called spirituality to be? And how do I know when I am being spiritual? Am I being spiritual only when I am having certain theological thoughts? Or am I spiritual when I am experiencing certain emotions about theological thoughts? Or is my spirituality to include only those times I call "prayer," whether that be personal or communal? And if this is the case, what do I call the rest of life? What about when someone is studying chemistry? Or playing sports? Or making love? Where does one draw the line on spirituality and understand "ordinary life" to have taken over?

Or is spirituality what gets me ready for what lies ahead? Is it concerned with another reality in another dimension? Is this life a test, or is it simply, as some suggest, the departure lounge? A question I need to ask myself is this: is spirituality a preparation for what is to come, or is it the context through which my present life is shaped?

I have already suggested that spirituality be understood as something that encompasses my entire life, seeking to understand it and integrate it through a faith context. Spirituality is my life lived in faith. Understood in this way, spirituality is the lens of faith through which I perceive all of my experiences, encounter all of my relationships, and make all of my choices. This means, of course, that every aspect of my life is potentially spiritual; every aspect of life has faith implications, positively or negatively. What I am describing is what is usually called holistic spirituality. This means that spirituality is not a segment of life, not even the most important segment of life. It means that spirituality is what life itself is all about.

My own perspective on dreams comes from this holistic understanding of spirituality as my life lived in faith. If all of the experiences of my life can be placed in a faith context, and within that context are seen as being spiritual in nature, that means all my experiences are potentially transformative. They are all open to grace and
they all have the possibility of transformation. Dreams, then, which
themselves are human experiences, are therefore transformative as
well. To me this means dreams are open to our Source of grace, and
therefore can in the very least be helpful sources of information for
the discernment process.

While this might seem to be just a bit of holistic logic, I find it verified again and again through the life experiences of countless
retreatants and directees. Our dreams, like our prayer and the working of our conscience, like our emotions and reason, our intuition
and sensation, are part of the accumulation of the inner voices that
speak to discernment. The voices I mention are, of course, metaphorical. None of them are inner voices in either the schizophrenic or the
angelic sense. Dream material, in other words, is neither abnormal
nor supernatural. A dream is a human experience, most often a
reflective event about other human experiences. But this simple
human experience, like so many others in our lives, has a power
within it that can amaze us.

I say that dreams are reflective events. This calls for some explanation and qualification. First of all, as I mentioned, in our everyday
parlance the term "dream" usually covers everything we do while
asleep. Not all experiences that happen while sleeping, however, are
reflective events. For instance, dreams can infrequently be paranormal, so on some rare occasions we might need to consider a parapsy-
chological perspective.[2] By and large, however, our dreams are what
could simply be called metaphorical. This means that dreams primarily use images, rather than concepts, as their means of expression
and reflection on the experiences of life. This is the opposite of how
we usually reflect on our experiences in waking life. Usually our
reflection during the day is conceptual. We "think through" problems, consider our alternatives, and plot out our course of action.
Actually, dreams are likely doing the same kinds of things, only they

are doing it through the language of imagery. To work with dreams, therefore, we must be able to "speak their language." We have to learn to think metaphorically.

A metaphor is, of course, an imaginative way of comparison. We compare something abstract with something else that is more concrete and tangible. We speak in metaphors all the time, and do not often pay them much attention. Rather than saying "I just had an insight," I might say, "The light just went on." Instead of describing all the common behavioral features two friends or siblings possess, I might simply say they are "like two peas in a pod." Dreams not only perform the same kind of comparative operation, but metaphors actually become their predominant structural mode. Dreams can have conceptual content, just as our waking life can be metaphorical, but concepts appear in a decidedly subordinate manner.

To clarify our thoughts on this, let me offer one more metaphor, and that is on the process of dreaming itself. My basic metaphor for understanding how most dreams work is what I call the minority report. We have all watched enough national news to know that when Congress holds important committee meetings, it brings in many experts and gathers vast amounts of testimony and evidence. When all has been received, the committee issues its final report. Frequently, however, it is accompanied by a minority report. A segment of the committee has understood the evidence differently than the majority of its members. They hold different values and see things from another perspective. They feel they must address the topic from their own vantage point.

What you are doing now is the majority report—consciousness. You are reading this paragraph, trying to understand it cognitively, and seeking to integrate its ideas with those you already hold. We do that throughout our day; we spend our waking hours processing information. But when we go to sleep, our unconscious offers to us its own perspective from the many minority voices that were not dominant enough to gain consciousness. We know what happens to a society that represses its minority voices. It ends up either in totalitarianism or in rebellion, or both. That in itself should suggest the value of paying attention to our dreams.

That will also give us some idea as to why dreams are helpful in a discernment process. They offer us a rich amount of information with perspectives that we would not otherwise receive. To extend our metaphor, a healthy society is governed by its majority. To give in to all the minority voices would lead to chaos. In our lives we need to make our choices from consciousness. But we also realize that our conscious ego can be selective, and conditioned, and prejudiced, and even obsessive. The minority report of our dreams can offer us stark honesty about our feelings, about our attitudes, and about our judgments.

More and more frequently, psychologists and other professionals who help people understand their dreams are moving away from the classic understanding of interpretation as the goal of dream work. In that understanding the dreamer was not capable of making sense of a dream. An expert was needed who could delve into the unconscious and arrive at the one correct interpretation of the dream's content. Today we are more aware that the dreamer is the one person who has the best chance of finding meaning in a dream, because it is that person's own unconscious material that the dream is expressing. This is not to say that professional people are not helpful, or even necessary, to explore a dream completely. It means that there is no "correct answer" to be found somewhere beyond the experiences of the dreamer.

The fact is that dreams are not the best place to go to look for answers at all. They do not have much interest in giving them. Dreams, however, are very good at raising questions. As I have suggested, when it comes to discernment, questions are far more important than answers. The minority report questions the presumptions of consciousness. It questions the smug certainty with which we go about living out our lives. It asks us to stretch our horizons, to look at paths we might not have otherwise noticed. The questions that dreams ask are not generally the kind that settle issues. They ask the kinds of questions that look not for answers but for responses. And I might discover that I have many different responses to a particular issue. It is not unlikely that some of them might be contradictory. The point is that they are all honest. I am never more honest with myself than when I am dreaming.

Because the dream is presenting few answers but a wealth of questions, and because my responses to these are frequently paradoxical, it is best to realize that most dreams are meant to remain to some degree open-ended. Rather than understanding the goal of dream work as interpretation, it is better to be seeking to form a relationship with the dream. If I am in relationship with the dream, I am in dialogue with it. I am hoping to deepen my understanding of what the dream is presenting, and to open myself more completely to the many voices that speak out of the minority report. To continue in relationship with the dream means that I desire to unlock its mystery and to learn from its wisdom.

Perhaps the greatest danger in dream work, therefore, is falling prey to what could be called premature closure. Premature closure is the experience of coming to conclusions on the "meaning" of a dream too soon. Because a dream will always remain to some degree mysterious, I run a risk when I close the book on it and say, "Well, now I know what that is all about." Even if my presumptions are correct, and I have a rather clear understanding of what issues in my life the dream is addressing, once I have made such a statement, the dream will cease speaking to me. I have ended the relationship, because I now know "what it means." Since my life itself is open-ended, dream issues (which are life issues) are also open-ended. Areas in my life that seem to be clearly resolved might open up again with the experience that awaits me just around the corner. It is not unusual that people who faithfully keep a journal of their dreams find themselves going back again and again to dreams of their past, which seem to have taken on new meaning with subsequent events.

One reason dreams are so open-ended is that they are symbolic. This means that the images that make up our dreams are far more complex than we might first assume. A symbol is an image that has taken on layer upon layer of meaning. My house is not just a house; it is a place that is a concrete expression of my deepest values. It is also a place where I feel secure. It is a place I own, and defend. It is a place I choose to welcome into or exclude from. My house is a place for family, for loving and for reproducing. If I have lived there for a long time, it is a place of memory, either positive or negative. It is like me. Just like me, it has an attic, where it stores memories. Like me, it also has a basement, where it keeps a lot of other things that are too shabby or dirty for display, but still can't seem to be discarded. It might also have some other rooms not often used, or rooms that no one has looked in lately. When I dream about my house, any or all of these meanings might be relevant. There might be many others as well.

Symbols are among the most powerful of human realities. They touch us at a place much deeper than conceptual reasoning ever will be able to. They impact on us both individually and communally. They have the power to move mountains, start wars, reconcile families, unite nations, divide neighborhoods, and bring disparate peoples together in a common faith. Symbols can capture us and hold us in bondage; they can also free us and enable us to free others. To think that I can practice discernment on a moment-by-moment basis and not make allowances for my own symbolic process is naive in the extreme.

Symbols appear in dreams in any number of ways, and anything in my life can be symbolized. This is true of aspects of life that I am aware of, as well as portions of my life that are buried or hidden. That is why I always urge people who are working with their dreams to remember what I call the principle of inclusion. This states that I cannot presume anything in my dream imagery is to be excluded from the possibility that it is also in my experience. While this seems like a simple enough statement, it is amazing the number of people who are ready to deny that issues emerging from their dreams have any place in their waking lives. "Anger? Oh no, I'm not angry at anyone." "An authority issue? Well, I used to have an authority issue, but now that's all behind me." One power that dream work offers is the ability to bring some of the dream's honesty into my discernment process as a balance to the conscious ego's tendency toward self-deception.

This ability of the dream to speak with ruthless honesty to the events of our lives brings us back to the dynamics of paradox. To grasp the importance of paradox in dreams, particularly in relation to discernment, we must once again return to Jung's understanding of the psyche, as mentioned in chapter four. For Jung, the psyche is interested in wholeness, which it perceives as the bringing together of oppositional pairs. This perception, however, is at first unattainable because initially consciousness knows only how to deal with one side of those pairings. The other side is pushed to some degree into the unconscious. The more the dominant side of the pair is esteemed by consciousness and the subordinate side is relegated to unconscious depth, the less capable the individual is of seeing the inherent wholeness present in both.

The accumulation of this repressed material in the individual's unconscious is a very basic understanding of the archetype that Jung called the shadow. Through the ego's monitoring, part of psychic content is withheld from consciousness. As it is withheld in subordination, it is also frequently placed under suspicion, distaste, or mistrust by consciousness. On the other hand, the material of the conscious side of the pairing tends to be idealized and reinforced. The unrecognized aspect, however, continues to work through the unconscious to receive its due. This work is not relegated only to dreams, by any means. It might also appear in slips of the tongue, in accidents, in embarrassing circumstances, or in various attitudes toward those to whom we relate. All this appears to be very subversive to consciousness, and through defenses such as repression, projection, and denial, the unwanted feature is pushed even further away and covered over. In effect, the shadow material is more or less placed under a pressure cooker in the closed system of the psyche. Rather than vanquish the unwanted material, however, it only creates the effect of giving it more energy. If enough pressure is applied to the unconscious material, it will occasionally burst out with great forcefulness. When people speak of having nightmares, attacks of anxiety, or disproportionate emotional outbursts, the venting of the shadow is most frequently involved.

Working with dreams allows some recognition to be brought to this struggle between conscious and unconscious material. When I begin to take the minority report seriously, I open myself to hear the other side of the story. I slowly permit material to come before me without the need to reject it. I begin to recognize traits and tendencies in me that I never knew were there before. The story is told in dreams through its symbolic structure, and because of this it is delivered with all the more power.

Discernment uses each piece of information the dream unveils. Each voice from the minority report gives a little different slant on the makeup of my life. Perhaps a dream has shown me an unrecognized strain of anger toward a particular issue of my life. Perhaps I discover it has its roots in other experiences from my past. As I seek to form a response to a coming event concerning that issue, that information will be very helpful. I will be attentive to my tendency to anger. I will be less likely to fall into unconscious judgments or uncharitable remarks. I will be able to make wiser choices without the ghosts of the past interfering.

The other advantage to using dream work in my discernment process is simply a matter of time. Exploring dreams, their emotions, and their symbols makes me aware of emerging life issues much more quickly than if I await the slow process of bringing material to consciousness through other means. In the example I just used, how long would it take me to recognize that hidden strain of anger, especially since I am usually so good at covering over what I do not want to see? How many meetings would I have to unconsciously sabotage? How often would friends and associates have to give me painful feedback? How often would I have to question my own dissatisfaction with my emotional responses? My dreams are usually the first place where life's revelations can be received, if I can listen to them with a discerning heart.

But this is still not the final stage of the drama. As I am called through my dream work to consciously face both sides of each opposite pairing within me, something has to happen, for the two cannot exist side by side for long without some effect. I could push one back into the unconscious. This is much simpler than might first be imagined. I might simply choose to forget. There are many things we quickly forget rather than deal with. I might also try to live with both. This could create what is called cognitive dissonance, where two awarenesses, both having some degree of consciousness, dwell side by side, frequently with accompanying psychic pain. Living with my own incongruence is difficult to maintain for very long. The other alternative is transforming consciousness, and the embrace of paradox. The steady process of bringing the shadow to consciousness leads, in fact, to the clear indication that transformation is waiting to happen. The two sides are within me, and the two are one. I need only let go of the hold that ego has on the situation to realize their oneness. A surrendering begins to come into place, if the opportunity provided by grace can be taken.

This might suggest that dreams have a role to play in a spirituality of paradox beyond their importance to discernment. They are also powerful tools for healing and the integration of life. Dream work will therefore be revisited in the coming chapter, as we look more closely at what might be keeping us from wholeness and transformation.

ENDNOTES

1. See, for instance, Joseph A. Tetlow, *Choosing Christ in the World: Directing the Spiritual Exercises of St. Ignatius Loyola According to Annotations Eighteen and Nineteen, a Handbook* (pp. 247-248).

2. Paranormal dreams are perhaps more frequent than we might first imagine. For instance, precognitive dreams, dreams that to some degree live out future events, are reported regularly in dream workshops I have conducted. Some of them are quite dramatic in nature. Still, the vast majority of dreams are not paranormal, and to treat them as such would close off many otherwise fruitful possibilities. I suggest that time itself is one of the best tests for precognition or other paranormal phenomena. I also suggest that a presumption be given to the idea that a particular dream is metaphorical, until events might prove otherwise.

VIII

Healing

A Story: Randall the Potter

There once lived a young potter named Randall. He resided in a small hamlet in the far corner of a large and expansive country. He had a wife and a baby daughter whom he loved very much. They were a poor couple, just barely making ends meet through the amount of income Randall made at his potter's wheel and what they could bring in from their own small garden. As quite often happened in those days, both Randall's wife and daughter became very ill one winter with an unknown disease that seemed to drain their strength and showed no signs of leaving. Randall did all he could think to do, and sought help from every quarter, but the two people he loved more than anything else in the world seemed to be wasting away before his eyes.

One day a mysterious visitor arrived at Randall's door. He had bright piercing eyes, which were basically all Randall could see beneath a great hat and a long dark cloak. The mysterious visitor spoke kindly, however, and produced a vial of medicine that he said would help the sick of the house recover. Randall pressed the stranger to find out more about who he was and where this new medicine came from. All the man would say was that he had been sent by the king of that country. Then he turned and was soon out of sight.

The medicine worked in a marvelous way. Almost overnight both his wife and daughter had made a complete recovery. But no one in the village could shed any light on who the visitor was, or how the far-distant king, whom Randall had never met, or even seen, would know about his family's sickness. All he knew was that he was overwhelmed with gratitude, and wanted somehow to express this to whoever was responsible for his family's recovery. He had no money, and why would a king need money anyway? All Randall had was his considerable skill at his potter's wheel. He decided to fashion the most beautiful pot he could make and, even though he felt it would be crude by royal standards, to give it to the king as a gift.

It took him a very long time to complete the project, because he wanted it to be as beautiful and as perfect as he could make it. Many attempts were smashed or reworked because they failed to capture the sense of total gratitude that Randall felt. Finally after several weeks he had created something that was truly a masterpiece by any standards, and all his neighbors assured him that the king would certainly appreciate his efforts. Carefully wrapping up his pot, he set out for the king's palace.

He did not really know the way, for he had never made the journey before, and soon he was lost. He realized he could wander forever, so he knew he would have to find someone who could point the way for him. This thought had no sooner come into his head than he overtook an old woman walking along the road. He was amazed to discover that she, in fact, could give him very specific directions to the king's palace. He hurried on his way, but in only a few steps he began to wonder if he had even thanked the woman. As he turned around, he could see no sign of her, but he did see the hat and dark cloak of his mysterious visitor slip away into a nearby wooded area.

When he arrived at the palace, he discovered that he had not been the only one to make the journey. There were a great number of people who had also come. All seemed to have received a great favor from the king. And all had brought gifts to the palace to present in their gratitude. The gifts were as varied as the individuals who brought them, and some were very exquisite. All had been created out of the humble resources of those the king had helped. As he looked at the variety of gifts, Randall was proud of his pot. It was not any more elaborate or beautiful than a number of the other gifts, but he felt that he had done his best and his gift would make a good showing among the others.

The many gift-bearers were escorted into the king's presence. Randall was awed by the grandeur of the king's stateroom and the splendid clothing that the king himself wore. Randall also noted that his mysterious visitor stood there, just to the right of the king. It took all he had to keep from rushing up to the man to offer thanks. Instead he waited as patiently as he could as, one after another, the gifts were presented to the king, who seemed truly touched by the gratitude each gift represented.

When it came time for Randall to present his gift, he stood silently before the king and brought forth his pot, wrapped in a firm sack. But as he removed it from the sack in order to present it to the king, his hand slipped and the pot fell to the floor. A very noticeable chip broke from the lip of the pot. As he saw the chipped pot laying at the feet of the king, Randall collapsed in embarrassment and sorrow, his composure completely destroyed.

In this state he did not notice all in the hushed room gather around him and the pot. It was not until Randall heard the mysterious visitor begin to recount the old prophecy that he once again became aware of what was happening around him. There would come one who bore a beautiful gift, the man pronounced, but his gift would be flawed. While his gift was flawed, his heart was not. He would be the heir to the kingdom.

Randall was immediately adopted by the king as his son, and soon afterward his wife and daughter came to live with him in the palace. Randall later discovered that many came to the palace with flawed gifts, and the king adopted them all, many daughters and sons who were heirs to his throne. The king could see the beauty that had been placed in each of their gifts, as well as the beauty that had been placed in each of their hearts.

The Nature of Healing from a Holistic Perspective

The word healing means many things to many people. Many understand healing to be something physical that happens to a body. I am sick and I get well. I have surgery, but I then recuperate. Some attribute such processes to medical science, some to the natural curative abilities of the human body, some to God, some to all three. Many people also understand healing in the human person to include areas other than physical. They speak of emotional healing, psychological healing, or spiritual healing. Again they attribute these processes to different sources. Many think that healing can also have communal implications. They speak of reconciliation and forgiveness. They call for national grieving and social amnesty.

For some people, healing is an ordinary thing. For some of them, it is something they have come to expect. When not healed to their satisfaction, they might presume some kind of incompetence on the part of their caregivers and look for compensation. For others, however, healing is an extraordinary thing, perhaps even a miraculous occurrence. For some, this says something about the marvelous nature of life. For others, it says something about God, who generously bestows healing grace. For still others, it says something about them, that they had the necessary faith to receive what God offered. When discussing healing, I think we need to recognize the diversity of all these understandings, although some might be more adequate perceptions of healing than others. I would, therefore, like to speak of healing in its broadest sense.

Healing should not be viewed in too narrow a perspective, in my opinion, because it is essentially bound up in holistic spirituality. In the last chapter I spoke of spirituality as my life lived out in faith. I said that this understanding was holistic because it did not divide life into compartments or segments, of which only a part would be spiritual, but it saw the entirety of life as transformable by grace. It is this same vision of life and of wholeness that I feel needs to be present in our understanding of healing.

This is seen even in the word itself. Healing has its linguistic roots in the Anglo-Saxon word *hal*. In that language this word carried the connotation of being vital or alive. When we hear English concepts such as healthy, or to heal, and we remember what it is like to be healthy and not sick, we too can sense their vitality. However, this same root word, hal, is where our English word whole comes from, as well as the word holistic. Wholeness, for our linguistic ancestors, carried that same sense of vitality and life. To complete the picture, it is this same Anglo-Saxon word that has evolved into our word holiness. To be holy is also to be vital. I do not mean that all these English words are identical in meaning. Their evolution points to the refinement of language and meaning that has taken place over a thousand years. I do mean, however, that they spring from a common root experience that our linguistic ancestors attempted to articulate. While not exactly identical, wholeness, healing, and holiness have a lot in common.

I do not think it is adequate to define healing as an absence of sickness. Nor can we simply characterize health as being present when everything is normal. This is, however, the common medical understanding. The presumption of medical science is that health is where we start from. Health is present when the body is functioning properly. An individual is healthy when he or she is symptom-free. The problem starts when the body begins to malfunction for some reason. This is usually recognized through the appearance of symptoms, and medical help is sought out. Medicine uses the symptoms to diagnose what is wrong and a cure is undertaken. This cure is evaluated through the alleviation of the symptoms, when the person is then again judged to be healthy. Even the contemporary tendency to advocate preventive medicine, which is certainly an advancement over waiting until things start going wrong, is still based on a static view of health. While trends in preventive medicine are usually more holistic than former approaches, they still frequently focus on keeping things from happening, rather than encouraging things to happen.

We have a similar understanding when we look at health from a psychological point of view. People are considered to be psychologically healthy if they evidence a lack of dysfunctional symptoms. Such a state is usually identified as adjustment, and is frequently a goal of therapy or counseling, particularly in schools of thought such as behavioral science, the predominant psychological influence in America. It is when things have begun to malfunction for an individual that a problem is recognized. This is again seen in symptomatic ways through behaviors recognized as debilitating. These problems can be solved or at least eased by teaching the individual certain skills that allow for adjusted behavior to return.

We could contrast this medical understanding of health with a spiritual understanding of holiness. Very few of us would be willing to attribute holiness to someone who merely showed a lack of evident dysfunction. We would not say they were particularly holy because they did not stand out (that they were, in other words, symptom-free). In fact, when the faith community tends to credit individuals with holiness, it is usually because they stand out in some very noticeable way. Individuals in the twentieth century who have been acclaimed as holy—Dorothy Day, Thomas Merton, Martin Luther King, Mother Teresa—were in fact stimulated to action by their lack of adjustment. There have been very few saints, and even fewer prophets, who could be considered adjusted. Holiness, unlike health, is usually understood as something one seeks out and approaches rather than something one has but might lose. What would it be like if we began to view health in the same way?

If we then consider true health not as a lack of sickness or an absence of symptoms, how would it be understood? How would healing be seen from a more holistic viewpoint? We could at least say that it would not be static. It would instead be associated with some kind of growthful movement. Health would then be seen as something through which I am continuously seeking to deepen myself. In other words, I would be invited into the healing process in much the same way as I am invited into holiness. In this sense, healing is no longer considered maintenance, but it is instead perceived more in terms of transformation.

But transformation of what? What is to be healed? Certainly the very word still suggests that something is not right or complete. Whether it is understood in a static sense or through holistic process, healing involves some kind of recuperative action. What is the focus of that action? From a holistic point of view the answer would be "all that stands in the way of what transformation offers to me." If I am sick of body or sick at heart, I am left fragile and incomplete. And I recognize that something greater calls out to me. I am called through grace to a deeper wholeness. I therefore am called to move beyond whatever it is that keeps this wholeness from taking place. Here, then,

I suggest a possible definition of healing. Healing is the removal of any pain, barrier, disease, or remnant of experience that keeps the self from graceful living.

This definition of healing might be a challenging one to many, because it implies the necessity that I become involved in my own healing process. It is no longer simply a matter of my going to someone to "find out what's wrong." To seek out healing in a deep and ongoing way now commits me, first, to a kind of discernment process that asks me to participate diagnostically with my various caregivers, and, second, to the kind of actions that help in the effort to bring about my healing. This is indeed a commitment, and it calls forth something more from within us. We tend to anticipate that life should be simple, straightforward, and uncomplicated, but this approach to healing will draw me into uncharted waters. In seeking health I will also come to learn much more about myself, my deepest pains, and my greatest joys. I will find greater purpose and meaning, and in the process discover what life is all about.

The Paradox of Healing

This perspective might seem rather profound if all I have is a headache. Is the healing process really this ultimate? One difficulty with the holistic understanding I have presented is that quite often the perspective on healing maintained by the majority of the medical community is correct and appropriate. Often an individual actually is in relatively good health and, for whatever reason, things start to go bad. This could be brought on by infection; it could be genetic; it might be from personal neglect; it could be accidental; it might simply be because of aging. Symptoms do flare up that medicine can treat, and, generally speaking, the disappearance of symptoms is a good indication of health returning to an individual. Also, from a psychological point of view, people who are maladjusted often do lead miserable lives. To offer them skills that can reduce their suffering is, to say the least, compassionate. Medical and behavioral science has never claimed to provide a path to transformation. It simply has sought to alleviate human pain.

When we take this perspective into account, healing presents us with something of a dilemma. On one hand, healing offers us a process that truly is potentially transforming, and on the other hand, it deals with the everyday suffering that is part of the human condition without much expectation of moving beyond that condition. This dilemma points to a basic paradox at the very center of our understanding of healing. It could be stated in an affirmation/negation dialectic this way:

- Affirming: healing is ultimately a transformation, since it involves a surrender in response to the working of grace, and is instrumental in creating a new reality at that graced level.

- Negating: healing is not ultimately transforming since what is restored to health is only temporary and is still subject to human decline and mortality.

- Reconciling: healing is a symbolic (sacramental) transformation because it enfleshes a transforming power that points to the more ultimate restoration that is found in the Reign of God.

This triad will, of course, need some explanation. The affirming statement asserts that healing always involves transformation. It understands this transformation in the way I have been using it throughout the book, as an event of transforming consciousness that represents a new reality brought about through an action of surrender in cooperation with grace. I have asserted that transforming consciousness is the result of paradox. This suggests that every healing would in some way be paradoxical, that it would be a reconciling reality overcoming polar opposites. So the affirming statement of our healing paradox already presumes another triad. This paradox within a paradox could be fashioned around the human experience of power or control. It would appear in this way:

- Affirming: I have control over my health. I have the power of my own will to seek ways of alleviating pain when I am ill or dysfunctional. This power varies depending on the nature of the ailment and the means of alleviation available to me. However, I specifically need the will to implement this power.

- Negating: I have no control over my health. I am at the mercy of my pain. My power is always limited, and sometimes may be nonexistent. There is a point at which I must recognize this limitation and detach from the need to control the healing process. I must rely upon a higher power.

• Reconciling: Healing is the result of cooperation between will, detachment, and grace. In this cooperation pain is resolved for me in some form of higher awareness.

At one end of a spectrum this understanding of healing could be recognizable in what we might call extraordinary healing, the kind of healing that produces dramatic results and at the same time is scientifically unexplainable. Is it not, however, also recognizable in the most mundane and simple treatment of pain? The positive effect of an individual's faith, for instance, is frequently noted by physicians as having a significant role in even an ordinary recovery process. In a psychological context, any health care professional knows that even the simplest positive growth in a client is an occurrence surrounded by mystery before which the caregiver can only humbly stand.

It is also important to note that in this understanding of healing, the cessation of pain is not promised. Of course, pain is frequently removed in healing, or at least lessened, but as we know from life's experiences, this does not always happen. That is why I defined healing as I did above: the removal of any pain, barrier, disease, or remnant of experience that keeps the self from graceful living. Healing is primarily a removal of what blocks the fruitfulness of life. We all know people who live with pain, disease, psychological trauma, and spiritual heartache but whose lives are grace-filled. They have received the healing they need. There is nothing that stands in the way of their further transformation. From a human perspective they might not be flawless, but their physical, emotional, or spiritual flaws have not kept them from pursuing the deeper path. Much like the flawed pot presented to the king in the chapter's opening story, the flaw itself might prove to be the path to adoption and transformation.

This brings us to the negating statement of our original triad: healing is not ultimately transforming since what is restored to health is only temporary and is still subject to human decline and mortality.

At face value this statement would seem to deny everything that has just been said. How can healing be considered a transformation, since no healing ever lasts? (What, after all, is the meaning of a temporary transformation?) A coronary bypass operation might be regarded as successful if it extends a person's life by so many years, but it will not allow that person to live forever. It cannot even guarantee that a diseased heart will not eventually be the very thing that brings about that individual's death. Someone who completes an extensive counseling relationship might be able to cope with life in ways that were never before available to that person. He or she might even find life unimaginably more enjoyable, but life will still present its problems, and new and possibly more severe problems are just over the horizon.

Healing by its very nature, therefore, is always what I will call "middle ground." By that I mean that healing is always something that happens in process. Furthermore, healing never completes that process; it simply allows us to continue it. This is consistent with the approach to healing that Jesus takes in the gospels, as I mentioned in chapter two. Jesus does not heal everyone, nor does he make healing the ultimate end of his ministry. Healing is a sign of the Reign, and it is a gift that prepares the way for the experience of conversion, which is ultimately transforming.

This is an important distinction because there are Christians who present healing as something ultimate. For them healing is not middle ground preparing the way for deeper faith, but a sort of spiritual litmus test that seeks to judge faith already present. This approach has a certain Christian "logic" to it that looks something like this:

- God is loving, therefore:
- God doesn't want us to suffer, therefore:
- Everyone should be healed, therefore:
- If you aren't, it's your fault…because you lack faith.

The outcome of this "logic" is, therefore, that the individual should pray for more faith. Faith, of course, is a good thing to pray for. The problem here is that faith is understood quantitatively, rather than qualitatively. It is a thing that I can acquire and possess in measurable amounts, rather than something that is both gift and decision. The other problem is that this "logic" is accompanied by full-blown judgment. It's not God's fault that the healing didn't happen, so it must be yours. Your faith was not strong enough to bring the healing about. People whose ego defenses are weak will hear this as an accusation: "There's something wrong with you; you failed again."

The further presumption here is that the "logic" already knows the healing that is necessary. This is what you should pray for; God obviously wants this to happen. The reality is that we do not always know the healing that is needed, because we cannot always recognize what it is that is blocking graceful living. Perhaps it is the identifiable disease, but perhaps it is my need to be perfect which is frustrated by the disease's presence. Perhaps it is my depression that needs to be healed, or perhaps it is a deep-seated anger resulting from a lack of forgiveness that is causing the feelings of depression in the first place. When healing becomes an ultimate thing, it runs the risk of becoming a block that keeps real healing from taking place.

Because this real healing is middle ground, it always seems to live in paradox. It carries with it a give-and-take reality. Healing offers us new possibilities, but these very possibilities seem to have implications we never planned on. If I give up my need for perfection, perhaps my disease will become manageable, even transforming. But once my illusion of perfection is surrendered, my whole self-image might be challenged. If I give up my hardness of heart and forgive the one I am angry with, I might discover my depression lifted. I might also discover, however, that there is a whole series of people to whom I must now make amends. In relation to healing, I believe the old spiritual adage rings true: be careful what you pray for, because you may get it.

This understanding of healing as middle ground leads us finally into the reconciling statement of our healing triad: healing is a symbolic (sacramental) transformation because it enfleshes a transforming power that points to the more ultimate restoration that is found in the Reign of God. To say that healing is symbolic does not mean that the healing is not real, as when some people might say that something is only symbolic. This reveals a lack of awareness of what the symbolic level of reality is all about. I said in the last chapter that something becomes symbolic when it takes on layer upon layer of meaning. That is the understanding of a symbol from a psychological point of view. A theological understanding of symbol adds another factor, however—that a symbol also in some way contains or manifests the reality it signifies. Traditionally this is called a sacrament. In the Church a sacrament is not merely a sign of some particular form of Christ's presence, but it is in some way the actual manifestation of that presence. This understanding of the faith community is based on the ultimate symbol of Christian belief, the Incarnation, the manifestation of the presence of God in humanity. The living Word of God is symbolized (revealed and made present in continuously deeper levels of meaning) in the human nature of Jesus.

Healing, then, manifests this kind of symbolic transformation. As a graced reality it is a transforming experience, but its real power is its ability to point to a greater transformation that the healing itself makes visible to some degree. I have used the phrase ultimate restoration to identify the Reign of God. The fact that our present reality is not the Reign means that some kind of healing of this reality must take place before it can fulfill the destiny that Jesus came to make possible. Every particular manifestation of healing, even the most ordinary and mundane, says to us again, "Yes, it is indeed possible. The Reign of God will yet come in its fullness with God's grace and our willing surrender." The healing is a sign of the Reign's presence, but it is also a sign of its absence. Because healing is a symbolic transformation, it is not necessary that it be ultimate in itself. Yet as a symbolic transformation it shares in the ultimate nature of what the Reign in its fullness will be.

As a symbolic event there is no need, therefore, for healing to meet perfectionist standards of human expectation. We tend to approach our pain and disease with a perspective that demands immediate and complete results. To some extent we have been conditioned by the medical establishment to this way of thinking. Many of the efforts of medical science have been geared to achieving the quick and permanent removal of our symptoms through technical and pharmaceutical advancement. The same kind of expectation could be said for certain approaches to spirituality as well. What is wrong with me that I have these spiritual symptoms? Why can't I pray right? I shouldn't be so easily hurt by others. What is wrong that I haven't yet attained perfection? I know I shouldn't have these doubts, but I can't seem to get rid of them. Our expectations of healing are frequently set so high as to be unattainable.

Every healing contains a kernel of the Reign, but no one healing can ever fully embrace what the Reign will mean for transformed reality. To say, for instance, "I prayed for healing in this area, but nothing happened" speaks of a kind of presumptive arrogance. First of all, I cannot presume to know what actually happened. All I know is that what didn't happen was what I expected—at least not yet. Since I might not really know what needed to be healed, I might not have solid ground upon which to base assumptions about what took place.

Nor does one person's healing always compare to another's. Because two people have common back pain and they undergo the same experience—surgery, medication, or prayer—doesn't necessarily mean that the results will be identical. Perhaps the body's recuperative powers are different in the two individuals; perhaps one's ability to deal with life stress is greater than another's; perhaps one is more successful at changing lifestyle than another; perhaps one's prayer was truly trusting and open, while the other's was approached in a formal or magical way. Or perhaps for the one, the real healing needed was the pain, while the other's healing needed to be more along the lines of a change in attitude. Much like any of life's transformations, there is a great deal about healing that remains surrounded by mystery.

The Healing Process

Because the Reign of God is a process already under way, the symbolic nature of healing manifests itself through process as well. Rather than say, "I have been healed," it is perhaps more accurate to say, "I am in the process of being healed." Since I do not always know the extent of the healing necessary in my life, I cannot really say that the healing is finally complete. Perhaps my pain has gone, but the healing has only begun. Or perhaps the healing has begun, and the pain seems all the worse. Perhaps I must first truly feel the pain (a frequent condition in healing within addictive behavior, for instance) before I can open myself to the ongoing power of the healing process.

In the process of symbolic healing, the awareness of the present moment becomes of primary importance. I do not know what this process will ultimately ask of me. I do not know God's intention; I do not know my own strength. I am not sure what means will eventually be made available to me that are not now possible. All I know is this present moment as I discern it. And as I discern this moment, this is the course I feel is best to follow. The results of my actions will be in keeping with what the moment offered and what I was able to accept. This will then open the next moment with new potential and new opportunities. I really cannot know any more than that, nor do I need to.

I think this is what Stephen Levine means by his phrase "just this much."

> The cost of crossing the river of forgetfulness, moving from the unhealed to the ever healed, is "just this much." In the worlds of healing, the coin of the realm is a merciful awareness focused in this very instant of life's unfolding. "Just this much" is the millisecond in which the truth is to be found. It means opening to our whole life. It is the very moment in which existence presents itself and is received. It is in "just this much" that our healing accumulates. All the work that is to be done is done in "just this much." (*Healing into Life and Death*, pp. 79-80)

Another way of saying something similar is to borrow a phrase from the Twelve-Step program. We could say that healing is "one day at a time." This phrase says something about both the past and the future. First of all, it says I cannot rest in the past. I cannot say that I have done enough now, I've achieved the healing that I wish. To say this is to lose the healing that has been granted to me. It is like saying that enough of the Reign of God is here to suit me. Such a statement would be to say that I do not know what the Reign is all about. There is still more to do. The process is only begun.

"One day at a time," however, also says something about the future. This is that the future is not yet here. We are impatient with process, and we fail to see the importance of timing as a spiritual principle. We want to be done with it all, so that we can get on with life. There is, however, no way to hurry the process, no way to shortcut the journey. The process is what life is all about. There is no life outside the journey. Yet this journey can only reveal itself as the step I can now take if I so choose. I do not have to burden myself with the decision as to whether I can walk in this same direction forever. Can I take one step in this direction now? If I can, perhaps then I can take another in the same direction, but that is for the next moment's discernment.

It is my sense that our desire to be done with it, to be through the process and finished with healing, is only partly concerned with impatience. It is also concerned with fear. As strange as it seems, I believe we frequently fear healing. It seems to me that we instinctively understand that healing is a process, and we are afraid of what that process might end up revealing to us. To use the analogy of playing the board game Monopoly, we would rather get the card that sends us directly to Go to collect an additional $200 than experience the dreaded unknown of working through the remainder of the board. We therefore come to think of healing in the same way. We hope for healing as a means of ending a process that has too many variables and too much pain, rather than seeing healing as the opportunity to continue the process in order to grow and be transformed. The fear that I have toward healing is the fear of coming to know who I really am. It is the fear that says, "If you really knew me, you wouldn't like me." More importantly, it is the fear that I wouldn't like myself. This fear, then, is a sign of my own lack of self-worth. It says, in effect, "I'm not good enough to be a whole person."

The effect of all this is to create within each of us, to some extent, a network of resistance. We so fear being healed that we find ways to sabotage the healing process. In *Addiction and Grace*, Gerald May spoke about this as a turning away from love. He said that from a psychological point of view, we do this in one of two general ways, through either repression or addiction. These two mechanisms, of course, have very different characteristics. Still, they have one common outcome. They push us away from our truest feelings. They inevitably lead us to try to find in isolation—isolation from God, and from others, but especially from ourselves—a kind of protection or insulation where we do not have to face who we really are.

To begin to reverse this network of resistance is itself one of the greatest healings that could take place in our lives. We could call it the healing of the inner self. It has all the characteristics of the healing process as I have described them so far, but it also reaches down to the very core of our being to release us from what blocks our acceptance of God's grace. I have referred to healing in general as the removal of any pain, barrier, disease, or remnant of experience that keeps the self from graceful living, but it is the healing of the inner self that most gives meaning to this definition.

The process of healing the self, like all else that is transforming, is wrapped in mystery. It is ultimately God's process, and not mine. I cannot orchestrate it; I can only respond to its invitation. Still, from our human perception, certain events characteristically happen in this process. They are, if you will, our part in what God wishes to do. These events are: 1. awareness; 2. forgiveness; 3. manifestation; and 4. commitment. They are not strictly time sequential, although awareness must logically come first, and commitment tends to follow the others. I would like to conclude my treatment of healing by briefly examining these events, and by making some suggestions as to how dream work can be particularly helpful in allowing us to work through them.

Awareness, first of all, is one of the most important fruits of discernment. This should alert us to recognize that, if I am living in an ongoing discernment process, as suggested in the last chapter, the opportunities for the healing of the inner self are never very far away. I come to awareness by continuously exploring my life as I seek to live consciously in the moment. If I am honestly doing this, it will not be long before I come to have a growing sense of what needs to be healed. This doesn't mean it happens automatically. It means that conscious living will make me aware of the spaces in my life inhabited by the wounds and pains that call out for healing.

This deepening awareness is greatly enhanced by my ability to recognize the paradoxical nature of my life experiences. What does life offer me? Joys or pains? Happiness or sorrow? It should not surprise me to find all of these mixed up together, even within a single experience. This realization could create either openness or apprehension; it could lead to either contentment or dissatisfaction—the choice is mine. When I discover that the pain and sorrow block me, when I recognize apprehension and dissatisfaction running as a pattern through my life, I have discovered an area of woundedness. I need to search further to understand its power and its source.

Awareness then becomes a call to further explore my past. This does not mean that all healing in my life is involved with past events. I can certainly need to be healed of the present as well. But the present is not so successfully hidden from me by repression and addiction as are my past experiences. I carry around within me the remnants of many hurtful experiences. John Bradshaw frequently speaks about the deeply rooted shame that is the by-product of life in family systems and in early socializing. (See, for instance, John Bradshaw's book, *Healing the Shame That Binds You*. The first three chapters set forth his understanding of toxic shame very well.) It can create within me an attitude of self-judgment and self-hatred. I can learn to disguise this with all sorts of perceptions and attitudes toward myself and others, but until I become aware of their roots, there is little I can do to find an alternative way of living.

These attitudes that I construct toward life are generally revealed in one of two broad life stances. I seek to hide my self-hatred either by becoming self-preserving or by becoming self-enlarging. The first takes on a general stance of fear and protection that colors a vast number of my behaviors and choices. The second seeks to hide behind pride and a willfulness that are constantly seeking the enhancement of ego. It is important to recognize that these attitudes are not simply behavioral patterns. They reach much deeper into what motivates me.

This deep-seated woundedness can affect just about any dimension of my life. It can be seen in my relationships, in how I function with family, with friends, and even with those I casually meet in passing on the street. I see it in how I perceive my own body and my sexuality. My woundedness affects my ability to work and to play. It keeps me from fulfilling my true potential, as well as admitting the limitations inherent in that potential. Ultimately it keeps me from dealing realistically with my own death. By that I do not simply mean the ending of my physical life. I am also unable to deal fruitfully with all the daily deaths I must face—my aches and pains, my losses, my failures, and my aging, just to name a few.

Dreams are most helpful in deepening awareness of my woundedness. Many of the voices of the minority report speak from some stance of pain. If ego has covered over that pain through self-preservation or self-enlargement, the many voices of the unconscious are not buying the package. Exploring the symbols in my dreams honestly will ask me to deal with perceptions and attitudes, behavioral patterns and personal characteristics that will reveal my deep vulnerabilities. Asking a simple question like, "What does this image in my dream remind me of?" can open doors of insight that will surprise me. "Where have I met this image elsewhere in my life?" "Does this dynamic in my dream match any past or present dynamics in my experience?" Once again, questions in dreams or in life are much more powerful than answers. These questions should be allowed to remain open-ended.

My understanding of the images of my dream will be monitored by the emotions connected to them. The emotions in a dream should not be underestimated. The emotions in my dream are the emotions in my life. That does not mean they are predominant emotions. They are quite likely the feelings of the minority report. But they are mine, and I need to own them. If I cannot own the fear or the anger, the shame or the selfishness I feel in my dreams, how do I expect to heal the areas of my life they refer to? To be able to admit to the emotions I have toward my life experiences is a key to movement in the healing process. It is the magical door that enables me to move from awareness to the event of healing that is forgiveness.

In chapter three I said that surrender was the fundamental spiritual experience, and I have referred to it throughout this book as something absolutely necessary to move us into transforming consciousness. Surrender is actually present in each of the four events that make up the healing of the inner self. Surrender, for instance, is necessary in the event of awareness or I will never be able to honestly deal with the memories and emotions that will inevitably arise.

Without bringing surrender to awareness, all I have is selective perception. I will hear only what is safe to hear. To hear what I need to hear requires the surrender of self-image.

Forgiveness, however, the second of the four events, is the one that is most directly dependent upon surrender. Without it, forgiveness is simply not possible. Forgiveness is one of the hardest things we can do in life, but at the same time it presents us with one of the most freeing opportunities we will ever have. The lack of forgiveness is perhaps the biggest barrier to healing. Usually it is our pride and our fear that most completely stand in the way of bringing forgiveness to a particular situation. Forgiveness is hard because it represents a loss of control. While pride and fear are not things we consciously work to acquire, they become important commodities for the ego because they can be used as strategies for maintaining control. In forgiving I must surrender them. The root understanding of forgive is "to thoroughly give"—in other words, to hold nothing back. If we are to forgive, there is the need to develop an attitude of not holding on.

I am not speaking only of forgiving others. Certainly, that is often a very hard thing to do. The forgiveness in question, however, is also the forgiveness I must extend to myself. While neither of these is easy, it is my experience that for most people self-forgiveness is the more difficult action. Most people are very hard on themselves, and hold themselves to standards that they are willing to forgo when it comes to others. This is particularly true of religious people, who have been taught throughout their lives to have mercy on others, but to hold themselves accountable. As an action of surrender, forgiveness therefore depends on a growing sense of trust within an individual, and this is first of all a sense of self-trust.

While forgiveness is difficult, we can take consolation in that it is itself a process. When dealing with other people, very few of us find that we can forgive immediately, or even overnight. Particularly when we feel we have been betrayed, it takes a long time to again build a trusting relationship. Some struggle with forgiveness for many years. When it comes to self-forgiveness, the process might be even longer, often because we might not even be able to identify our self-hatred. In either case, we might wish to be further along in the process, but the most important thing is that we are in the process. To be in the process is to open ourselves to God's grace, and that is the most important thing. For those who do not know how to begin, therefore, I usually recommend that the intention to forgive and the exercise of prayer are the best place to start.

We must, however, be cautious of false forgiveness. There are a number of experiences that might go by the name of forgiveness but actually are something else. One of these is excusing. Many people excuse others for the hurt that has been done to them without really bringing forgiveness to the situation. This is a frequent occurrence in codependency. It is similar to another false forgiveness, tolerating. Tolerating can be a form of appeasement that basically hopes the cause of my pain will just go away. Both of these are really living a lie, for they are pretending that forgiveness is present when it really isn't. There are two other forms of false forgiveness as well: ignoring and condescending. When people say things such as, "Oh, I just don't pay any attention to her," or "Well, what can you expect from him," they might feel they are in a forgiving mode, but they really are not. All of these are forms of the ego holding on to something.

Dream work gives us an excellent opportunity to further the process of forgiveness. There are two ways in which this can happen. On some occasions the images in a dream might suggest that forgiveness has already occurred within the unconscious. This might be observed in images of reconciliation or resolution. Dreams of resolution are often a signal from the unconscious that we have come to terms with some opposition in our lives. There are dreams that can reconcile, heal, or lead to integration. Some of these can be very powerful, and leave us with overwhelming feelings of awe or peace.

Often, however, our dreams simply point out the need for forgiveness that has not yet happened. We might see this in dream images that seem to be asking something from us. Frequently dreams will even hint at a solution and then seem to turn the process over to the conscious self. In these situations it is not the dream but the dream work that follows where the necessary actions of forgiveness will have to take place. In regard to both kinds of dream experiences, it is probably true to say that forgiveness must eventually take place at both the conscious and the unconscious level for it to be complete.

Our dream work might very well prepare us for the third event of the process of healing the inner self, that is, manifestation. I distinguish between this third event and the fourth, commitment, through the following analogy. It is the difference between creating a plan of action and actually putting the plan into effect. Manifestation is an important aspect of seeking to externalize my woundedness. Through awareness I have come into touch with the material of that woundedness, its causes, the pain it has produced, the attitudes it has created, and the various effects it has had on my life. As I seek forgiveness of myself or others, I begin to realize that all this cannot continue to remain inside. I must begin to manifest my pain. This involves opening my woundedness to others and sharing my pain with them. This is not yet the sharing of pain with those who might have caused it. That would be a possible action of the fourth event. Here I manifest my pain to someone I know I can trust, a close friend, a spiritual director, a confessor, or a faith-sharing group. If the event of forgiveness shows us the dangers of holding *on*, the event of manifestation reveals that a lack of healing is often connected with holding *in*.

Sharing our dreams can be an important vehicle for manifesting our pain. Through the images and the emotions of our dreams we can find honest yet safe ways of laying out our burdens before those we trust. Hearing another's dream can be a very intimate thing, because we realize that we are receiving an uncensored look into the heart of this person. That is why dream sharing should always be done in the context of confidentiality. This is presumed in sacramental reconciliation, and should go without saying in a professional relationship such as spiritual direction. It is helpful, however, for members of a sharing group to periodically remind each other of the expectation of confidentiality because of the more informal atmosphere in which the group's meetings might occur.

Once the forgiveness process has begun and I have manifested my woundedness to those whose trusting presence can support and advise me, I am ready to face the fourth event of the healing process, commitment. This is where I undertake the necessary action that completes and reinforces the healing. It is necessary because without it I cannot completely integrate the healing into my life. Healing is a symbolic transformation, and therefore depends upon an incarnational principle for its completion. The healing must be enfleshed in concrete action.

The kinds of actions I commit myself to can vary widely from simple symbolic ritual actions that dramatize my desire for a complete integration of this part of my life to much more risky actions such as confronting individuals who have caused me pain or harm or making public amends with those I might have harmed. The nature of the action is not to be based on my desire for safety or lack of complication. It is established because it is the action that seems to best offer me the chance to finally bring the pain to resolution. Our dreams might very well hint at what the nature of this action might be, but it will be up to the conscious self to choose the best way to incarnate this final event of healing.

The kind of healing process I have been describing, however, is not the end of the story, by any means. The greater integration of self and the release of transforming power that the healing establishes produces yet another invitation to move me further toward the next steps of transformation. It is, first of all, an invitation to even deeper healing, because there are probably many more blocks in my path. Even more importantly, it is an invitation to conversion, for once the blockage is removed, I will be asked to go deeper in faith. Finally it is an invitation to express my praise and gratitude through prayer and mutual presence with the One who has truly brought the healing about.

IX

Action: Lighting a Fire on the Earth

In concluding my remarks on the healing process in the last chapter I suggested that healing is not totally complete until it is concretized in action. But action is not simply something important to healing. Action is, in fact, the bottom line by which everything else can be assessed. It is the litmus test of our spirituality. Despite what our own system of values might tell us runs the world, it is ultimately run on action. The world does not run on money, or power, or information. The world does not run through government, or through the church, or through the military-industrial complex. It does not run from either a liberal or a conservative agenda. Your world and mine run on action.

Action presumes energy. We could say that energy is the potential to act; so energy is pretty basic as well. In fact, a contemporary understanding of physics would suggest that energy is really all there is. The theory of relativity is essentially a theory about energy, and how energy comes to be converted into physical mass as we perceive it. But even though energy might be all there is, it is only important as it relates to action. This is because reality is not about what could be, but about what is. The same thing could be said about spirituality. Spirituality is about what is and about our ability to recognize it. Transforming consciousness, therefore, the fruit of living through paradox, is primarily about our ability to act and about our ability to perceive action that is taking place.

In the framework of the enneagram, action is the most basic of virtues. It is called essential action. Essential action, as I choose to speak of it, is not just activity; it is activity that proves itself to be graceful. By that I mean it has the power to bring forth some aspect of the Reign of God. Because it is grace, however, it is only partly mine. It is at one and the same time an action of the Spirit and my action. That is, if you will, the first paradox of action.

So this essential action is envisioned as always being transforming. This would indicate that it is the outcome of a reconciliation of some sort of opposition. These polar opposites could be referred to as activity and inactivity. Notice that activity is not the same as essential action. Neither activity nor inactivity is in itself essential, that is, graceful. We can easily see that from our perception of life around us. Too often activity or inactivity is put forth as a substitute for real living. A great deal of action, for instance, can take place around us. Our local, national, and international news is filled with it. Each of us, as well, goes through each day involved in a lot of activity. Much of all this enacted energy is dissipated. On the other hand, to choose inactivity as an alternative is not necessarily any more fruitful. What benefit would it be to you, or me, or our world to simply fall into the innumerable forms of inactivity—laziness, complacency, or passivity, to name a few—even if it is to get away from the "craziness," as our active world is now sometimes referred to?

We might again look at the image of essential breath that began this book. There the paradox of breath was suggested in the inhaling and the exhaling. But now we could think of both inhaling and exhaling as actions. They are opposite actions, but actions nonetheless. Life is contained in the rhythm that exists between them. But that rhythm is only possible because something else is present in the process. It is necessary that there also be nonaction in order that life might be sustained. Nonaction here is the space between inhaling and exhaling. Without this nonaction, inhaling could not become exhaling, or vice versa. But breathing is not in the activity or nonactivity; it is in the rhythm of both, and depends on both. Every breath is process, even though every breath is the same. Essential breath is in the paradox between change and inertia.

So essential action is in the paradox between an affirming principle of action and a negating principle of nonaction. Sometimes essential action is in the grace given to activity, and sometimes in the grace given to nonactivity. Sometimes it is in the grace given to both at the same time. We might use as an example the essential action of peace. I mentioned earlier that peace is problematic, because it is understood as many things that are not really peaceful. But there is surely such a thing as essential peace. Yet what is it, an activity or a non-activity? "Blessed are the peacemakers, for they will be called children of God." (Mt 5:9) Are these peacemakers actively working for peace? They certainly are. But are they not also refraining from action, action that unduly disturbs and causes division and harm? Can they not do one while also doing the other? Such a paradox is also evident in prayer, where action and nonaction are both present in every moment of openness to mutual presence with God.

It seems clear that the essential action I am referring to demands a discerning heart. I must be discerning of what happens around me and of what I myself do in order to recognize the movements of grace. It is also true that action is the logical outcome of discernment. Discernment that leads to effective action is a fruitful use of energy. Discernment that does not lead to some form of action is dissipated energy. The action that is the fruit of my discernment is itself an energy released into the world. It is the rediscovery of fire, again and again.

Paradox or Pitfall?

Every paradox, that is, every graceful reconciliation of life's opposite poles, is an essential action. To recognize this and actively participate in it is to live in transforming consciousness. From here grace abounds, and the veil that covers God's presence in the world is lifted to some degree. Essential action has the capacity to bring about two similar kinds of events, conversion and transformation. While the two might not be identical, they stem from the same source. I offer here some brief definitions.

- Conversion: a decisive process that brings me to a new state of being through the liberation of rooted sinfulness. Its end is the freedom of self, enabling me to respond to God's grace and fulfilling my longing for God's presence.

- Transformation: a significant strengthening in the awareness of my essential being that allows for the experience of a deepening relationship with God as well as a greater interconnectedness with all reality.

Moving from these definitions, we recognize that the two experiences are very close. One could say that to some extent they are mutually causative. The liberation that comes from conversion will bring about a transformed awareness, while the awareness itself results in greater liberation. It is my understanding that conversion and transformation always involve the embrace of paradox and the invitation to transforming consciousness, even though we do not always see it. Sometimes, even in our graced moments, we do not clearly see what is being offered. This is particularly true in the earlier stages of life, and in times when our own busyness has distracted us from our center. We begin to see the paradox in the midst of reality only when our "eyes of faith" have enabled us to do so.

Faith grows and deepens within us. James Fowler's work on faith development has sought to delineate the various stages that we pass through in the life cycle. (See *Stages of Faith: The Psychology of Human Development and the Quest for Meaning*, pp. 197ff.) In Fowler's model we see the achievement of paradoxical thinking as coming to the individual in the last two stages of faith development, what he calls the stages of conjunctive faith and universalizing faith. In conjunctive faith we come to the point where we have a heightened awareness of life's opposite poles and we struggle to unify these opposites in our mind and through our experiences. We are able to develop an ironic imagination, and we come to live with the possibility that our understanding might not be sufficient to grasp reality's transcendence. In universalizing faith there is a final resolving of paradox through a moral and ascetical actualization that comes with the ability to apprehend universal truths. Paradox is no longer something we strive to understand, but it is a reality we live with.

Fowler sees relatively few people arriving at universalizing faith. It is my hope that our capacity for it is much more encompassing than we might initially suspect. An intention that lies behind this book is to challenge us to move beyond the wall of our contradictions and begin to recognize the presence of the universal truths that surround us. It is also my intention to suggest that this move is not something that just happens when we have lived on this earth long enough, for it is true enough that many people never seem to arrive there. Our ability to move to conjunctive faith and then to universalizing faith is greatly dependent on our ability to take essential action, particularly the essential action of surrender. The movements that bring us to these new levels of faith development, we could say, are themselves transformations.

Trying to live surrounded by the presence of reality's problems and difficulties can be overwhelming if all I see is duality. Life seems to be endless contradictions. Problems seem to seek us out. We live in a world that is immersed in suffering, one that becomes increasingly meaningless and absurd. But it is not easy to move from contradiction to paradox. We have ways of disguising the contradictions of life to make them seem either as if they are not there or are not really a problem. We can put on a kind of mask or disguise that hopes to buffer us from the pain and suffering of life. Some of these disguises are recognizable defense mechanisms. At times they are even necessary in order to supply us with the appropriate ego boundaries we need in the face of crisis. But some are simply ways of entrenching ourselves against life's challenge. We could call them pitfalls in our dealings with life's contradictions.

These pitfalls more or less lie within the realm of the three responses that are characteristically made toward contradictions: extremism, compromise, and indecision. These were discussed in the first chapter. The pitfalls mentioned here are generally "refinements" of these three. Some of our pitfalls are:

• Observation. This is a form of indecision where I try to take on a stance of cool objectivity. It allows me to become bemused by life's problems. I can easily slip into cynicism or disinterest. There is also a tendency toward critical judgment. The problem with most examples of such "objectivity" is that I become non-participative. From this position, no essential action is possible, because real graced action presumes involvement in life's experiences.

• Moderation. This form of compromise always seeks to find the "golden mean," the point in the middle that one hopes will silence both poles. Moderation frequently is effective, at least when seeking a majority's support. Because of this, moderation is frequently counseled as an appropriate response to opposite poles. But moderation, usually a measured intellectual response, seldom embraces passion. Also, when moderation becomes the principal criterion for discernment, discernment is seldom complete.

• Distraction. Here is another form of indecision. It plays up to our culture's love of options. If I can see so many kinds of possibilities that lie in other directions, I never have to deal with the contradiction at hand. There is a kind of denial built into distraction, because it tends to devalue the contradiction for the good that lies "over the rainbow."

• Inertia. This form of indecision simply causes me to shut down. Inertia means that I maintain the state I presently am in. In other words, I deal with the contradiction by declaring it not a problem, or by simply ignoring it. Maybe the contradiction will go away. There is no possible chance here for graced action.

• Perfectionism. This is a very common form of extremism. It holds the position that there must be one correct way to meet each problem, and I have to discover that one right way. Once I have arrived at my position, I can become unyielding. I restructure the problem in terms of black and white, and I usually end up being filled with judgment, on myself and on everybody else.

• Projection. This is a form of extremism where from the position of one pole I gather all my fears and apprehensions and cast them onto the opposite pole. The problem is perceived to be not with my position, but with the other position. While it seems like a very gross action, projection can really be quite subtle. While we can find blatant projection in hate groups, it is present in a more carefully disguised manner in even the most insidious forms of ideology—racism, nationalism, ageism, sexism, religious prejudice, and so on.

Perhaps thoroughness would suggest that each of these ideologies should be addressed, since hooking into an ideological framework is one of the most frequent ways we attempt to avoid facing contradiction. However, I am going to confine my remarks to one in particular. I want to spend a little time dealing specifically with the ideology of sexism, because it has some impact on how we have historically perceived paradox itself. I do not wish to imply that sexism is necessarily more pervasive, or dangerous, or evil than the others. But sexism, unlike the others, has found its way into the very understanding of what we believe paradox to be. Masculinity and femininity are one of our most basic pairings, and they deal with regions of human experience that no one can escape.

Classically, male and female have frequently been used to name opposite duality. Perhaps the most prominent instance of this is in the Taoist concept of yin and yang. There yang is not only identified as the active, bright, and firm principle of existence; it is also frequently identified as male. Yin, in the same way, is not only representative of receptive, dark, and yielding forces, but is also characterized as female. The question is, does identifying male and female in this categorical way actually further prejudicial judgments rather than resolve them and bring them to transformation? Are all males active and firm? Are all females receptive and yielding? Are such generalizations even possible?

Another important area of concern can be found in classical Jungian psychology. Jung's original concepts of *anima* and *animus* were established around the belief that each person had both a masculine and feminine side to one's personality, one being dominant and the other recessive. Actually this is quite evident if we can understand dream figures of the opposite sex as being representations of the minority voice, the recessive personality, within us. There is, so to speak, a feminine side within the man and a masculine side within the woman that each of us needs to get in touch with in order to move ourselves beyond a personal impasse. In Jungian theory the two sides of the personality are complementary. The question is, however, are they also opposite?

There are clearly physiological differences between men and women. There are also quite observable psychological differences between them. A debate has raged over whether they are there by nature, or from socializing patterns, or both. It is also debatable as to how much we can view these "gender-oriented" traits as deterministic, conditioned, or freely chosen, or whether they are gender-oriented at all, or based on other cultural or social factors.

Realizing that the debate will continue on long after my brief comments, let me at least state a general premise. First of all, men and women are complementary in that we need each other to be whole. This is evident simply in the fact that our species (and every other one) has so well and so long endured. Second, it is also clear, and for the same reason, that we are not opposites. We are not living, breathing, walking opposite poles to each other. We do not repel each other, nor are we totally incomprehensible to each other. The biological product of our union is not a transformed third reality, but is another fragile member of the human species like ourselves. Even at the most basic biological level our very chromosomes are not opposites; they do, however, contain opposite elements. So we are, perhaps, a mixture of like and not-like. As such, we are a complicated composite of same and different. This accounts for our intense attraction toward each other and at the same time for the great mystery that we remain to each other. This suggests to me one more paradox triad.

- An affirmation: men and women are essentially the same, and our differences are largely due to cultural conditioning. A reduction in our cultural gender dependency will reduce tensions in relations between the sexes.

- A negation: men and women are essentially opposite. They think differently (they use the brain differently), and they will always basically be contradictions to each other. Ongoing tension between the sexes is to be expected.

• A reconciled perspective: men and women are simultaneously same and different, and this sameness and difference can be met in the present moment and transformed into graced relationships.

Therefore, my suggestion is that we recognize our unique (and somewhat paradoxical) situation. We can generally understand the nature of polar opposites: up/down, black/white, presence/absence, active/receptive, and so on. We cannot treat male and female the same way, at least not without expecting to get skewed results. That is why I believe we cannot understand yang and yin as, strictly speaking, a male and female principle. That is also why we cannot understand anima and animus as polar opposites of the dominant conscious personality. We can, however, recognize opposition within us, and we can in many circumstances find the presence of opposite traits in males and females. Furthermore, the opposition that we sense between male and female has all the dynamic potential for paradox, surrender, essential action, and transforming consciousness as do all the other graced opportunities of our lives.

The fact, however, that we are walking paradoxes, same and different in the same moment, means that we probably should treat our sexual diversity differently than other opposite pairings we may encounter. It also means that we must seriously critique our systems, be they political, cultural, or religious, that too easily establish a male/female opposition as a basis for actions. We must critique them from the point of view that ideological projection might in fact be keeping them from the essential action that would fulfill their potential for transforming reality. We must also critique the systems that too readily presume no significance to gender difference, for this is simply another form of dualistic moderation.

Morality in Paradoxical Tension

Throughout this book I have attempted to tie paradox to both conversion and transformation. Whenever we deal with conversion and transformation, we must also invariably deal with morality. Conversion in its movement from rooted sinfulness to liberation presupposes a substantial level of moral decision making. Transformation, with its emphasis on deepened awareness and heightened interconnectedness, recognizes increasing levels of maturity, of which moral and ethical maturity is a substantial part. To live and act from the desire to dwell in God's presence while also being at one with all people and all of creation, and at the same time being fully aware of the dynamic energies in my own life, I must understand and incorporate into my life the vast implications of moral choice. To presume otherwise is little more than an illusion.

As paradox is concerned with conversion and transformation, so it is also involved with knowledge, specifically the kind of knowledge that comes with the recognition of paradoxical structure within experience. And knowledge is in turn directly connected with morality. How I know and interpret an event or experience will determine how I choose to act toward it. As Parker Palmer suggests in *To Know as We Are Known*, "To put it in somewhat different terms, our epistemology is quietly transformed into our ethic. The images of self and world that are found at the heart of our knowledge will also be found in the values by which we live our lives." (p. 21) Our knowledge and recognition of paradox, or their lack, will greatly influence what it is we feel is the "right thing to do."

Accordingly, morality is also directly connected with discernment. We could even understand moral decision as discernment that in any way touches on whatever is relevant to right and wrong action. While all discernment is concerned for what is fruitful in regard to the Reign, not all discernment has direct moral implications. But much of our discernment does have moral value, probably much more than we are ready to admit. If all our actions deserve their proper and complete discernment, this is all the more true of actions with moral weight. We cannot eliminate morality and still say that our discernment is complete.

Morality, however, is traditionally challenged by paradox. This is particularly true in what could be called categorical frameworks of morality that are looking for one right answer that is always true, in every event, under every circumstance. Such a moral framework wants to have little to do with paradox, and in fact is usually threatened by it. Rigid moral frameworks do not prefer questions; they look instead for clear and certain answers. They are not interested in a process of growing moral awareness. They feel more comfortable with definitive ethical axioms that evoke immediate adherence.

Jesus, the embodiment of paradox, was not often friendly toward such frameworks. Nor was moral rigidity friendly toward the Good News that Jesus preached. That Gospel proclaimed a Reign that had a place for sinners and prostitutes, for foreign collaborators and repentant thieves, for the outcast and the misshapen, for both the denier and the betrayer (if the betrayer would only seek it). But to provide a place for all of these, they would need to be welcomed in with all their contradictions and incompleteness. True, Jesus did not give them the message that everything is fine just the way it is, but they were encouraged to enter into the process of the Reign of God that would ultimately make all things new. While the enemies of Jesus, all part of the social and religious establishment, were scandalized at what they perceived to be the shocking laxity of his message, Jesus showed the kind of compassion and understanding that encouraged true repentance on the part of sinners.

If the moral framework of society and religion in first-century Hebrew-Greek-Roman culture was so thoroughly shaken by the preaching of Jesus, will our own contemporary Christian moral framework fare any better? There is cause to hope so, for it is the teaching of Jesus that is supposedly the foundation upon which that morality is based. But in actual practice we also recognize that in some quarters Christian morality can be just as rigid, just as demanding, just as uncompromising as was the ethical framework of those who felt compelled to try eliminating Jesus once and for all. Jesus rose, but it seems the moral world view of his enemies has never quite left us.

What changes in morality when an understanding of paradox is present in our moral decisions? Nothing and everything. Nothing changes because paradox does not eliminate a single one of our moral values. But everything changes because paradox gives us a new vantage point from which we can view those values, and it gives us a new process through which we can proceed in our quest to arrive at mature moral decision making. The process can be challenging because it first asks us to be aware of life's duality, but it also maintains that the moral good is not to be found in extreme adherence to either of these poles. Moral good, instead, is arrived at through the process of reconciling and transforming the duality, and finding our course of action through a response to a new moral reality.

This approach of paradox can be seen in the broadest view through the ways in which we tend to structure moral choice in the first place. A number of structural approaches could be cited, but let us take the way we arrive at personal moral action as an example. It could be presented through the following triad:

- Premise: morality is a personal decision.

- Counterpremise: morality must be legislated (no personal decision; some form of objective communal imposition).

- Reconciliation: moral action is arrived at through the graced interplay of personal and communal will.

Let us take a moment to explore this triad. There are, of course, scriptural reasons to support both viewpoints. Clearly, the New Testament affirms personal choice. Our personal decision is honored by the very fact that discipleship itself requires individual acceptance. With personal choice also flows personal implication. We hear in John's gospel that we shall know the truth, and the truth will make us free (8:32). Does Paul not clearly say that we have no righteousness through the law, but only in our personal faith in Jesus? (Rom 3:19–26) And certainly, as has already been mentioned, there are a number of passages that would suggest Jesus took a negative view of a law that left no room for individual decision. He chastised those who would load people with heavy burdens while making no effort to ease them. (Lk 11:46) Legal institutions were not to be seen as ends in themselves. Jesus said that the Sabbath was made for humans, and not the other way around. (Mk 2:27)

Still, the opposite statement seems to have just as much support. Jesus also said that he did not come to abolish the law, but to fulfill it. (Mt 5:17) Jesus tells the rich young man to keep the commandments if he wishes to enter into life. (Mt 19:17) Even the call to love one another, a call placed by Jesus on a par with the love of God, is

viewed in the gospels specifically in terms of its nature as a com-
mandment. (Mk 12:31; Jn 15:12) Paul recognized this very com-
mandment of love for others as a basis for affirming and fulfilling
the law received from Moses. (Rom 13:8–10) The presumption of a
clearly stated objective moral code of Christian living is scattered
throughout the writings of Paul in his advice to the young communities he labored with, and it is found just as clearly in the other New
Testament writings as well.

Still, the starkness of the first two statements of the triad is striking.
The potential abuses of either of these extremes can be vividly imagined. Personal choice can easily deteriorate into a libertine stance that
abides no responsibility and cares little for how one's actions have an
impact on others. Rigid moral legislation, on the other hand, is little
more than enslavement. It denies the personal dignity and freedom
that have always been recognized at the heart of God's plan as
revealed in Jesus. We would presume, therefore, that all would rush
to embrace the third statement of our triad: moral action is arrived at
through the graced interplay of personal and communal will.

The reality is, however, that in the practical nitty-gritty of life we
seldom allow ourselves or others to pursue this line of thought. Our
residual duality causes us to hear it as a threatening statement. For
many, the interplay of personal and communal will is perceived as
too risky. What if the law gets voted down? What if the communal
will is rejected? Isn't this just an invitation for "anything goes"? For
others, the fact that I might have to let go of my own chosen direction for the sake of some standard outside of me is unacceptable.
This is all the more true because each of us firmly believes that our
discernment is the proper one, even though we can clearly see poor
personal choices being made by others. Those who would seek to
curtail my choices have no doubt misunderstood the circumstances
that have led me to my conclusions. So we are frequently left with
the inconsistent reality that while we abhor the extremes of the triad,
we still choose to live in them.

The reason for this is that to do otherwise would require a transformation. Or more properly, it would require a surrender. When it
comes to moral choosing, most of us are unwilling to let go of our

preconceived moral axioms. To do otherwise would seem to be relinquishing control of something. Supporters of the law presume that it is legislation itself that keeps moral relativism, or even chaos, at bay. Proponents of personal responsibility feel that it is individual choice itself that constitutes freedom. To give an inch would be to give a mile. But without surrender we cannot speak about transformation in the first place. To come to transforming moral action we have to pass through an interplay of personal and communal will that is graced, that is, open to an activity of God's Spirit to which we in turn are willing to surrender. That means we have to enter into moral discernment with openness and trust, and not with preconception and rigidity from either side of the spectrum. This is a challenge to our society, to our churches, and to ourselves as well.

Personal and Communal Action

Every mature human being is called to a life of discernment. This includes not only moral discernment, but also that wider sense of discernment that seeks to recognize the overall holiness of life. As I mentioned in chapter seven, discernment should be involved in the moment-by-moment journey of life. Every dimension of my life has a faith context, and discernment is the ongoing process through which I discover that context and choose to act out of it in response to the events that constantly happen around me. It is my discernment and the surrender it calls forth that enable me to cooperate with God's Spirit, to move beyond duality, and to embrace an action that precipitates a transformation within me or around me. This kind of action, therefore, is at the very center of transforming consciousness.

Essential action is transforming action, an action that is both a response to grace and a cooperation with it. It is both an action of the Spirit and my action. As I said earlier, it has the power to bring forth some aspect of the Reign of God. This means that it is action that furthers the divine will. I do not mean this in the sense that whatever happens, no matter what it is, is perceived as God's will (a manipulation of God). Nor do I mean the opposite, that God already has everything mapped out, and all we are doing is going through the motions (God's manipulation of us). The divine will is dynamic, creative, and open-ended. Our cooperation with it is just that—a co-operation. What we discern and choose to act on either furthers the Reign of God, or it doesn't. If our choice bears fruit, a creative moment dawns and God's presence is actualized in a new way, in part through our action. If our choice is not fruitful, a possible direction the Reign might have taken will not materialize. It is closed to actuality—at least for now. Does that mean that the Reign is irreparably damaged? No, the paschal mystery of Jesus has already brought its definitive establishment. But the role we could play in its manifestation is that much diminished, and the possibilities we might have opened up must be approached by the Spirit from another avenue.

From this point of view, everything we do, everything in which we involve ourselves, everything we refrain from, has implications for the Spirit's presence in the world. Nothing we do is insignificant. Every action and every event is potentially transforming, not just for us individually or communally, but also for the transformation of all creation. Conversely, there is no way that we can really absent ourselves from the world. Our presence and participation will matter, for better or for worse, whether we wish it so or not. Our choice is really very simple. We can either choose to live in duality and contradiction, or we can move through paradox into transformation.

The actions we take happen on two different levels. We perform personal actions and we undertake communal actions. Each of us is exercising both of these kinds of actions constantly, although we might not be aware of it. There are three things to say about these different kinds of action. First, because I am performing certain actions, it does not necessarily mean that I am choosing to do so. Second, a corollary to this statement, because I have a "reason" for what I do, it does not necessarily mean I understand my motives for doing it. And third, merely because I am aware only of personal implications to what I do, it does not mean my action is not also in some way communal. Allow me to briefly explain.

Choice implies freedom, and to be fruitful it usually requires complete discernment. I perform many actions in the course of a day. If you were to stop me and ask if I were choosing to do the things I do, I would quickly say yes. But upon closer examination I might realize that much of what I do is automatic. I am not doing it because I chose to do it; I am doing it because I have been conditioned to do it. Even some of the "good" things I do are done, not because of a free initiative, but because these actions are set patterns within me. Free actions, however, have much more potential for fruitfulness than conditioned ones. Transforming consciousness requires the exercise of freedom because I cannot move automatically through paradox.

A further distinction must be made between reasons and motives. I understand a reason to be a consciously held explanation for a course of action. A motive, however, indicates a deeper drive or intention beneath that course. I can call to mind the reasons I do things, but I might not be clear on all the motivation that underlies and supports (or sometimes contradicts) my conscious intentions. Some of my motives, particularly those that lie within the unconscious recesses of the shadow, might not be available to me at all. They still affect my actions, and in fact sometimes can work directly at odds with my rational intentions. Frequently the effort to come to transforming consciousness through essential action will bring these deeper motivations to the surface. They can shock me, but it is a healthy shock, and their appearance usually brings me to a deeper realization of the presence of paradox in the midst of the events of my life.

Finally, it is necessary to make some comments on the intricate interconnection between my personal and communal actions. By communal action, I mean action that is taken by a community of people at some level. This could be the action of a family, a neighborhood, a church, a nation, or the world in general. Perhaps the word "community" implies too much. Is a neighborhood really a community? Perhaps it once was, but is it today? Can we really speak of the community of our nation? Or of the world as a whole? Some would even question whether most families today still qualify as communities. But despite our dire social predictions, and even despite an abundance of existing evidence, all of these social entities, and many others as well, are communities; they simply might not be fruitful examples. I believe that all human groupings have the potential for experiencing the dynamic and transforming power of community life at their various levels. That they do not is not the result of their being too big or too small, too simple or too complex, too progressive or too conservative, too diverse or too homogeneous. That they do not experience their own potential for communal power is because they are not sharing in the power of the Reign of God.

Most communities (probably all, to some degree) live out their experiences in duality and contradiction. In fact, it might be said that, if it is difficult for individuals to break through into paradox and the fruits of transforming consciousness, it is all the more difficult for communities to do so. Communities have the added burden (and it is a tremendous one) of moving a communal will forward. The greater the population of the community, the more difficult it is to shape a willing response. We can, in fact, look on community at our national and global levels, and marvel that any kind of fruitful response from fragmented and divided populations can take place at all. When society does seem to advance, it does so with painstaking slowness. And what seems to be termed an advancement for one generation is often called into question in the next.

Still, we could look at our world today, and claim something of a triumph over the ages that have gone before us. With a few notable exceptions, are not the nations of the earth moving to democracy? Surely this could be seen as a positive development. While that is true, we must still recognize the limits of democratic rule. In nations that operate at this level (in the best of circumstances, where democracy is more than just a meaningless term governments ascribe to themselves), duality continues to reign supreme in what is usually called "majority rule." It is our "advancement" of democracy to allow the polar opposite with the greatest following to establish the direction and the pace. By any comparison of governmental forms that preceded it, this is indeed an advancement, an improvement over every other kind of social contract humans have ever devised to date. It has proved to be a workable system, but it is not a particularly transforming one. Prejudice, injustice, and inequality continue, while the minority voices are pushed into the shadow regions of the collective psyche.

We can hope that at smaller levels, communities have a greater chance for actualizing transforming consciousness. Families, church congregations, and neighborhoods have greater potential for discernment, surrender, and essential action. But even here it will not just happen automatically. Small communities are just as likely to fall into the traps of dualistic and patterned thinking as individuals are, probably more so. If our dualistic nature could be viewed as a call to conversion on the part of individuals, that is also true when it comes to communities. We do not often think of conversion as something that is called forth at a social level, but it is in fact a very appropriate response on the part of communities of any size. Just as individuals are held in bondage by the nature of addictive sinfulness,[1] so are communities. If each person needs to experience liberation and transformation, so do communities. The dynamics of rooted sinfulness at a social level, while they might be more diffused and less easily named, are very much like those found in the individual.

On infrequent occasions a "spontaneous" conversion of a community can happen. Such an event could be said to have occurred to the Hebrew people at Sinai. We could also look to the Pentecost experience of the earliest followers of Jesus as a similar event. On occasion whole families or congregations might find some similar movement of the Spirit in their midst. These are always highly charged events. Such occurrences are not simply emotional experiences, for those kinds of experiences where groups are worked up into either positive or negative emotional hysteria can be easily induced. Their long-term fruitfulness can be seriously called into question. Real conversions of communities are always accompanied by profound surrender, and followed by concrete essential action. They have deep and lasting results.

Still, it is much more likely that communal conversion will take place gradually over a longer period of time in the intricate interactions of the community's members. It is when a number of individuals who are experiencing deep breakthroughs in life begin to interact from their new levels of awareness that the group as a whole can begin to see some effects. In this sense it could be said that every individual's conversion is also in some way a conversion of each communal entity that the person belongs to. We cannot presume that conversion is ever merely a private matter. This is true even when the individual is not consciously thinking about his or her community bonds, or when the implications of individual conversions upon various communities are not recognized, or even imagined.

Conversion involves liberation from sinfulness. Sinfulness, however, is not something that is confined to individuals, even though that is what we tend to think of first. Communities at every level can also be perpetrators of the kind of sinfulness that keeps humanity and all of God's creation far from living in the Reign. The reality is that social sinfulness is often the hardest to name, and even harder to uproot. It is the task of Christian discipleship to continue to work for the liberation of the human community, and for the liberation of our broken world as a whole. This work involves reconciliation, peacemaking, compassion, and prophetic witness. But first of all, it requires recognition. We cannot act upon what we do not see. So recognition is itself the first essential action. To be able to recognize the reality of what it is in communities that does violence, what it is that perpetrates injustice, and what it is that couches these actions in gross deception is to arrive at a great breakthrough into truth.

Once we see the ways in which communities hold themselves, their members, and other groups in bondage, we are then ready to break out of what Charles Tart, in *Waking Up: Overcoming the Obstacles to Human Potential* (pp. 85ff), calls the consensus trance that communities tend to live in. What is frequently discovered in this process, however, is that consensus trance, the self-hypnosis that groups unconsciously agree to accept and uphold, relies almost totally on dualistic thinking to maintain itself. We're good because they're bad. We're in favor of life, but they have no regard for the value of human life. We're supporters of the Gospel of Jesus, while they are the antichrist incarnate. To enter into paradox, on the other hand, destroys the illusion that dualistic thinking is an adequate tool with which to create a world view. It is harder for me to maintain that your group is evil when I see what is in you is in us as well. When I begin to think paradoxically, I begin to look beyond obvious disagreements for ways that both sides can pursue to enable transformation to happen. Rather than resort to violence, which we will inevitably do if we live in either pole of opposition for very long, we will begin to seek out ways of peace and reconciliation. Dialogue and mutual respect will take the place of name calling and vindictiveness.

From transforming consciousness, continuously checking our presumptions about reality, morality, culture, and the human community, we are then free to act in prophetic and compassionate ways to rebuild our communities anew. Our actions are done with boldness and trust, rather than tentatively. This is because once we have entered into paradox, we are no longer hampered by fear. We have seen both sides of reality, and so there is nothing further that can threaten us. We can then surrender what is necessary to release ourselves from the barriers of our own thinking, and we can choose to move with a transforming consciousness that sees reality in a different way. Here we discover that we have a new agenda for social change, and a new platform from which to act. Moment by moment and stone by stone we can work with God's Spirit to slowly and deliberately rebuild the earth.

Take a deep breath, and as the air passes into your lungs, imagine that you are being filled with God's Spirit. It is the promise of continued life. But to try to hold on to the Spirit indefinitely is inevitably to collapse. You will have to let go of It, so that the Spirit can flow out of you again. When It does, It goes out into your world, creatively and passionately. But at that moment you are left depleted and empty. It is the Spirit's return that saves you. That returning can be seen as pure gift, and so you receive your next breath with renewed gratitude.

Essential breath is a gift, but it is a gift that we have worked hard to receive. Isn't that strange, for how can a gift truly come from something we have had to do of necessity? It is the paradox of freedom. The best things in life are free at a terrible price. Without the price the freedom isn't really there. Freedom, without transforming consciousness, is ultimately an illusion.

The Reign of God is seen only with eyes that are free. It is seen only with eyes that are loving, trusting, and open, with eyes that are not afraid to envision letting go of what I have despite the fear that nothing will come back. The Reign of God is experienced only by those who have learned to breathe as an essential action. This essential breath is the fulfillment of our greatest potential and our deepest loss. It opens us to our Truest Desire, the longing of our hearts.

ENDNOTES

1. When referring to sinfulness in this chapter and elsewhere, I am not simply speaking of things we choose to do or not do that could be considered wrong and for which we can be held culpable. I am referring to a rooted sinfulness that lies at the heart of our human nature. I refer the reader to my previous book, *Conversion and the Enneagram*, pp. 121ff.

Cited Works & Further Reading

Abrams, Jeremiah, and Connie Zweig, eds. *Meeting the Shadow: The Hidden Power of the Dark Side of Human Nature*. New York: G.P. Putnam's Sons, 1991.

Bailey, James L., and Lyle D. Vander Broek. *Literary Forms in the New Testament: A Handbook*. Louisville: Westminster/John Knox Press, 1992.

Bennett, J. G. *Transformation*. Charles Town, WV: Claymont Communications, 1978.

Berne, Patricia H., Louis M. Savary, and Strephon Kaplan Williams. *Dreams and Spiritual Growth: A Christian Approach to Dreamwork*. Mahwah: Paulist Press, 1984

Bradshaw, John. *Healing the Shame That Binds You*. Deerfield Beach, FL: Health Communications, 1988.

Capra, Fritjof. *The Tao of Physics*. 3rd ed. Boston: Shambhala, 1991.

Capra, Fritjof, and David Steindl-Rast. *Belonging to the Universe*. San Francisco: HarperCollins, 1991.

Colledge, Edmund, and Bernard McGinn, ed. & trans. *Meister Eckhart: The Essential Sermons, Commentaries, Treatises and Defense*. The

Classics of Western Spirituality Series. Mahwah: Paulist Press, 1981.

Cousins, Ewert H. *Bonaventure and the Coincidence of Opposites.* Chicago: Franciscan Herald Press, 1978.

Cousins, Ewert H., ed. *Bonaventure: The Soul's Journey into God; the Tree of Life; the Life of St. Francis.* The Classics of Western Spirituality Series. Mahwah: Paulist Press, 1978.

Crossan, John Dominic. *Cliffs of Fall: Paradox and Polyvalence in the Parables of Jesus.* New York: Seabury Press, 1980.

De Mello, Anthony. *The Song of the Bird.* Garden City, NY: Image Books, 1984.

Dennis, Marie, Cynthia Moe-Lobeda, Joseph Nangle, and Stewart Taylor. *St. Francis and the Foolishness of God.* New York: Orbis Books, 1993.

Dillard, Annie. *Pilgrim at Tinker Creek.* Toronto: Bantam Books, 1981.

Erikson, Erik H. *Identity: Youth and Crisis.* New York: W. W. Norton & Company, 1968.

Feinstein, David, and Stanley Krippner. *Personal Mythology: The Psychology of Your Evolving Self.* Los Angeles: Jeremy P. Tarcher, Inc., 1988.

Finley, James. *Merton's Palace of Nowhere: A Search for God Through Awareness of the True Self.* Notre Dame, IN: Ave Maria Press, 1978.

Fowler, James W. *Stages of Faith: The Psychology of Human Development and the Quest for Meaning.* San Francisco: Harper & Row, 1981.

Fox, Matthew. *Breakthrough: Meister Eckhart's Creation Spirituality in New Translation.* New York: An Image Book, Doubleday, 1980.

Garfield, Patricia. *The Healing Power of Dreams.* New York: A Fireside Book, Simon & Schuster, 1991.

Hawking, Stephen. *A Brief History of Time: From the Big Bang to Black Holes.* New York: Bantam Books, 1990.

Henry, Patrick. *The Ironic Christian's Companion: Finding the Marks of God's Grace in the World.* New York: Riverhead Books, 1999.

Hillman, James. *A Blue Fire*. New York: Harper Perennial, 1991.

Hopkins, Jasper. *Nicholas of Cusa's Dialectical Mysticism: Text, Translation, and Interpretive Study of de Visione Dei*. Minneapolis: The Arthur J. Banning Press, 1985.

Ichazo, Oscar. *Between Metaphysics and Protoanalysis: A Theory for Analyzing the Human Psyche*. New York, Arica Institute Press, 1982.

John of the Cross. *The Collected Works of St. John of the Cross*. Kieran Kavanaugh and Otilio Rodriguez, trans. Washington: Institute of Carmelite Studies, 1973.

Johnson, Robert A. *Inner Work: Using Dreams and Active Imagination for Personal Growth*. San Francisco: HarperCollins, 1986.

Jung, C. G. *Memories, Dreams, Reflections*. Aniela Jaffe, ed. New York: Vintage Books, 1965.

———. *The Portable Jung*. Joseph Campbell, ed. New York: The Viking Press, 1971.

Keller, Edmund B. *Some Paradoxes of Paul*. New York: Philosophical Library: 1974.

Kurtz, Ernest, and Katherine Ketcham. *The Spirituality of Imperfection: Storytelling and the Journey to Wholeness*. New York: Bantam Books, 1992.

Lao Tzu. *Tao Te Ching*. Victor H. Mair, trans. New York: Bantam Books, 1990.

Leclerc, Eloi. *The Canticle of Creatures, Symbols of Union: An Analysis of St. Francis of Assisi*. Chicago: Franciscan Herald Press, 1970.

Levine, Stephen. *Healing into Life and Death*. New York: Anchor Books, Doubleday, 1987.

Lifton, Robert Jay. *The Broken Connection: On Death and the Continuity of Life*. New York: Basic Books, Inc., 1983.

Magill, Frank N., and Ian P. McGreal, eds. *Christian Spirituality*. San Francisco: Harper & Row, 1988.

May, Gerald G. *Addiction and Grace*. San Francisco: Harper & Row, 1988.

McGinn, Bernard, ed. *Meister Eckhart: Teacher and Preacher*. The Classics of Western Spirituality Series. New York: Paulist Press, 1986.

Merton, Thomas. *New Seeds of Contemplation*. New York: New Directions Books, 1962.

————. *The Way of Chuang Tzu*. New York: New Directions Books, 1965.

————. *A Thomas Merton Reader*. Thomas P. McDonnell, ed. Garden City, NY: Image Books, 1974.

Moore, Thomas. *Original Self: Living With Paradox and Authenticity*. San Francisco: HarperCollins, 2000.

Nicoll, Maurice. *Psychological Commentaries on the Teaching of Gurdjieff and Ouspensky*. Boston: Shambhala, 1984.

Norris, Kathleen. *The Cloister Walk*. New York: Riverhead Books, 1996.

Osborne, Kenan B. ed. *The History of Franciscan Theology*. St. Bonaventure, NY: The Franciscan Institute, 1994.

Ouspensky, Peter D. *In Search of the Miraculous*. New York and London: Harcourt, Brace, Jovanovich, 1977.

Palmer, Parker J. *The Promise of Paradox: A Celebration of Contradiction in the Christian Life*. Notre Dame, IN: Ave Maria Press, 1980.

———— *To Know as We Are Known: Education as a Spiritual Journey*. San Francisco: HarperCollins, 1993.

Peck, M. Scott. *The Road Less Traveled: A New Psychology of Love, Traditional Values and Spiritual Growth*. New York: Touchstone, 1978.

Perri, William D. *A Radical Challenge for Priesthood Today: From Trial to Transformation*. Mystic, CT: Twenty-Third Publications, 1996.

Poundstone, William. *Labyrinths of Reason: Paradox, Puzzles, and the Frailty of Knowledge*. New York: Anchor Press, 1988.

Quenk, Alex T., and Naomi L. Quenk. *Dream Thinking: The Logic, Magic, and Meaning of Your Dreams*. Palo Alto, CA: Davies-Black Publishing, 1995.

Rohr, Richard, with John Bookser Feister. *Jesus' Plan for a New*

World: The Sermon on the Mount. Cincinnati: St. Anthony Messenger Press, 1996.

Ross, Robert R. N. *The Non-existence of God: Linguistic Paradox in Tillich's Thought.* New York: E. Mellen Press, 1978.

Russell, D. S. *The Gospel in Creative Tension.* Louisville, KY: Westminster/John Knox Press, 1990.

Sanford, John A. *Dreams and Healing.* New York: Paulist Press, 1978.

Sawicki, Marianne. *Seeing the Lord: Resurrection and Early Christian Practices.* Minneapolis: Fortress Press, 1994.

Shah, Idries. *Wisdom of the Idiots.* London: The Octagon Press, 1989.

———. *The Way of the Sufi.* London: Arkana, 1990.

———. *Tales of the Dervishes.* New York: Penguin/Arkana, 1993.

Shaw, Marvin C. *The Paradox of Intention: Reaching the Goal by Giving Up the Attempt to Reach It.* Atlanta, GA: Scholars Press, 1988.

Singer, June. *Boundaries of the Soul: The Practice of Jung's Psychology.* New York: Anchor Books, 1994.

Slater, George R. *Bringing Dreams to Life: Learning to Interpret Your Dreams.* Mahwah: Paulist Press, 1995.

Smith, Cyprian. *The Way of Paradox: Spiritual Life as Taught by Meister Eckhart.* Mahwah: Paulist Press, 1987.

Speeth, Kathleen Riordan. *The Gurdjieff Work.* New York: Pocket Books, Simon & Schuster, 1976.

Standish, N. Graham. *Paradoxes For Living: Cultivating Faith In Confusing Times.* Louisville: Westminster John Knox Press, 2001.

Stella, Tom. *The God Instinct: Heeding Your Heart's Unrest.* Notre Dame, IN: Sorin Books, 2001.

Tart, Charles T., ed. *Transpersonal Psychologies.* New York: Harper & Row, 1975.

Tart, Charles T. *Waking Up: Overcoming the Obstacles to Human Potential.* Boston: New Science Library, Shambhala, 1987.

Tetlow, Joseph A. *Choosing Christ in the World: Directing the Spiritual Exercises of St. Ignatius Loyola According to Annotations Eighteen and Nineteen, a Handbook.* St. Louis: Institute of Jesuit Studies, 1989.

Thompson, Helen. *Journey Toward Wholeness: A Jungian Model of Adult Spiritual Growth.* Mahwah: Paulist Press, 1982.

Tickerhoof, Bernard. *Conversion & the Enneagram: Transformation of the Self in Christ.* Denville, NJ: Dimension Books, 1991.

Welch, John. *Spiritual Pilgrims: Carl Jung and Teresa of Avila.* New York: Paulist Press, 1982.

Wheatley, Margaret J. *Leadership and the New Science: Learning About Organization from an Orderly Universe.* San Francisco: Berrett-Koehler Publishers, Inc., 1994.

Wilber, Ken, ed. *The Holographic Paradigm and Other Paradoxes:*

Of Related Interest...

New Paths to God
Moving Forward on the Spiritual Journey
Catherine M. Harmer

The author suggests some paths to a closer relationship with God, a deeper sense of the sacred, and a fuller meaning to life—in other words, a spirituality for today.

1-58595-154-4, 128 pp, $10.95 (X-15)

The Ongoing Work of Jesus
His Mission in Our Lives
James A. Krisher

Looks at the work of Jesus as reflected in the gospels, and offers readers a guide to continuing Jesus' mission and ministry in their lives.

1-58595-210-9, 96 pp, $10.95 (X-27)

Spiritual Surrender
Yielding Yourself to a Loving God
James A. Krisher

The author focuses on surrender as a choice we make repeatedly no matter what the circumstance: in suffering, pleasure, joy, or prayer.

0-89622-721-9, 104 pp, $9.95 (M-94)

A Handful of Fire
Praying Contemplatively with Scripture
Carole Marie Kelly

People on their spiritual journey, the every-day reader, or anyone looking to get more deeply in touch with Scripture will find this a real treasure.

1-58595-126-9, 192 pp, $12.95 (J-78)

TWENTY-THIRD PUBLICATIONS
185 WILLOW STREET • PO BOX 180 • MYSTIC, CT 06355
TEL: 1-800-321-0411 • FAX: 1-800-572-0788
Bayard   E-MAIL: ttpubs@aol.com • www.twentythirdpublications.com